The Educated Person

The Educated Person

Toward a New Paradigm for Liberal Education

D. G. Mulcahy

ROWMAN & LITTLEFIELD PUBLISHERS, INC.
Lanham • Boulder • New York • Toronto • Plymouth, UK

ROWMAN & LITTLEFIELD PUBLISHERS, INC.

Published in the United States of America
by Rowman & Littlefield Publishers, Inc.
A wholly owned subsidiary of The Rowman & Littlefield Publishing Group, Inc.
4501 Forbes Boulevard, Suite 200, Lanham, Maryland 20706
www.rowmanlittlefield.com

Estover Road
Plymouth PL6 7PY
United Kingdom

British Library Cataloguing in Publication Information Available

Library of Congress Cataloging-in-Publication Data:
Mulcahy, D. G. (Donal G.)
  The educated person : toward a new paradigm for liberal education / D.G.
Mulcahy.
    p. cm.
  Includes bibliographical references and index.
  ISBN-13: 978-0-7425-6121-2 (cloth : alk. paper)
  ISBN-10: 0-7425-6121-6 (cloth : alk. paper)
  ISBN-13: 978-0-7425-6122-9 (pbk. : alk. paper)
  ISBN-10: 0-7425-6122-4 (pbk. : alk. paper)
  1. Education, Humanistic. 2. Education--Aims and objectives. I. Title.
  LC1011.M78 2008
  370.11'2--dc22

                                                    2008008813

Printed in the United States of America

∞™ The paper used in this publication meets the minimum requirements of
American National Standard for Information Sciences—Permanence of Paper
for Printed Library Materials, ANSI/NISO Z39.48-1992.

To the Memory of my Parents,
Daniel and Mary Mulcahy.

Contents

Acknowledgments   ix

Introduction   xi

1 Liberal Education in Context   1

2 Newman: Liberal Education as Cultivation of the Intellect   35

3 Adler: Liberal Education for All   71

4 Martin: Gender-Sensitive Liberal Education   107

5 Liberal Education as a Preparation for Life   147

6 Toward a New Paradigm for Liberal Education   177

Bibliography   197

Index   211

About the Author   221

Acknowledgments

I wish to thank many people for enabling me to undertake and complete this work. They include my colleagues at Central Connecticut State University: library personnel for their unfailing assistance, Dean Mitch Sakofs and my colleagues in the Department of Teacher Education for their interest and support, and the Board of Trustees for granting me sabbatical leave in 2007. They also include those at Rowman and Littlefield with whom I worked, especially the reviewers of my manuscript and my two editors, Alex Masulis and Art Pomponio, who along with their production staff were courteous and most supportive at all points along the way in bringing this work to publication.

Parts of this book draw on a number of earlier publications. A section of Chapter 2 draws heavily on "Newman's Retreat from a Liberal Education," *Irish Journal of Education* 7, no. 1 (Summer 1973): 11–22. Chapter 3 is a development of "Is the Nation at Risk from *The Paideia Proposal?*" *Educational Theory* 35, no. 2 (Spring 1985): 209–221. Chapter 4 draws on *Knowledge, Gender, and Schooling: The Feminist Thought of Jane Roland Martin* (Westport, CT: Bergin and Garvey, 2002) and on "Jane Roland Martin and Paul Hirst on Liberal Education: A Reassessment." *Journal of Thought* 38, no.1 (Spring 2003), 19–30. And chapters 4 and 5 first appeared in an earlier and more summary form in chapter 3 of *Curriculum and Policy in Irish Post-Primary Education* (Dublin: Institute of Public Administration, 1981).

It is impossible to pay thanks to the many former teachers, colleagues, and students who have helped shape my thinking on the subject matter of this book over the years but I do wish to acknowledge their contributions if only in general terms. Two of these stand out: the late Harry S. Broudy at the University of Illinois and my first-ever academic advisor, the late F. X. Martin, O.S.A., formerly Professor of Medieval History at University College, Dublin.

I am especially indebted to friends and colleagues who gave freely of their time to read various parts of the draft manuscript and to make valuable suggestions for improvement: Ronnie Casella and Tim Reagan at Central Connecticut State University, Padraig Hogan at The National University of Ireland, Maynooth, Alan McClelland, Emeritus Professor at the University of Hull, Bill Schubert at the University of Illinois at Chicago, Doug Simpson at Texas Tech University, and Kevin Williams at Mater Dei Institute in Dublin. I am especially indebted to Jane Roland Martin, the influence of whose thinking is evident even in the title of this book, for her encouragement from an early stage, for her support along the way, and for her comments on parts of the draft manuscript. Needless to mention, weaknesses and any errors that remain are my responsibility alone.

Most importantly, I wish to acknowledge the support and assistance of my family. Thanks to Cara, Donal, and Brendan for contributing in their different ways and for their unfailing interest in what I do. Thanks to Mary for her patience, generous support, and guidance when all else fails.

Introduction

Accompanying the liberating and expansionist thinking of the post–World War II era, several powerful new social forces brought their particular influences to bear on educational thought and practice. The first and perhaps most tangible of these is a massive central government involvement and intergovernmental cooperation in the affairs of schooling. The second is changing patterns of work and family structures that have far-reaching implications for schools and society. The third, imperceptible at first—and perhaps ultimately the one to dominate—is our system of mass communications and entertainment, notably television, the personal computer, the Internet, mobile devices, and a staggering array of software applications.

Today, one cannot reasonably engage in a discussion of the curriculum or of almost any facet of school or college life without taking account of these powerful forces. Yet just as these influences are changing the educational landscape and demanding imaginative and flexible thinking about education, the debate is increasingly encumbered by a societal disorientation toward educational values and priorities. At the same time, a broad social critique has emerged that sees the interests of the wealthy and the powerful going unchecked, aided wittingly or unwittingly in the educational sphere by cumbersome governmental directives, legislative mandates, and constraints imposed by testing and grading imperatives. Betwixt and between, we find ourselves saddled with an expensive yet debilitated decision-making apparatus. Educational decision makers and practitioners at the local levels are rendered incapable of exercising judgment or imagination out of fear of committing transgressions great or small—or even miniscule.[1]

Meanwhile, the enormous challenges and possibilities presented by a revolution in communications technology go largely unheeded and the ambivalence of many adolescents toward schooling remains a puzzling challenge.[2] Sadly, in an age of distraction where the jailing of Paris Hilton is as much in the spotlight as the unjailing of Scooter Libby, an age characterized by towering disparities in wealth and by glamorized and even officially sanctioned violence, it is with the distractions that we are preoccupied. The actual needs of students and communities remain unattended, and difficult solutions to real problems go unexamined. In a sort of postmodernist state of euphoria, the lack of a compass and of clearly articulated, carefully justified, and widely agreed core educational understandings and values is coming home to roost.

The aim in this study is not to tackle all of these problems but to focus on one, bearing in mind the others. It is a problem as old as education itself: to what end do we educate the young, or, stated a little differently, what does it mean to be an educated person? In responding to this question, schools and colleges have been heavily influenced by the idea of a liberal education even as its conceptualization has changed over time. But liberal education has fallen on hard times, and with it a guideline long relied upon in the shaping of school and college programs. Is it because—actually or apparently—liberal education has lost relevance to social issues, the reality of mass schooling and higher education, the communications revolution, and the sense of frustration and powerlessness felt by many?[3] Or is it because it has lost touch with the lives of students? Whatever the reason, no longer is liberal education the answer of first or even of last resort in determining the purposes and content of a school or college education.

For these reasons, I approach liberal education not as an answer but as a question. It can be variously stated as follows: What do we understand by the education of the young; by what purposes and values is it to be guided; and what are the implications for the curriculum and its pedagogy, including its attitude toward the existing knowledge and experience of the learner? In what ways—if any—and how does liberal education speak helpfully to social and educational challenges we face today? In what ways is the idea itself in need of change, or should it be abandoned altogether, a relic of times past?

In undertaking this work, I first set out to think about liberal or general education in a way that would address the considerable curriculum challenges we face at a time of unremitting social change, when it is easy to lose one's way in education. Eventually, the project outgrew its original intent, as two formidable if theoretical objectives that I had not pondered at an earlier stage gradually emerged. The two objectives are, first, to bring practical education, traditionally seen as beyond the bounds of liberal education, within the concept of a liberal or general education, and second, to incor-

porate into the idea of liberal education a pedagogical dimension historically foreign to it.

The products of the ongoing discussion surrounding liberal education,
these additional objectives held out the prospect of addressing more vigor-
ously the connection between school and society, between teacher and student. They similarly held out the prospect of articulating, finally, a comprehensive new paradigm for liberal education that both supports innovative
practice and gets beyond the question of the continued usefulness of liberal
education itself. It would be the first such articulation since at least the mid-
nineteenth century, when the still dominant formulation was set in stone.

The upshot of all of this is that I have attempted to sketch in broad terms
a new idea. It is new not so much in its constituent parts as in its recombination of elements from different sources that will be obvious to the reader.

NOTES

1. Here one is reminded of the view of Deborah Meier that the elimination of
small schools and the growth of the federal bureaucracy in education in the United
States have actually undermined good judgment. See Deborah Meier, "NCLB and
Democracy," in *Many Children Left Behind*, ed. Deborah Meier and George Wood
(Boston: Beacon Press, 2004), 66–78.

2. One of the more sustained responses to this challenge and to the perceived
wastefulness of the final year of high school has come from the Bill and Melinda
Gates Foundation. A particular beneficiary of this response has been the middle college movement, aimed at smoothing the transition from high school to college and
expediting college completion. See Kathleen M. Carter, "Secondary-Postsecondary
Partnerships: An Analysis of the Educational, Cultural, Economic and Political
Characteristics of Blended Institutions" (EdD diss., Central Connecticut State University, 2007).

3. Al Gore, *The Assault on Reason* (New York: Penguin Press, 2007) may be read as
a timely reminder and an implicit commentary on how disengaged from social and
political life education has become.

1

Liberal Education in Context

In his consideration of the nature and role of liberal education in a knowledge society, Carl Bereiter asks, "What should it mean to be an educated person in the twenty-first century?"[1] This is the central question to be examined here.

Liberal education has long been a fascination for scholars in a variety of disciplines. Seen at one time as a matter to be dealt with by colleges and universities, over the years it has increasingly become central to the debate surrounding education in high school and even the earlier grades.[2] In approaching the subject, many have waxed lyrical, some have searched for true meaning, and others have even sought practical applications. More than a few, including institutions, have prescribed particular programs. Yet so many and varied are the uses of the term 'liberal education' that features once considered central to it are sometimes lost sight of and new meanings have been added on. According to Charles Wegener, the term is so overloaded with meanings that "it is a good question whether it should be retained."[3] Much the same is true of 'general education,' a term often used interchangeably with liberal education. While these terms have had rich historical meanings, the question now arises of whether and how liberal education is any longer a useful construct. And even if it is, how does it still speak helpfully to educational challenges we face today? How can it be a guide as we search for a better way to think about education in the age of distraction? How does it assist us in addressing the question of what it means to be an educated person in the twenty-first century?

Those who engage in this discussion are, by and large, of the view that liberal education does have a continuing relevance. Drawing on roots that go back over two thousand years to Greece and Rome, educational theorists

1

of the twentieth and twenty-first centuries representing different philosophical, religious, and political perspectives have elaborated variations on
the core features of liberal education.[4] The conceptualization of the issues
and the justifications provided have often differed considerably, but, in the
final analysis, on the crucial issues of purpose and curriculum, the primacy
of intellectual goals and academic content long remained more or less constant across competing philosophical perspectives. Up until and even beyond the mid-twentieth century, the scholarly standpoint in varying guises
appeared to prevail, as educational programs in schools and colleges remained primarily academic in their orientation. Programs that were less so
and institutions where goals were more vocational or less keenly academic
in nature did exist, it is true, but these were not normally seen as engaged
in liberal education. They also tended to be held in much less esteem and
were not seen as routes to positions of power and status in society.[5]

As we moved through the second half of the twentieth and into the
twenty-first century, scholars and educational theorists were increasingly
joined and even overtaken by others in the educational debate. Philosophizing about the curriculum enjoyed a special prominence in the mid-
twentieth century, when challenges such as those presented by the launching of Sputnik in 1957 forced Americans to focus on education in a new
way. Since then, theorizing aimed at establishing broad models of curriculum for general education of the kind found in the 1960s and 1970s has de-
clined. In its place, we find influential contributions from new entrants into
the debate. These have included governments—increasingly central
governments—aided and abetted by corporate and other interest groups,
frequently those on the right of the political and religious spectrums. For
these relatively new participants, the continuing relevance of liberal education is a less pressing matter. The belief in the value of academics, notably
in mathematics and the sciences, persists. But there is also a keen eye on the
linkage between education and the economy, to the degree that education
is seen less as an end in itself and more as a vehicle for promoting economic
growth and even personal wealth, as distinct from personal development.[6]
Religious, cultural, and political constituencies have in some cases been
more anxious to promote their religious and moral values than the historically academic values of liberal education. At the level of higher education
especially, differences of viewpoint surrounding issues of cultural diversity
have given rise to heated and intense debate.

Alongside these new participants in the debate, other distracting and
seemingly aimless players are now given a platform by an array of communications technologies and service providers willing to open the airwaves to
any and all sources of easy revenue in exchange for loud talk, televised
shouting matches, and grotesque displays of human frailty. Viewed from
the relatively sedate perspective of the scholars and theorists, such compet-

ing and unruly influences have muddied the clear waters considered necessary for a vision of priorities. Viewed from the hustle and bustle of contemporary life, it is the way things are! Like it or not, this confusion of views, and the challenges presented by sometimes invasive government legislation and policy directives, are a reality. These, too, must now be borne in mind by those wishing to reassert the continuing relevance of liberal education or seeking an alternative and more compelling vision of education as we move through the twenty-first century.

To pursue the question of the continuing relevance of the idea of liberal education and its potential contribution here, I chose for special consideration three very different theorists of liberal education around whose positions those of other contributors may also be viewed. While addressing central questions with which advocates of liberal education have been concerned over the centuries, each of these theorists approaches the subject from varying historical, religious, cultural, and educational standpoints. The three highlight aspects of the concept of liberal education that have shaped our understanding of it, draw attention to new possibilities within it, and challenge it to redefine itself.

John Henry Newman's nineteenth-century presentation of the core elements of liberal education as centered on the notion of cultivation of the intellect remains the prevailing conceptualization of the idea. Throughout the twentieth century, Mortimer Adler elaborated on the implications of democratic citizenship for the idea of liberal education, which he popularized and presented to a worldwide audience through his association with *Encyclopedia Britannica* and the *Great Books of the Western World*. Jane Roland Martin has infused the idea with a twenty-first-century feminist sensitivity, exposing gender bias in the historical idea and pointing to imaginative new possibilities for the future. Not only do these writers highlight and uncover important new dimensions of the idea of liberal education; all are deeply committed to identifying the most valuable form of liberal education conceivable. Yet there are strong points of difference in their positions, reminding us that there is no one monolithic concept of liberal education. It may even indicate that the concept is best seen as a construct to be used in addressing recurring questions.

DEFINITIONS

From the outset, I want to be as clear as I can on my use of the terms 'liberal education' and 'general education,' both in regard to how these terms have come to be understood and in regard to how I use them here. As I have just indicated, there is no overall consensus on the precise meaning of these terms, meanings that have evolved over the years. In *The Uses of Schooling,*

Harry Broudy uses the terms interchangeably[7] as do Harold Henderson and Barry Smith when they speak of "the problem of general or 'liberal' education" as being "one of the central controversies in educational thought."[8] I too shall normally use the terms interchangeably in referring to what they have come to mean.[9] I also use them interchangeably but, for obvious reasons, rather differently when I call for a new conceptualization of both. To keep confusion to a minimum, I shall usually use just the one term, 'liberal education,' except where using the other or both together more accurately reflects the context (such as when referring to the terms as used by another writer).

What I understand by 'liberal education' and 'general education' when I call for a new conceptualization I trust will be made clear throughout the course of this book. By the term 'liberal education' as it has come down to us, I understand an education defined by Newman as cultivation of the intellect, the object of which is "intellectual excellence,"[10] and elaborated by Paul Hirst and R. S. Peters as knowledge and understanding in depth and breadth.[11] The concept therefore has a two-sided nature: the development of intellectual skills and the understanding of a broad range of knowledge, once characterized by Newman as knowing enough on all subjects to be able to converse with ease and sense on any of them.[12] This range of knowledge has usually been equated with what are considered to be the core academic disciplines and it has excluded practical subjects and an applied, vocational, or professional orientation. The term 'liberal education' has also connoted an education pursued for its own sake, that is, as a leisure pursuit for self-cultivation as opposed to some ulterior purpose, such as vocational preparation. But as both Broudy and Nel Noddings have pointed out, in practice if not in intent, programs of liberal education in schools and colleges are actually vocational in function, serving as a form of preparation for a career or further studies.[13] I have largely avoided using the term in this sense.

The term 'general education' sometimes refers to a range of subjects that may include but reaches beyond the academic disciplines and a range of skills that similarly extends beyond the academic.[14] But it is also used in much the same way as I have just described liberal education. In his writings, Robert Hutchins saw general education as being committed to the cultivation of intellectual excellence, just as Newman did liberal education, and to the promotion of knowledge and understanding in depth and breadth, as Hirst and Peters later would. In speaking of the great books of Western civilization, Hutchins spoke of liberal education as conversation, much as Michael Oakeshott does. In the Great Books program introduced into the undergraduate curriculum in general education at the University of Chicago during his Presidency,[15] Hutchins fashioned his ideal of a liberal education in programmatic form. General education as envisaged in the report of the faculty of Harvard University, *General Education in a Free Society*,[16] may also be seen as a program of liberal education aimed at intellectual formation based on a study of core academic subjects. The conceptualization of general education presented by Broudy, B. O. Smith, and Joe R. Burnett is essentially that of a liberal education in terms of its perceived purpose and content.[17] In addition, general education requirements widely employed by colleges and universities have also normally been understood to provide a liberal or liberal arts education. As these examples testify, then, 'general education' is often used to refer to a form of education that may reasonably be seen as liberal education. Hence my use of these terms more or less interchangeably here.

ORIGINS

It may be difficult to be sure as to the exact origins of the idea of a liberal education, but it is reasonable to ascribe it to antiquity and specifically to Athens of old. Whether Plato relied on the term or not, the plan he laid out for the education of the ruler did provide for what may reasonably be considered a liberal education. Aristotle distinguished between liberal and illiberal subjects and used the term 'liberal' to characterize knowledge that one may seek for its own sake or out of intellectual curiosity. Though Aristotle did not object to teaching useful knowledge, in identifying some knowledge as liberal he further characterized other knowledge as mechanical because it was sought for some purpose beyond itself.[18] And so we find the origins of a distinction between liberal knowledge and professional knowledge and later between liberal education and professional or useful education. The one, liberal education, is directed toward a person's inherent potential to know and to enjoy knowledge. The other is directed toward promoting the knowledge and skills needed to carry out useful tasks, such as practicing law, conducting the affairs of state, or tending to the sick or the affairs of the soul. Arising from this distinction, liberal education has been open to the charge of having little use, being, as Martha Nussbaum bemoans it, "too costly to indulge in the apparently useless business of learning for the enrichment of life."[19]

Still, not all are enamored of the idea of a useless education or the pursuit of knowledge for its own sake. Even Plato seemed to take the view that philosophers should get off of their perches and do something for the betterment of others, and Cicero felt obliged to convince his fellow Romans that the liberal arts had their uses. Ironically, to assuage his listeners, Cicero had recourse not to the inherent qualities of the liberal arts but their utility. If a knowledge of all the liberal arts was not self-evidently a worthwhile accomplishment, it did, at least, provide the orator with a deep fund of knowledge upon which to draw so as to captivate and sway listeners by eloquence and grace in words and movement.

By the time the once powerful empires of Greece and Rome were fading, there had emerged certain broad understandings of the idea of liberal education and its relationship to professional or useful education. It was an understanding highlighted by some of the last great minds of the era of classical antiquity, notably St. Augustine and St. Jerome, both of whom accepted that for the clergy a knowledge of the classics laid an important basis for a deeper theological understanding. What was largely an idea prior to the arrival of the Dark Ages in the fifth century A.D. would appear in the form of bricks and mortar, and even regulation and ritual, with the emergence of the medieval university in the twelfth century. Here the idea gained a firm footing, as all those entering the university were required to do so through the faculty of arts. Similarly, the course of study leading to the B.A. degree came to be considered a prerequisite for admission to any of the three great professional schools of the medieval university, namely, medicine, law, and theology. And so the idea of liberal education as a necessary foundation for the professional studies became a reality by the Middle Ages. Once firmly in place, it would not be easily dislodged.

While the idea of liberal education was challenged from time to time in different ways, it would take centuries for the most serious advocates of competing educational philosophies to raise their voices most effectively. When they finally did so in the nineteenth century, in conjunction with other revolutionary changes in education, they met stiff resistance. This resistance was found most notably in the United States in the *Yale Report of 1828*[20] and in England in a work that has become a classic treatment of the subject of liberal education, Newman's *Idea of a University*. By the mid-1800s, the impact on education of the Industrial Revolution was also becoming evident. Going hand in hand with this development was a growing involvement by governments who were just now dipping their toes in the largely uncharted waters of mass or public schooling. This involvement would grow continuously during the next one hundred and fifty years and would be accompanied by a consequential decline in the influence of the hitherto primary champions of education, the churches. A major attraction for governments and others would be the economic benefits to be derived from government-supported popular schooling. This would lead in time to an emphasis on the basic, useful education essential to life in the new industrial workplace—the three Rs, as it became known.[21]

In the upper reaches of the educational structures, the emergent notion of the economic usefulness of education raised questions regarding the continuing suitability of the then-dominant form of university education, liberal education rooted in the classics. Prominent among those raising the questions were various combative contributors to the *Edinburgh Review* who took direct aim at Oxford University, alleging that its curriculum and traditions were obsolete; another party leading the charge for change in this sphere was an upstart institution: the University of London. Tracing its origins to the 1820s, the innovative thrust of the University of London represented at least two serious challenges to the status quo in higher education everywhere. It rejected the idea of a set course of studies rooted in the classics, and it rejected a close relationship between religion and education, features with which liberal education had become closely entwined.

It was these rejections that set the course for Newman's line of argument in defense of liberal education. Not surprisingly, Newman was not alone in defending religion, the classics, and liberal education in the university.[22] Prevalent in the many defenses presented was the view that a college or university education was to provide students with a broad education, as distinct from a specialized or merely vocational education. Consequently, for Newman the emphasis was upon a broad knowledge and understanding in the humanities and the sciences, well-developed intellectual skills, and mental discipline. Some ambiguity surrounded the place of moral character and the social skills befitting the gentleman, with Newman, for example, appearing to attribute at least some such developments to the influence of college and university life rather than liberal education, strictly speaking.[23] With this important qualification, such acquisitions were considered defining characteristics of the person of liberal education and a necessary foundation for anyone wishing to enter professional studies, as they often still are by supporters of liberal education to this day.

By century's end, attention in the United States was also focused upon the college preparatory curriculum in the high school, where many of the beliefs concerning the academic focus of the college curriculum remained prominent. Such was the case with the Committee of Ten, established by the National Education Association in 1892 to address the question of the school curriculum at a time of expanding enrollments in high schools. A particular difficulty facing high schools was the varying entrance requirements of colleges and universities. There was also the challenge of preparing students for life after high school when some were intending to go to college and others were not. The Committee of Ten came down firmly in support of a common curriculum for all students regardless of whether they were college-bound or not. It also proposed four different courses of study ranging from more classical and traditional to less so. Foreign language, mathematics, science, English, and history were included in all four courses. Classical languages were not, setting a new direction for the future.[24]

Before long, discontent regarding the established purposes and curriculum of the high school resurfaced, leading to the creation within thirty years of another committee by the National Education Association. In 1918, this committee issued its famous report, *Cardinal Principles of Secondary Education*.[25]

Here we find quite a different view of the nature and purpose of education and of the task of curriculum design. This view of education, upon which many would pour scorn for years to come,[26] traced its roots to a position championed by English social philosopher Herbert Spencer in the mid-nineteenth century.[27] It also reflected the influence of the social efficiency movement in America of the early twentieth century. Accordingly, in the *Cardinal Principles of Secondary Education*, the objectives of education are seen to be determined by the demands and everyday activities of living with little regard to the classics or the hallowed traditions of liberal education. These demands included, among others, earning a living, being a citizen, and being of ethical character.

One may detect a distinct utilitarian streak in American schooling dating back at least as far as the emergence of the academy initiated by Benjamin Franklin in the late eighteenth century. Yet the rhetoric surrounding education and the justifications set forth to guide it have generally been more humanistic in character at the upper levels and, by and large, influenced by the traditions of liberal education. To that extent, the thinking outlined in the *Cardinal Principles of Secondary Education* and a number of subsequent writings, such as that of Florence Stratemeyer[28] and her colleagues, may be seen as being in a lesser motif, if not quite an aberration.

Not surprisingly, therefore, before a further thirty years had passed, the quest for equilibrium would be joined by yet another prestigious body, the faculty of Harvard University. Published in 1945, *General Education in a Free Society*, the report of the faculty, accepts many of the traditional principles associated with liberal education: General education is distinguished from specialized education. There is a core of general knowledge to which all should be exposed, and there are basic intellectual skills to be acquired. The knowledge core recommended for all included the study of the humanities, the natural sciences, and the social sciences.[29] The intellectual skills considered fundamental included effective thinking, communication skills, judgment, and discrimination among values.[30] The recommendations made in *General Education in a Free Society* were not accepted by Harvard University itself. The thinking in the report, while hardly original, did have considerable influence in the broader debate on the curriculum of high schools and colleges, however, and once again traditional claims modified for the changing times were reasserted.

These changing times would usher in a new global recognition of the importance of education for the individual as well as for social development and prosperity. Powerful new educational mantras to emerge following World War II included investment in education and equal educational opportunity for all. At least in the developed world,[31] mass education was coming of age—and talk of rising costs, accountability, and excellence was not far behind. Neither was another new phenomenon: an emerging hesitancy to identify and articulate core educational values and priorities, what has been referred to as "a missing dimension in the educational conversation."[32] In the place of these values, there began to appear a sort of marketplace of noises beckoning those who listened—or even unavoidably heard them—in sometimes disconnected directions. Ambiguity of purpose opened the door to the loudest voices.

At the onset of this trend, an unlikely event sharpened the focus in the United States on excellence as a guiding theme: the launching of the Soviet satellite Sputnik in October of 1957. Taken by surprise, Washington responded by looking to the schools as both culprit and cure. Throughout the 1950s, prominent critics such as Arthur Bestor and Admiral Hyman Rickover[33] expressed concern over the decline in academic rigor in America's public schools. By the mid-1950s, scholars were also developing new approaches to the teaching of mathematics to gifted children that collectively became known as the new math. Within a year of Sputnik, the push for improved teaching in mathematics and science was given a huge boost, the National Aeronautics and Space Administration (NASA) was established, and the National Defense Education Act of 1958 was on the books. Whether or not it represented an early signal that difficult times lay ahead for the arts, humanities, and social studies, the act was aimed primarily at improving education in mathematics, science, and foreign languages, subjects considered central to the national defense. Thereafter, the new reform movement, buoyed by an early glow emanating from the new mathematics projects, spread to almost all subjects as the nation was caught in the grip of the first excellence in education movement of the second half of the twentieth century.

The various points of intersection among these seemingly unrelated forces, all of which have had a profound and enduring effect on curriculum work, is captured with reference to the notion of eminent domain by J. Dan Marshall and his colleagues.[34] As is shown in Marshall's work, in the push for excellence and curriculum renewal, a little book authored by Jerome Bruner, *The Process of Education*,[35] helped shape the course of curriculum reform and textbook design by highlighting the concept of the structure of knowledge as a guiding principle. Ironically, Bruner was also at the forefront of the reaction against the emphasis on excellence, a change of course he advocated in *The Relevance of Education* in 1971.[36] The excesses of the quest for excellence, he argued, had pushed aside the needs of those neglected by the system: the poor and the underprivileged. The federal government had already begun moving in that direction, beginning with the passage of the mammoth Elementary and Secondary Education Act of 1965 inspired, it was said, by the War on Poverty. But in the early 1970s, new forces took control of national and international events: the oil crisis of 1973 and the subsequent global recession. These would lead governments to lose confidence in the capacity of educational institutions to engage in worthwhile reform and ease the momentum for investment in education. This, in turn, ushered in another loss of confidence in schooling. Yet, when the clamor grew loud enough once more, a scramble for reform led to the second excellence in education movement aimed at state-supported or public schools. Beginning in the United States in the early 1980s, following the lead of Britain, this movement was less keenly focused and more marked by aimless bursts of energy of which the accompanying cacophony remains symptomatic.

The two excellence reform movements emerging in the public schools during the second half of the twentieth century did retain some common orientations. It would be claiming too much to say that these movements were inspired by the ideals of liberal education, but they did hearken back to those principles, and a number of influential theorists directly invoked the core values of liberal education. These included Philip H. Phenix and Broudy, Smith, and Burnett during the 1960s,[37] and later Adler[38] and Martin.[39] In England, Peters and Hirst,[40] were especially prominent; their ideas had a decisive impact on deliberations on the curriculum and curriculum theorizing there and beyond. At the college level, appeals to liberal education were omnipresent. Characteristic of the movement in higher education in the United States were appeals by writers such as Harry Levine, Ernest Boyer, and Allan Bloom, and in England, the emerging views of Michael Oakeshott.[41] To say that there was a lack of a shared understanding here would be a gross oversimplification of developments commonly referred to as the culture wars. At the same time, at least as argued by Bruce Kimball,[42] new commonalities were being forged across even bitter divides by a renascent pragmatism in the curriculum renewal efforts of American institutions of higher education in the closing decades of the twentieth century.

Martin is of particular interest among later writers on liberal education, even if most of her innovative work has not been focused directly on higher education. Offering a cautionary feminist note on the subject, she attempted to widen the range of discourse surrounding the idea of liberal education. As others such as Noddings have also done, Martin draws attention to the potential if not actual gender and cultural exclusions of liberal education, whether born of its origins and development in the midst of largely, white, dead, European males or elsewhere. These cautionary considerations aside for now, the contributions of those such as Hirst and Peters in England and Adler and Martin in the United States, while differing on important points, did seek direction for school programs from varying conceptions of liberal education. In doing so, they bring clear ideas, deep understanding, and competing perspectives to the fundamental and age-old but continually evolving question of what constitutes a good education.

WHITHER LIBERAL EDUCATION?

There is sufficient substance in the positions of Newman, Adler, and Martin, three central figures in this study, upon which to build in rethinking liberal or general education. They are not, of course, the only such positions, as there is a wide world of rich theory and practice that may also be explored and drawn upon. For this reason, it will be helpful to engage the broader ongoing discussion of liberal education as well as other influences that intersect with it, sometimes in novel and productive ways. These influences, too, can be brought to bear on the analysis of whether and how the historical ideal of liberal education may be useful in working toward the transformation of education in the twenty-first century. In some cases, these influences grow out of a conflict between the ideals of and a disenchantment with the public schools, the trend toward privatization of education, and the preoccupation with testing. Other influences draw on sources of social commentary that along with the critique they contain may, in fact, be pointing to important new ways to redefine liberal education in the twenty-first century.

Purpose and Pedagogy

At whatever level, whether school or college, the debate regarding liberal education is defined and treated, two aspects dominate the discussion: aims (or purpose) and curriculum (or content). At one time a fundamental question in the philosophical discussion of education, consideration of aims has been neglected in recent years.[43] This is a point that has already been raised and is one to which Noddings has forthrightly drawn attention in her writings on schooling,[44] commenting that "without continual, reflective discussion of aims, education may become a poor substitute for its best vision."[45] With his sights fixed firmly on the ongoing debate regarding liberal education at the college level, W. B Carnochan also attempts to bring the spotlight back to the primacy of aims. This he sees as necessary to any successful resolution of the problems arising from the culture wars—and their attendant casualty, civility in the discourse—that have been given so high a profile in the debate. Carnochan is especially insistent that it is the question of purpose rather than content that should be our starting point: "the big question is not the abstract ideal of liberal education and its derivative strategies but the specific purpose of whatever it is, educationally, that we are trying to do. What is any requirement, or set of requirements, actually for?"[46] If we can answer these questions, we may then be able to move on more productively to the question of content and other matters pertaining to the means necessary to achieve our purposes or aims.[47]

Like many who contributed to the curriculum theorizing of the 1960s and onwards, Noddings' focus does not end with the consideration of aims. She too has a philosophy of curriculum for general education as she understands it, set out broadly in *The Challenge to Care in Schools* and followed up in two subsequent books.[48] But her stance is in several respects at a remove from the thrust of the dominant curriculum theorizing of the 1960s and 1970s. For Noddings, in a sentence, ". . . liberal education is a false ideal for universal education."[49] Rather than pursuing the notion of liberal education for all, Noddings suggests that we ask what kind of education each of us wants for our children.

In asking how we would wish our children to be educated, Noddings acknowledges that she is embarking on quite a task. Gardner's seven intelligences, she says, is a useful point of departure for discussing capacities, with interests rather than testing suggesting where these capacities may lie. But other elements are needed also: one is a concern for moral development and acceptability; others include common human tasks, such as health and preservation, and spiritual development.[50] Nodding acknowledges that, by arguing for human activities as the organizing principle of curriculum, Franklin Bobbitt helped promote a 'human tasks' approach,[51] but she argues that his principle sometimes led to mere lists of things to be done. What we need, Noddings believes, is a scheme that speaks to the "existential heart of life—one that draws attention to our passions, attitudes, connections, concerns, and experienced responsibilities."[52] She goes on to suggest themes of care as a way forward. Care, she writes, "can be developed in a variety of domains and take many objects."[53] She also notes that because our perspectives differ depending on race, nationality, sex, class, and religion, people will have different priorities regarding these various domains of care and of what it means to care.[54] Similarly, while it is the issue of caring that dominates for Noddings, she is also attentive to individual differences and developmental issues. These have not always been highlighted at the level of higher education and, his likely protestations to the contrary notwithstanding, neither have they been given much attention by Adler at the school level.

Linked to the notion of caring, and a feature of Boyer's curriculum stance at both the high school and college levels, is the notion of service. This is a theme that has emerged amidst mild controversy as a curricular innovation in liberal education. Joseph L. DeVitis, Robert W. Johns, and Douglas J. Simpson[55] have argued that in Richard Pratte's ideal civic curriculum, "community service provides an integrative vehicle for practicing freedom with responsibility."[56] And in John Dewey's view, as DeVitis, Johns, and Simpson see it, every place where people meet is by its nature a schoolhouse: shops, factories, churches, political caucuses. Yet not all forms of service-learning would be educative. To be fully Deweyan in their eyes, one must also see the student as a participant in "'the formation of the purposes which direct his activities in the learning process.'"[57] They quote Richard Guarasci to the effect that complexity, ambiguity, and nuance make up our daily lives and that it is reciprocity and mutuality that make life worthwhile.[58] And they are taken by Boyer's vision of higher education as contributing to social betterment by focusing on pressing social needs. Here undergraduates participate in field projects and relate ideas to real life, classrooms and laboratories reach out to become health clinics and youth centers, and faculty members build partnerships with practitioners and are committed to improving the human condition.[59]

Speaking for themselves, DeVitis, Johns, and Simpson raise themes that resonate with critical pedagogy, feminist theory, and education viewed as preparing one for the callings or vocations of life. They "envision a rich linkage between liberal and service-learning that will permit students to be critically reflective participants in whichever settings or callings they choose to enter." It is one in which students will learn to critically examine even such notions as service, helping, and intervention[60] as they have the opportunity to investigate social institutions, power relations, and value commitment. As they see it, the key values of autonomy and service to community are not taught through didactic methods alone. These values are learned, in part, by experiencing the consequences of confronting individual and group challenges. In fact, in a way that separates them from others such as Nussbaum, DeVitis, Johns, and Simpson feel that one must experience citizenship at a deep level of involvement and participation to learn it. Clearly committed to citizenship as a goal, Nussbaum appears much less enamored of practical involvement of this kind. Showing instead the pluralistic tendencies toward which she inclines, Nussbaum writes that there may be detractors, traditionalists who are defenders of the older idea of a gentleman's education who want acculturation rather than accepting cultural pluralism along with socratic and universalistic goals. But, she continues, we ask "a higher education to contribute a general preparation for citizenship."[61] Then Nussbaum strikes the discordant note, one for which she has been taken to task by Martin because of its preoccupation with observation rather than participation.[62] For this "general preparation for citizenship" is to be accomplished largely through courses such as Enlightenment thought, by learning about the experience of women and about racial and other differences, and by gaining reflective understanding of topics such as human sexuality. It is therefore very urgent right now, Nussbaum adds, "to support curricular efforts aimed at producing citizens who can take charge of their own reasoning, who can see the different and foreign not as a threat to be resisted, but as an invitation to explore and understand, expanding their own minds and their capacity for citizenship."[63]

Before leaving DeVitis, Johns, and Simpson,[64] reference must be made to
at least one of the chapters of their book that reports on the experience of
service-learning in a particular college setting, making clear that there is a
pedagogical as well as a content dimension to this general way of approaching the curriculum.[65] According to Oren W. Davis and Jennifer
Dodge, at Trinity College of Vermont service-learning means students learn
by participating in "thoughtfully organized service experiences that meet actual community needs and that are coordinated in collaboration with the
college and community."[66] It is learning that is "integrated into the student's academic curriculum and provides structured time for students to engage in critical reflection about what they did and saw during the actual service activity." Service-learning is seen as providing students with
opportunities "to use newly acquired skills and knowledge in real-life situations in the community. It enhances what is taught by extending student
learning beyond the classroom into the community and helps to foster the
development of a sense of caring for others."[67]

There is faculty opposition, of course, some arguing that community service would be an artificial element in their courses, and service-learning
cumbersome, "left wing," "just another distraction from serious intellectual, academic pursuits" and not at "the heart of the 'true' liberal arts."[68]
Opposition notwithstanding, the undergraduate course at Trinity College of
Vermont is an effort to integrate traditional methods with service-learning.
The particular course that Davis and Dodge discuss deals with liberation
theology. Here exponents of contemporary philosophical principles of
hermeneutics, phenomenology, deconstruction, and existentialism, in their
interpretations of the Bible and in their critique of social and political
events, "raise their questions and develop their theories from a concrete,
lived perspective."[69] Their theologies and theories, Davis and Dodge continue, "rise from the ground; they are 'local' theologies. It is this emphasis
on the lived experience of the poor that allows community service-learning
to become such a powerful instrument in teaching and learning about the
liberation of all human beings."[70] To enhance their theoretical understanding, students are engaged in community service that involves them directly
with individuals. Through this they are challenged to develop and articulate
ways to assist in liberation, for "the community service project helps students recognize that liberation involves more than theories—it also involves action, doing, praxis. In fact, theology itself, as conceived by Gustavo
Gutierrez, is a 'critical reflection on Christian praxis in light of the word of
God.' The students are doing theology."[71] And so, through an academic
course in liberation theology, "consciousness of oppression is raised; learning is enhanced by these practical, concrete experiences; and moral and
civic values are reinforced."[72] To call it an academic course, given what we
are told of it suggests a meaning for academic that reaches beyond mere observation into participation.

Finally, and as if to verify this, the point of view presented in Davis and Dodge brings into perspective the criticism of service-learning as "behavior" or activity that has nothing to do with education. It is clear from what they write that service—for which we may read participation for Martin or "everyday social application" for Dewey[73]— allows one to accomplish even more than contributing something tangible to the community and maybe developing caring and interpersonal skills not normally associated with liberal education. According to Dodge herself, a student at Trinity College of Vermont, service heightened her understanding—as is intended by Adler through a combination of studying the Great Books and socratic teaching—in a way that "no book or lecture can elicit."[74]

Critical Pedagogy

As was seen earlier, caring is central for Noddings. But she is also committed to the notion of critical thinking, a stance that is underlined and elaborated in *Critical Lessons*. In her approach to critical thinking, as in the work of DeVitis, Johns, and Simpson, there is also an undercurrent of the kind of theorizing we have come to associate with critical pedagogy. Influenced by the progressive educational thought and activism of Paulo Freire, Henry Giroux, Peter McLaren, and Joe Kincheloe, to mention a few, have expounded the central tenets of critical pedagogy energetically and in compelling fashion. Here, however, it is the contribution of Ira Shor that I largely wish to draw upon to indicate the possibilities that critical pedagogy holds out for a merging of crucial elements of liberal education, critical thinking, participation, and personal experience. This is because of the manner in which Shor elaborates on the interactions between such a pedagogy, the curriculum, and the development of students as critical thinkers— and as activists to boot.[75] Before doing so, nonetheless, attention to some elements of critical pedagogy highlighted by Giroux is warranted if we are to appreciate fully the implications for the direction and content of liberal education and its possible enrichment by addressing pressing social, political, economic, and personal issues.

Henry Giroux: Positivism and Corporate Culture

Central to Giroux's position is his concern regarding two overpowering tendencies in contemporary culture: what he terms the culture of positivism and technical rationality[76] and the corporate culture.[77] The culture of positivism and technical rationality relies on the belief that the methods of investigation and proof exemplified in the natural sciences, logic, and mathematics—as is borne out by their applications in technology—represent in today's world the proper path to knowledge and truth. These rational methods are characterized as objective and value free. Knowledge as contained in other disciplines and forms of inquiry lacks this objectivity and is value laden. As such, the conclusions drawn in these disciplines are unreliable and more akin to hunches.

This is an erroneous account, according to Giroux, because scientific knowledge is not value free, but also has its subjective elements and underlying beliefs. These are kept out of sight, presumably by keeping the focus on those aspects of the methodology that are open to scrutiny and freely available to all seeking to verify scientific claims. This position is also misleading in its account of the humanistic or non-scientific disciplines and forms of inquiry. In this characterization of them, Giroux holds, the humanities are stripped of their concern with ends and ethics, which were a central feature of the classical Greek notion of theory. Such a stripping is the inevitable outcome of Auguste Comte's definition of scientific theory "when he insisted that theory must be 'founded in the nature of things and the laws that govern them, not in the imaginary powers that the human mind attributes to itself.'"[78] The culture of positivism and technocratic rationality is kept in place by a vast array of control mechanisms, notably modern means of mass communications technology, advertising, and other devices employed by governments and powerful elites in society. These mechanisms lead to a form of cultural amnesia and the acceptance of technology as the method for solving problems of all sorts, including those of a social and political kind that are not in fact amenable to technological solution.

The adverse effects of the culture of positivism on the public at large are many and varied. One effect in which those who view education as committed to social justice have a particular interest is its tendency to substitute *what is* for what *should be* by intimating that society has a life of its own, independent of the will of human beings, who are merely passive creatures. As a consequence, "we are left with a mode of reasoning that makes it exceptionally difficult for human beings to struggle against the limitations of an oppressive society."[79] It is a mode of reasoning accepted as much by the oppressed as by the oppressors.

Under the force of mass culture, teacher training institutions, and the influence of the state, schools serve in a variety of ways to further the culture of positivism and the subjugation of critical thought pervading society at large. School knowledge, with history being a good example, is often viewed as unproblematic, preordained, and independent of human involvement in bringing it into existence in the first place. Further promoting the culture of positivism is "the way classroom teachers view knowledge, the way knowledge is mediated through specific classroom methodologies, and the way students are taught to view knowledge."[80] Moreover, if we are to grasp the way in which knowledge, power, and ideology are to be understood, knowledge itself will need to be seen "not only as a set of meanings generated by human actors, but also as a communicative act embedded in specific forms of social relationships."[81] Hence the value of a Freieran pedagogy that not only emphasizes the interpretive dimensions of knowing but also highlights "the insight that any progressive notion of learning must be accompanied by pedagogical relationships marked by dialogue, questioning, and communication."[82] To this one could add the view of Pamela Bolton Joseph, a view long associated with the humanities, that "humanistic study is characterized by the idea that human beings have choices, that they may be tested and have opportunities to demonstrate courage and persistence."[83]

So how are our schools and we to respond to the culture of positivism and technocratic rationality? More recently than the critique advanced above, Giroux expressed the view that critical pedagogy could learn from feminist theory the need to go beyond critique to a language of possibility.[84] But even here Giroux himself does have such a language concisely expressed as "a commitment to change the nature of the larger society."[85] An important aspect of the kind of change needed brings us to the second of Giroux's criticisms of contemporary society, his critique of corporate culture and his appeal for a world characterized by openness to more humanistic forms of inquiry and to social justice for all.

Serious questions have been raised as to whether the failure of the public schools is real or imaginary,[86] but this has not stopped efforts by those who maintain it is real from pursuing a path of privatization, sometimes with the support of governments and politicians.[87] This in turn has generated charges of private interests topping public good, of putting profit before children, and of the federal government being an accomplice. In large part a critique of unbridled corporate greed, Giroux's analysis of corporate culture takes aim at its manifestations in schools and the manifold deleterious effects on the quality of public life which the beneficiaries appear content to undermine. These effects, he claims, are to be found in their disregard for the education of the young, the advancement and protection of basic civil rights, and the health and economic needs of the poor and consumers alike. The historic purposes of public schooling in America, Giroux argues, are now under threat from the forces of privatization and market-oriented school reforms, forces that issue in Bill Schubert's concerns about "The Big Curriculum" and which Grace Roosevelt argues also pose a serious threat to liberal education in higher education.[88] As commercial culture replaces public culture through the corporatization of our schools, the role of schools shifts from "creating a 'democracy of citizens [to] a democracy of consumers'"[89] as schools themselves are reduced to investment opportunities.

Giroux's analysis of corporate culture may be characterized as a critique of unbridled corporate greed whose effects are found in its profound disregard for education, civil rights, and the needs of the poor and consumers alike. Public schools, long a part of a proud tradition, are now under threat from forces for the privatization of schools and market-oriented school reforms. Little is said, Giroux points out, of the politics of social indifference, the relationship between choice and economic power, school failure, and the impact of joblessness, poverty, racism, schools that are falling down, and unequal school funding. Absent a vocabulary of ethics and values powerful enough to override opposing value systems, the corporate takeover of schools, according to Giroux, is made legitimate by appeals to school vouchers, privatized school choice plans, and excellence.

What is to be done, Giroux asks, to preserve schools as forces for democracy and social justice in the face of this assault?[90] There are roles for the public at large and for educators as public intellectuals. We need to address the problems of schooling in the realms of values and politics. We need to reinvigorate the politics of schooling by analyzing "how power shapes knowledge, how teaching broader social values provides safeguards against turning citizenship skills into work-place training skills, and how schooling can help students reconcile the seemingly opposing needs of freedom and solidarity."[91] Teachers and other educators for their parts must assert the crucial role of the teacher as public intellectual, rather than robotic classroom technician serving the will of controlling corporate interests at the expense of the public good. They are called as both teachers and citizens to the moral and political role of nurturers of the young, imparting the core values of democratic citizenship and not mere consumer citizenship. To this end, educators must engage in policy and enlist the support of diverse communities to support the schools themselves, for "educators must reclaim public schools as a public rather than a private good and view such a task as part of the struggle for democracy itself."[92]

Ira Shor: Education that Empowers

Taken together, the two critiques show Giroux challenging the philosophical and economic underpinnings of the culture of positivism and technocratic rationality, the corporate culture and, with particular reference to the public schools, the attack on the public good by private interests. Between them, Giroux's analyses make for a two-pronged critique of the forces aimed at undermining historical goals of liberal education such as critical and creative thought and democratic citizenship. Adopting the broad critical stance of Giroux and others, Shor, like Freire, considers in detail how the practitioner educator might respond. Although Shor is speaking as a professor in an institution of higher education,[93] his thinking is also applicable at other levels, supporting the idea that education can be addressed at various levels from much the same theoretical perspective. In Shor, moreover, there are strong strains of Freire and of Dewey's progressive approach to subject matter and student involvement. Like Dewey, Shor believes students need to be introduced to serious academic content. But content in isolation is not the central issue. The issue for Shor, as it was for Dewey, is how best to do it, that is how to enable students to grow in subject matter knowledge and understanding of the relations between knowledge and power so as to become agents for social justice for all.

The goals of empowering or critical education as understood by Shor are to relate personal growth to public life, "by developing strong skills, academic knowledge, habits of inquiry, and critical curiosity about society, power, inequality, and change."[94] It is unlike the approach of E. D. Hirsch, Shor points out, which provides "a Eurocentric canon of information, works, and usage for teachers to transfer to students," and which along with other "traditionalists" presents standard canons of knowledge as "universal, excellent, and neutral."[95] In contrast, problem posing, a method favored in critical education, views all subject matter as open to question, not as universal wisdom to be accepted. Unlike the banking education of Hirsch and others, critical education is not "exclusionary rather than inclusive."[96] It is also more motivating and more successful than traditional, didactic forms of education, Shor maintains. There are, moreover, associations between social class and various forms of pedagogy that may be pertinent. Drawing on research of the past quarter century that has found that powerful literacy is difficult for working-class children, Patrick J. Finn has this to say: "Progressive methods, empowering education, and powerful literacy tend to go together. Traditional methods, domesticating education, and functional literacy tend to go together."[97]

Shor recognizes that knowledge has always been a site where competing interests vie for power. Because standard knowledge as defined by the curriculum has been created by powerful interests, it needs critical study and not blind acceptance as "a bogus common culture."[98] In problem-posing teaching, students do not discard the academic subjects; they study them critically. They ask why the official textbook and syllabus are organized the way they are, why assigned readings were chosen, and what readings are omitted.[99]

For Shor, there are three roads to critical thought: generative, topical, and academic themes. Generative themes make up the primary subject matter. They arise from student culture and "express problematic conditions in daily life that are useful for generating critical discussion."[100] The topical theme, reminiscent of Broudy's notion of molar problems,[101] is a social question of importance locally or globally and is raised in class by the teacher. The academic theme also is raised by the teacher, "but its roots lie in formal bodies of knowledge studied by specialists in a field."[102] It responds to the need to recognize both the experience of the student at one end of the experiential continuum and that of organized disciplined knowledge at the other, a point well captured by Richard Pring in his discussion of the place of commonsense discourse in defining the curriculum. The curriculum, Pring writes, "should aim at the systematic reflection upon the commonsense beliefs of the pupil and student, and, in doing this, should draw upon those areas of enquiry which have extended the commonsense thinking of mankind into definite traditions of disciplined enquiry."[103]

Empowering education as presented by Shor is dialogic pedagogy. Fending off likely criticism from purists and those to which Davis and Dodge referred, for example, Shor explains the academically demanding criteria of the dialogic teaching he endorses. The dialogic teacher "cannot abandon structured content, the empowering class must have expert knowledge, and the democratic curriculum must be a rigorous process," he writes.[104] For a general and critical introduction to a field, students do not need "blackboards full of charts." Such detailed knowledge is inappropriate for the general education that most students need. Comprehensive knowledge of a subject may be appropriate for upper-level and graduate students. When it comes to general education, students should encounter relevance, subjectivity, and provocative debate, "not orthodoxies of information."[105] Critical thinking, Shor continues, is an analytic and imaginative habit of mind. It reflects on material in a meaningful context. It is not "a warehouse of data."[106]

According to Shor, the critical-democratic class frequently crosses the boundaries of the academic disciplines and as such challenges the dominant structure of education. This leads to the last of the eleven values of his agenda: activism. It is a value shared by Giroux, Martin, and DeVitis, Johns, and Simpson but it has been historically absent in the tradition of liberal education and in contemporary proponents such as Nussbaum and Adler. Critical-democratic pedagogy, Shor writes, "is cultural action against the educational limits of the status quo," just as dialogic problem solving, "is a pedagogy Freire called 'cultural action for freedom.'"[107]

Adopting the view that students' discourse is informed by students' backgrounds and personal histories, the teacher needs to engage students by means of a language that is legible to them, in a discourse that Shor calls the third idiom. Here Shor depicts a place where the two ends of Dewey's progressive organization of subject matter meet: in between the one idiom of the teacher and the other of the student. "The dialogic third idiom," he writes, "is simultaneously concrete and conceptual, academic and conversational, critical and accessible"[108] and its process overcomes the noncommunication of students. It transforms the separate idioms of student and teacher into a new discourse, "which relates academic language to concrete experience and colloquial discourse to critical thought. Everyday language assumes a critical quality while teacherly language assumes concreteness."[109] Once again Shor is at pains to assert the rigorous academic nature of the process, for mutual dialogue is not "a know-nothing learning process." Neither is it permissive, nondirected, or unstructured. It is interested in skills development and systematic knowledge. If it is to work properly, the teacher must be well informed and must actively use his or her knowledge in a dialogic way.[110]

Knowledge Production, Practices, the Practical, and Pragmatism

In a chapter on critical teaching and classroom research in *Empowering Education,* Shor proposes research in classrooms, where all too often it is lacking, separating researchers from school teachers and students. He cites Schniedewind and Davidson to give examples of such classroom research.[111] The examples serve the purpose of showing a further dimension of Shor's critical pedagogy, but they also introduce a question that is brought to our attention in more dramatic terms by Carl Bereiter. In "Liberal Education in a Knowledge Society,"[112] Bereiter argues that the survival of liberal education—assuming it is not already dead—will require a careful synthesis of new ideas and enduring principles. The essence of Bereiter's resolution of the difficulty we face lies in his notion of the knowledge society, a society organized around the production of knowledge just as agrarian society was once organized around agricultural production. "My proposal," he writes, "is that the school should be a productive part of that society, a workshop for the generation of knowledge."[113] At the root of his idea are the new vision of understanding taking shape in cognitive science and the notion of designing knowledge-based organizations so that everyone is a contributor to the generation of knowledge. These two, coupled with "the enduring vision of a liberal education, do give us an idea of what education for the twenty-first century should be."[114] Together, they suggest that schools, like research laboratories, should become knowledge-building organizations and that the daily activities of the classroom should undergo a cultural shift "from classroom life organized around activities to classroom life organized around the pursuit of knowledge."[115] While students remain learners, learning is no longer their job: now "their job is producing knowledge."[116]

For Bereiter, going forward, knowledge production is essential to liberal education. In the past, understanding what others knew of the known world may have been thought to constitute a liberal education. The proposal to make knowledge building the principal activity in schooling by contrast "would mean enlarging liberal education so as to encompass both the grasping of what others have already understood and the sustained, collective effort to extend the boundaries of what is known."[117] Aside from the kind of knowledge production that Bereiter suggests be brought within the ambit of liberal education, the question arises as to what would be the content of this new form of liberal education, in particular that which relates to "grasping of what others have already understood."

To elaborate on this aspect, Bereiter relies on a distinction between the knowledge an individual possesses and knowledge as it exists independently of one's mind, in a sort of world of ideas. The knowledge-building classroom embodies such a conception of knowledge and "it thus presents a miniature of the knowledge society into which students are to become enculturated."[118] To develop and explain his position more fully, Bereiter draws on the philosophy of Karl Popper, specifically Popper's theory of objective knowledge in which things are classified by Popper as belonging to World 1, World 2, or World 3. World 1 refers to objects of a material kind in the world. Knowledge in the first of the two senses alluded to by Bereiter, namely, the knowledge that an individual possesses, belongs to World 2 as classified by Popper, Bereiter explains. That which belongs to World 3 is objective knowledge found in the world of ideas. With these clarifications, Bereiter continues, we may now define the role of the school: "it is *to enculturate students into World 3,*"[119] which consists largely of the world of the academic disciplines or systematic knowledge. According to Bereiter, World 3 also includes cultural artifacts from literature and the arts, folk knowledge and culture in the anthropologist's sense of the word.

Thus far for Bereiter, therefore, there appear to be two distinct elements in liberal education in the knowledge society: knowledge production and existing objective knowledge. But does Bereiter go so far as Shor and call for students to engage in action research? Citing Daniel Solorzano, Shor writes, moving the focus from mere research to action, that Solorzano also offered the classroom as a research and action center. In regard to action, "Solorzano reported that 'to understand the problem posed and to empower students, one must take action on the problem and reflect critically on the action taken.'"[120] For his part, Bereiter, while sharing with critical pedagogy a disinclination to teaching in the traditional sense of merely conveying information, appears to stop short of action research. Given the loud, protracted, and often divisive debate as to what merits inclusion in the curricular canon, Bereiter adds an important clarification. While cultural variety around the world provides great richness, distinctiveness, and vitality, the contents of World 3, he insists, are culturally neutral. As he puts it, "there are not culture-specific sciences, mathematics, literary or historical theories,"[121] and to proceed otherwise is to jeopardize invaluable educational possibilities. To finish the point, he continues that "the largest cultural divide, cutting across the whole world with great consequence, is that which separates people who are at home in World 3 from those who are not."[122]

In "Liberal Education in a Knowledge Society," arguing the case for liberal education to incorporate knowledge building by students as central to its meaning and to its survival, Bereiter does not make explicit reference to the similar proposals emanating from critical pedagogy. Neither does he link his proposal to an explicit commitment to two other areas potentially transforming liberal education in the same general direction. The first is an interest in the practical and in practices and their implications for education; the second is what Kimball sees as the emergence of pragmatism as a feature of the intellectual evolution of liberal education.

Under the influence of Alasdair MacIntyre and Michael Oakeshott, philosophers of education have come to focus on the educational significance of social practices. The beginnings of this can be dated to about 1993, which saw the publication of Joseph Dunne's epic study *Back to the Rough Ground* and Hirst's retraction of his forms of knowledge theory of liberal education.[123] This also saw the emergence of Hirst's newfound emphasis on the educational significance of initiation into social practices. Ever since, there has been a continued interest in the matter. The central focus of this attention was recently restated by Hirst in a discussion of the philosophy of education as an exercise in practical reason. Drawing on Aristotle's concept of *phronesis*, he argues that the value of philosophy as a guide to good educational practice originates not in the application of theory to educational situations. Rather, it is to be found in the very practice of education itself through our ability to "discern in actual situations what activity is constitutive of some particular human good."[124]

The reliance on Aristole here, as in MacIntyre, is reflected in a related if slightly different focus in recent work of John White, in which White draws attention to the overall aims and character of general education as being concerned to promote "a person in the round, a person with a life to lead, a path to follow through all its conflicts, opportunities, contingencies," as one "who lives the life." Highlighting what he calls "the primacy of the practical," White too draws on Aristotle in support of his own contention that practical rationality is at the heart of the good life. From there he proceeds to argue that we ought to "begin our thinking about the curriculum with the human being as agent, not the human being as knower." This may lead us to "a more practically oriented curriculum" of general education as distinct from one premised on the acquisition of knowledge which leads to the neglect of "thinking about ends and means, planning and evaluating one's actions."[125]

In their advocacy of the practical, White and others represent well what Kimball sees as the growing influence of pragmatism in education and liberal education in particular.[126] It is not that White wishes to renege on general education or throw in his lot with the forces of vocationalism, for this is not his intent nor what Kimball understands by pragmatism influencing liberal education. This can be seen in Kimball's skillful sketch of the wide sweep of the gradually evolving force of pragmatism, which embraces many of the themes introduced in this overview and to which he draws attention in "Toward Pragmatic Liberal Education."[127]

In the introduction to his work, Kimball states the relationship concisely: pragmatism and general education, he says, seem to be converging for "pragmatism is now exerting an influence on liberal education in a number of ways." This, he suggests, can be seen in a widespread reliance upon pragmatism, pragmatists, and progressivism by those who comment on liberal education, a reliance that is accompanied by "intellectual and cultural influences that are subtle and indirect." These developments in liberal education may appear to be unconnected, but in their responses to changes of an economic, demographic, and disciplinary nature, they are interrelated through their cultural roots. "Though perhaps individually prompted by such changes," Kimball continues, "these recent developments exhibit a collective pattern that is shaped by the historical and cultural context in which they occur." It is from this that he concludes the influence of pragmatism which he detects "lies in providing a deeply-rooted rationalization, or intellectual justification, for recent changes and reforms in liberal education." This might not be called "pragmatic" or be considered to be a coherent philosophy, as pragmatism may be. Yet he suggests that pragmatism "provides an intellectual framework within which recent developments in liberal education 'make sense during the current era.'"[128]

In talking of pragmatism as being an intellectual framework influencing the evolution of liberal education, Kimball is clearly not referring to pragmatism in the strict sense of a rigorous philosophical system. He employs the word in a more ideological sense that, when applied to education, means an education that is shaped with an eye to its general usefulness and general viability. In a final chapter, Kimball elaborates on the recent developments he sees as exhibiting the collective pattern to which he refers. In all, he identifies seven such developments, adding that, "pragmatism provides an intellectual and historical framework within which these developments collectively 'make sense.' It is in this regard that pragmatism is exerting the most widespread and significant influence on liberal education. It might even be said that pragmatism is now infusing liberal education."[129]

Presenting the seven developments in summary form constitutes an appropriate end point to this overview. They are as follows: First, an affirmation of multiculturalism both in student body and in curriculum, based on a consensus justified by the pragmatic view that "belief, meaning, and knowledge depend on perspective and context."[130] Second, a new attention being given to values and service in liberal education, reflecting "the pragmatic capacity to address, if not to reconcile, the tension between fact and value."[131] Third, an emphasis on community and citizenship, drawing on the "pragmatic notions of community and communal conceptions of truth and knowledge."[132] Fourth, a similar emphasis on general education—as seen in hundreds of colleges and universities in the 1980s and 1990s—to the one that marked the impact of pragmatism in experimental higher education back at the beginnings of pragmatism in the 1920s and 1930s. Fifth, a closer cooperation between schools and colleges (including the "middle colleges" idea), reflecting Dewey's view that divisions among educational levels are potentially mischievous. Sixth, a reconceptualization of teaching in terms of learning and inquiry, of which Kimball says, "consequently, the sixth development, like the fifth, stems from the idea that all learning and inquiry follow an experimental pattern. The liberal arts teacher should stimulate and facilitate the student's learning and cannot, in fact, teach in the traditional sense of conveying information."[133] And seventh, assessment in liberal education. This reflects the view of pragmatism that testing of hypotheses and solutions is integral to the cycle of reflective inquiry.

Those responding to Kimball's thesis are noncommittal on whether they agree with him or not that pragmatism is catching up with liberal education. Neither do they address the question of whether we may be on the verge of a redefinition that challenges the parameters set down in the mid-nineteenth century debate between the *Edinburgh Review*, representing the forces of the moderns, and Oxford University, representing the ancients. Not that it matters, for the debate will take its course. And it is into this debate that we now enter more directly in what may be seen as a search for guiding principles to imbue our curriculum theorizing with a greater degree of coherence. In doing so it must be borne in mind that, while the education of the young takes place in schools and colleges, these are not the only places of education. What is educationally desirable, moreover, may not always be attainable within formal educational institutions. At the same time, an understanding of the purposes of education is essential in reflecting upon the work of schools and colleges, for it is on the basis of such understandings that the policies and practices affecting them take shape.

NOTES

1. Carl Bereiter, "Liberal Education in a Knowledge Society," in *Liberal Education in a Knowledge Society*, ed. Barry Smith (Chicago: Open Court, 2002), 11.

2. See, for example, Mortimer J. Adler, *The Paideia Proposal: An Educational Manifesto* (New York: Macmillan Publishing Co., Inc., 1982), and Jacques Maritain, *Education at the Crossroads* (New Haven, CT.: Yale University Press, 1943), who treat liberal education in the context of schooling without departing from core principles. Adler made a special effort to relate these principles to the reform of public schooling in the United States as we entered the closing decades of the twentieth century.

3. Cited in W. B. Carnochan, *The Battleground of the Curriculum: Liberal Education and American Experience* (Stanford: Stanford University Press, 1993), 115.

4. Bruce A. Kimball, *Orators and Philosophers: A History of the Idea of Liberal Education*, 2nd ed. (New York: College Entrance Examination Board, 1995). This is an

expanded edition of the original published in 1986 by Teachers College Press. This work remains an authoritative source on the subject.

5. See, for example, Nancy Stewart Green, "Training for Work and Survival," in *Cultures of Curriculum*, by Pamela Bolotin Joseph, Stephanie Luster Bravmann, Mark A. Windschitl, Edward R. Mikel, and Nancy Stewart Green (Mahwah, NJ: Lawrence Erlbaum Associates, Inc., 2000), 29–49.

6. While it was hardly the original cause, the highly influential report of the U.S. Department of Education *A Nation at Risk* (1983) undoubtedly added to such a perception.

7. Harry S. Broudy, *The Uses of Schooling* (New York: Routledge, 1988), 9–10.

8. Harold Henderson and Barry Smith, "Introduction: A New Definition of Liberal Education," in *Liberal Education in a Knowledge Society*, ed. Barry Smith (Chicago: Open Court, 2002), 1.

9. For an earlier and more extended treatment of this general point, see D. G. Mulcahy, *Curriculum and Policy in Irish Post-Primary Education* (Dublin: Institute of Public Administration, 1981), 73–97.

10. John Henry Cardinal Newman, *The Idea of a University Defined and Illustrated*, ed. Charles Frederick Harrold (New York: Longmans, Green and Co., 1947), 107.

11. P. H. Hirst and R. S. Peters, *The Logic of Education* (London: Routledge and Kegan Paul, 1970).

12. John Henry Cardinal Newman, *An Essay in Aid of a Grammar of Assent*, ed. Charles Frederick Harrold (New York: Longmans, Green and Co., 1947), 42.

13. Harry S. Broudy, B. Othanel Smith, and Joe R. Burnett, *Democracy and Excellence in American Secondary Education: A Study in Curriculum Theory* (Chicago: Rand McNally & Company, 1964), 36; and Nel Noddings, *The Challenge to Care in Schools* (New York: Teachers College Press, 1992), 34.

14. See Arthur D. Roberts and Gordon Cawelti, *Redefining General Education in the American High School* (Alexandria, VA: The Association for Supervision and Curriculum Development, 1984).

15. Robert M. Hutchins, *The Higher Learning in America* (New Haven: Yale University Press, 1936), 59–87; Robert M. Hutchins, *The Great Conversation: The Substance of a Liberal Education*, vol. 1, *Great Books of the Western World*, ed. Robert M. Hutchins (Chicago: Encyclopedia Britannica, 1952); and Michael J. Oakeshott, *The Voice of Liberal Learning: Michael Oakeshott on Education*, ed. Timothy Fuller (New Haven: Yale University Press, 1989). For an account of the Great Books program at the University of Chicago, in which Hutchins co-taught alongside Mortimer Adler, see *The Great Ideas: The University of Chicago and the Ideal of a Liberal Education*, An Exhibition in the Department of Special Collections, the University of Chicago Library, May 1, 2002 – September 6, 2002, at www.lib.uchicago.edu/e/spcl/excat/ideas3.html (accessed July 25, 2007). On this point, see also Carnochan, *The Battleground of the Curriculum*, 79–87.

16. Harvard University, *General Education in a Free Society* (Cambridge, MA.: Harvard University Press, 1945). On this point, see also Carnochan, *The Battleground of the Curriculum*, 88–99.

17. Broudy, Smith, and Burnett, *Democracy and Excellence*.

18. *Aristotle on Education: Extracts from the Ethics and Politics*, trans. and ed. John Burnet (Cambridge: Cambridge University Press, 1903), 108. It is an indication of

the many interpretations of liberal education that the meaning of 'liberal' even in this context is seen in different ways. See, for example, Jacques Maritain, "Thomist Views on Education," in *Modern Philosophies and Education*, vol. 1, 54th Yearbook of the National Society for the Study of Education, ed. Nelson B. Henry (Chicago: The University of Chicago Press, 1955), 77–83; R. S. Peters, "Ambiguities in Liberal Education and the Problem of its Content," in *Ethics and Educational Policy*, ed. Kenneth A. Strike and Kieran Egan (London: Routledge and Kegan Paul, 1978), 3–21; Mortimer J. Adler, *Reforming Education: The Opening of the American Mind*, ed. Geraldine Van Doren (New York: Macmillan Publishing Co., Inc., 1988), 283; Jane Roland Martin, *Changing the Educational Landscape: Philosophy, Women, and Curriculum* (New York: Routledge, 1994), 181–182; Martha C. Nussbaum, *Cultivating Humanity: A Classical Defense of Reform in Liberal Education* (Cambridge, MA: Harvard University Press, 1997), 293–301; Lars Lovelie and Paul Standish, "Introduction: Bildung and the Idea of a Liberal Education," *Journal of the Philosophy of Education* 36 (2002): 317–340; and James V. Schall, "Liberal Education and 'Social Justice'," in *Liberal Education* 92, no. 4 (2006): 44–47. For a comprehensive historical treatment that draws attention to the many nuances and interpretations of the term 'liberal education' and others related to it, see Kimball, *Orators and Philosophers*, and Sheldon Rothblatt, *Tradition and Change in English Liberal Education* (London: Faber and Faber, 1976).

19. Nussbaum, *Cultivating Humanity*, 297.

20. *The Yale Report of 1828*, Part I, at http://collegiateway.org/reading/yale-report-1828/ (accessed July 25, 2007). Also in G. H. Willis, W. H. Schubert, R. Bullough, C. Kridel, and J. Holton, eds., *The American Curriculum: A Documentary History* (Westport, CT: Greenwood Press, 1993), 27–37. This book makes readily available a valuable collection of original sources relating to the history of curriculum in America.

21. For an interesting discussion of basic education, see Jane Roland Martin, *Educational Metamorphoses: Philosophical Reflections on Identity and Culture* (Lanham, MD: Rowman and Littlefield, 2007), 37–39.

22. See, for example, Carnochan, *The Battleground of the Curriculum*, especially 22–50.

23. This matter is treated more fully in chapter two. For now, it will suffice to refer to this important article which has attracted a good deal of commentary over the years: Timothy Corcoran, "Liberal Studies and Moral Aims: A Critical Survey of Newman's Position," *Thought* 1, no. 1 (June 1926): 54–71.

24. Committee of Ten on Secondary School Studies, *Report* (New York: Published for the National Education Association by the American Book Company, 1894).

25. Commission on the Reorganization of Secondary Education, *Cardinal Principles of Secondary Education* (Washington, D.C.: United States Bureau of Education Bulletin, no. 35, 1918). For a helpful account of the context in which the report was produced, see Herbert M. Kliebard, *The Struggle for the American Curriculum, 1983–1958* (New York: Routledge, 1992), 111–115.

26. One example of a particularly caustic treatment of the *Cardinal Principles* is found in Richard Mitchell, *The Graves of Academe* (Boston: Little, Brown, 1981). It is noteworthy that Nel Noddings has recently expressed a more supportive stance. See Nel Noddings, *Happiness and Education* (Cambridge: Cambridge University Press, 2003), 77.

27. On the significance of the educational thought of Herbert Spencer, see the important contributions of Kieran Egan in *The Educated Mind: How Cognitive Tools Shape Our Understanding* (Chicago: The University of Chicago Press, 1997) and *Getting It Wrong from the Beginning: Our Progressivist Inheritance from Herbert Spencer, John Dewey, and Jean Piaget* (New Haven: Yale University Press, 2002).

28. Reference here is to the second edition, which appeared ten years after the first. Florence Stratemeyer, Hamden L. Forkner, Margaret G. McKim, and A. Harry Passow, *Developing a Curriculum for Modern Living* (New York: Bureau of Publications, Teachers College, Columbia University, 1957).

29. The notion of the core curriculum, which is still with us, received a good deal of attention in the years following the publication of *General Education in a Free Society*. The work of Harold Alberty was particularly important in this regard. See, for example, Harold Alberty, "Designing Programs to Meet the Common Needs of Youth," in Willis et al., *The American Curriculum*, 335–353.

30. Harvard University, *General Education in a Free Society*.

31. It was a different matter in the developing world. For an account of the times, see Philip H. Coombs, *The World Educational Crisis* (New York: Oxford University Press, 1968).

32. Noddings, *Happiness and Education*, 74.

33. See Arthur E. Bestor, *Educational Wastelands: The Retreat from Learning in Our Public Schools* (Urbana, IL: University of Illinois Press, 1953), and Hyman G. Rickover, *Education and Freedom* (New York: Dutton, 1959).

34. For a fuller account, see J. Dan Marshall, James T. Sears, Louise Anderson Allen, Patrick A. Roberts, and W. H. Schubert, *Turning Points in Curriculum: A Contemporary American Memoir* (Upper Saddle River, NJ: Pearson Education Inc., 2007), especially 34–52.

35. Jerome S. Bruner, *The Process of Education* (New York: Vintage Press, 1960).

36. Jerome S. Bruner, *The Relevance of Education* (New York: Norton, 1971).

37. See, for example, Broudy, Smith, and Burnett, *Democracy and Excellence*, and Philip H. Phenix, *Realms of Meaning* (New York: McGraw Hill, 1964).

38. See, for example, Adler, *The Paideia Proposal*.

39. See, for example, Martin, *Changing the Educational Landscape*.

40. See, for example, R. S. Peters, *Ethics and Education* (London: Allen and Unwin, 1966), and P. H. Hirst, *Knowledge and the Curriculum* (London: Routledge and Kegan Paul, 1974). It should be added that Hirst subsequently recanted the theory of a liberal education espoused in *Knowledge and the Curriculum*. See P. H. Hirst, "Education, Knowledge and Practices," in *Beyond Liberal Education: Essays in Honour of Paul H. Hirst*, ed. Robin Barrow and Patricia White (London: Routledge, 1993), 184–199.

41. See, for example, Ernest L. Boyer and Arthur Levine, *A Quest for Common Learning* (Washington, DC: Carnegie Foundation for the Advancement of Teaching, 1981); Ernest L. Boyer, *College: The Undergraduate Experience in America* (New York: Harper & Row, 1987); Allan Bloom, *The Closing of the American Mind* (New York: Simon & Schuster, 1987); Oakeshott, *The Voice of Liberal Learning*. See also Adler, *Reforming Education*, in which Adler takes serious issue with Bloom.

42. The confusion created in the labeling of this book raises questions about the competence of the College Board to be involved in conducting examinations on the

scale it does, or any scale for that matter. I offer my best shot at referencing it. The book consists of an introduction and a substantial lead essay by Kimball followed by some twenty-four essays commenting on Kimball's essay. Robert Orrill is executive editor and has written a preface. See Bruce A. Kimball, "Toward Pragmatic Liberal Education," in *The Condition of American Liberal Education*, ed. Robert Orrill (New York: College Entrance Examinations Board, 1995), 3–122.

43. One notable exception is the work of John White. See, for example, J. White, *Education and the Good Life* (New York: Teachers College Press, 1991). A classic treatment of the role of objectives in curriculum theorizing is Ralph W. Tyler, *Basic Principles of Curriculum and Instruction* (Chicago: University of Chicago Press, 1949). See also Decker F. Walker and Jonas F. Soltis, *Curriculum and Aims* (New York: Teachers College Press, 1997).

44. Noddings, *Happiness and Education*, 74–93.

45. Noddings, *Happiness and Education*, 76.

46. Carnochan, *The Battleground of the Curriculum*, 115, 117–19, 126. See also W. B. Carnochan, "On the 'Purposes' of Liberal Education," in *The Condition of American Liberal Education*, ed. Robert Orrill, 182–188.

47. This said, important contributions to the considerations of aims and curriculum and the interplay between them, accompanied by a discernible commitment to investment in education in many countries, was a feature of a good deal of curriculum theorizing in the post–World War II environment. See, for example, Broudy, Smith, and Burnett, *Democracy and Excellence*; Phenix, *Realms of Meaning*. Important works by English scholars of the same period include Peters, *Ethics and Education*; R. F. Dearden, *The Philosophy of Primary Education* (London: Routledge and Kegan Paul, 1968); Hirst and Peters, *The Logic of Education*; J. White, *Towards a Compulsory Curriculum* (London: Routledge and Kegan Paul, 1973); Hirst, *Knowledge and the Curriculum*; and Robin Barrow, *Common Sense and the Curriculum* (London: George Allen and Unwin, Ltd., 1976).

48. Noddings, *The Challenge to Care in Schools*. See also Noddings, *Happiness and Education*, and Nel Noddings, *Critical Lessons: What Our Schools Should Teach* (Cambridge: Cambridge University Press, 2006).

49. Noddings, *The Challenge to Care in Schools*, 28.

50. Noddings, *The Challenge to Care in Schools*, 46.

51. See Franklin Bobbit, *How to Make a Curriculum* (Boston: Houghton Mifflin Company, 1924).

52. Noddings, *The Challenge to Care in Schools*, 46–47.

53. Noddings, *The Challenge to Care in Schools*, 47.

54. Caution is needed on several fronts in dealing with the issue of caring. See D. G. Mulcahy and Ronnie Casella, "Violence and Caring in School and Society," *Educational Studies* 37, no. 3 (June 2005): 244–255. See also Audrey Thompson, "Caring in Context: Four Feminist Theories on Gender and Education," *Curriculum Inquiry* 33, no. 1 (Spring 2003): 9–65.

55. Joseph L. DeVitis, Robert W. Johns, and Douglas J. Simpson, "Introduction," in *To Serve and Learn: The Spirit of Community in Liberal Education*, ed. Joseph L. DeVitis, Robert W. Johns, and Douglas J. Simpson (New York: Peter Lang, 1998), 6–18.

56. DeVitis, Johns, and Simpson, "Introduction," 9.

57. DeVitis, Johns, and Simpson, "Introduction," 10.

30 Chapter 1

58. DeVitis, Johns, and Simpson, "Introduction," 13. The reference to Guarasci is to Richard Guarasci, "In Search of an Ethical Voice," *Pulteney St. Survey* 21 (Winter 1994): 2.

59. DeVitis, Johns, and Simpson, "Introduction," 13.

60. DeVitis, Johns, and Simpson, "Introduction," 13.

61. Nussbaum, *Cultivating Humanity*, 294.

62. Jane Roland Martin, *Coming of Age in Academe: Rekindling Women's Hopes and Reforming the Academy* (New York: Routledge, 2000), 139.

63. Nussbaum, *Cultivating Humanity*, 301.

64. In passing, it should be said that DeVitis, Johns, and Simpson do not present an argument so much as an articulate statement of their belief in the contribution of service-learning to liberal education.

65. See Oren W. Davis with Jennifer Dodge, "Liberationist Theology through Community Service-Learning at Trinity College of Vermont," in *To Serve and Learn: The Spirit of Community in Liberal Education*, ed. Joseph L. DeVitis, Robert W. Johns, and Douglas J. Simpson (New York: Peter Lang, 1998), 92–101.

66. Davis with Dodge, "Liberationist Theology," 93. As understood by Dewey, meeting actual community need is a condition of students being acquainted with "everyday social application." See DeVitis, Johns, and Simpson, "Introduction," 10.

67. Davis with Dodge, "Liberationist Theology," 93–94.

68. Davis with Dodge, "Liberationist Theology," 94–95.

69. Davis with Dodge, "Liberationist Theology," 97.

70. Davis with Dodge, "Liberationist Theology," 97.

71. Davis with Dodge, "Liberationist Theology," 97.

72. Davis with Dodge, "Liberationist Theology," 97.

73. See DeVitis, Johns, and Simpson, "Introduction," 10.

74. Davis with Dodge, "Liberationist Theology," 98.

75. Ira Shor, *Empowering Education: Critical Teaching for Social Change* (Chicago: University of Chicago Press, 1992).

76. Henry Giroux, *Pedagogy and the Politics of Hope* (Boulder, CO: Westview Press, 1997), 3–34.

77. Henry Giroux, "Education Incorporated?" in *The Critical Pedagogy Reader*, ed. Antonia Darder, Marta Baltodano, and Rodolfo D. Torres (New York: Routledge-Falmer, 2003), 119–125.

78. Giroux, *Pedagogy and the Politics of Hope*, 10.

79. Giroux, *Pedagogy and the Politics of Hope*, 14.

80. Giroux, *Pedagogy and the Politics of Hope*, 21.

81. Giroux, *Pedagogy and the Politics of Hope*, 23.

82. Giroux, *Pedagogy and the Politics of Hope*, 24.

83. Pamela Bolotin Joseph, "Connecting to the Canon," in *Cultures of Curriculum* by Pamela Bolotin Joseph, Stephanie Luster Bravmann, Mark A. Windschitl, Edward R. Mikel, and Nancy Stewart Green (Mahwah, NJ: Lawrence Erlbaum Associates, Inc., 2000), 61.

84. Henry Giroux, "Modernism, Postmodernism, and Feminism: Rethinking the Boundaries of Educational Discourse," in *Postmodernism, Feminism, and Cultural Politics*, ed. Henry A. Giroux (Albany, NY: State University of New York Press, 1991), 52.

85. Giroux, *Pedagogy and the Politics of Hope*, 28.

86. In this connection, see David C. Berliner and Bruce J. Biddle, *The Manufactured Crisis: Myths, Fraud, and the Attack on America's Public Schools* (New York: Basic Books, 1995), especially 164–168.

87. Bush-led governments at the state and federal levels have been particularly active in this regard. President George H. W. Bush twice presented to Congress his *America 2000* bill, which included elaborate proposals for financial aid in support of private school choice, without success. While the proposal for private school choice failed to pass Congress, shortly after Jeb Bush became Governor of Florida, a broadly similar plan was introduced in that state as the first statewide plan in the nation. At the same time, proposals for private school choice met with widespread rejection in public referenda across the country. Privatization measures at the federal level were finally introduced in the *No Child Left Behind* (NCLB) act signed into law by President George W. Bush in early 2002. Although they were reportedly toned down for fear of rejection in Congress, these privatization measures nonetheless now have statutory force. See Alfie Kohn, "NCLB and the Effort to Privatize Public Education," in *Many Children Left Behind*, ed. Deborah Meier and George Wood (Boston: Beacon Press, 2004), 87, and Alex Molnar, "What the Market Can't Provide," in *The Critical Pedagogy Reader*, ed. Antonia Darder, Marta Baltodano, and Rodolfo D. Torres (New York: RoutledgeFalmer, 2003), 126–141.

88. W. H. Schubert, "THE BIG CURRICULUM," *Journal of Curriculum and Pedagogy* 3, no. 1 (2006): 100–103, and Grace Roosevelt, "The Triumph of the Market and the Decline of Liberal Education: Implications for Civic Life," *Teachers College Record* 108, no. 7 (July 2006): 1404–1423.

89. Giroux, "Education Incorporated?," 120.

90. To what extent schools serve as forces for democracy rather than autocracy has itself been questioned. See, for example, W. H. Schubert, *Curriculum: Perspective, Paradigm, and Possibility* (New York: Macmillan Publishing Company, 1986), 417, where Schubert's observations may well have a bearing on the puzzle over the disenchantment of schoolgoers with schooling.

91. Giroux, "Education Incorporated?," 122.

92. Giroux, "Education Incorporated?," 125.

93. Much the same may be said of the work of Yusef Waghid in the area of citizenship education. See Yusef Waghid, "Action as an Educational Virtue: Toward a Different Understanding of Democratic Citizenship Education," *Educational Theory* 55, no. 3 (August 2005): 323–342, and Yusef Waghid, "University Education and Deliberation: In Defence of Practical Reasoning," *Higher Education* 51, no. 3 (April 2006): 315–328.

94. Shor, *Empowering Education*, 15.

95. Shor, *Empowering Education*, 32. Other such traditionalists could include Allan Bloom, Dianne Ravitch, and Chester Finn.

96. Shor, *Empowering Education*, 32.

97. Patrick J. Finn, *Literacy with an Attitude: Educating Working-Class Children in Their Own Self-Interest* (Albany, NY: State University of New York Press, 1999), x–xi.

98. Shor, *Empowering Education*, 35.

99. Shor, *Empowering Education*, 35–36.

100. Shor, *Empowering Education*, 55.

101. See Broudy, *The Uses of Schooling*, 103–106, and Broudy, Smith, and Burnett, *Democracy and Excellence*, 233–236.

102. Shor, *Empowering Education*, 55.

103. Richard Pring, *Knowledge and Schooling* (London: Open Books, 1976), 88.

104. Shor, *Empowering Education*, 144.

105. Shor, *Empowering Education*, 145.

106. Shor, *Empowering Education*, 146.

107. Shor, *Empowering Education*, 188.

108. Shor, *Empowering Education*, 255.

109. Shor, *Empowering Education*, 255.

110. Shor, *Empowering Education*, 247.

111. Shor, *Empowering Education*, 181. The reference to Schniedewind and Davidson is to Nancy Schniedewind and Ellen Davidson, *Cooperative Learning, Cooperative Lives: A Sourcebook of Learning Activities for Building a Peaceful World* (Dubuque, IA: William C. Brown, 1987).

112. Bereiter, "Liberal Education," 11.

113. Bereiter, "Liberal Education," 12.

114. Bereiter, "Liberal Education," 16.

115. Bereiter, "Liberal Education," 18.

116. Bereiter, "Liberal Education," 19.

117. Bereiter, "Liberal Education," 25.

118. Bereiter, "Liberal Education," 27.

119. Bereiter, "Liberal Education," 28.

120. Shor, *Empowering Education*, 184. The reference to Solorzano is to Daniel Solorzano, "Teaching and Social Change: Reflections on a Freirian Approach in a College Classroom," *Teaching Sociology* 17 (April 1989): 218–225.

121. Bereiter, "Liberal Education," 30.

122. Bereiter, "Liberal Education," 30–31.

123. Joseph Dunne, *Back to the Rough Ground* (Notre Dame, IN: University of Notre Dame Press, 1993), and Hirst, "Education, Knowledge and Practices." See also Joseph Dunne, "What's the Good of Education?" in *The RoutledgeFalmer Reader in the Philosophy of Education*, ed. Wilfred Carr (London: RoutledgeFalmer, 2005), 145–160.

124. P. H. Hirst, "A Response to Wilfred Carr's 'Philosophy and Education'," in *Journal of Philosophy of Education* 39, no. 4 (November 2005): 617.

125. J. White, "Conclusion," in *Rethinking the School Curriculum: Values, Aims and Purposes*, ed. J. White (London: RoutledgeFalmer, 2004), 184. See also J. White, *Education and the End of Work: A New Philosophy of Work and Learning* (London: Cassell, 1997), especially 69–96.

126. While actually describing it as utopian, MacIntyre himself appears to adopt a remarkably traditionalist stance in regard to the subjects of the curriculum. See Alasdair MacIntyre and Joseph Dunne, "Alasdair MacIntyre on Education: In Dialogue with Joseph Dunne," in *Education and Practice: Upholding the Integrity of Teaching and Learning*, ed. Joseph Dunne and Padraig Hogan (Malden, MA: Blackwell Publishing, 2004), 13–14.

127. Kimball, "Toward Pragmatic Liberal Education." There is yet another dimension to the question of education in the knowledge society, namely, the impor-

tance of ensuring continued open access to the frontiers of knowledge. On this point, see John Willinsky, "Just Say Know? Schooling the Knowledge Society," *Educational Theory* 55, no. 1 (February 2005): 97–111.

128. Bruce A. Kimball, "Introduction," in *The Condition of American Liberal Education*, ed. Robert Orrill (New York: College Entrance Examinations Board, 1995), xxii-xxiii.

129. Kimball, "Toward Pragmatic Liberal Education," 89.

130. Kimball, "Toward Pragmatic Liberal Education," 89.

131. Kimball, "Toward Pragmatic Liberal Education," 90–91.

132. Kimball, "Toward Pragmatic Liberal Education," 91.

133. Kimball, "Toward Pragmatic Liberal Education," 97.

2

Newman: Liberal Education as Cultivation of the Intellect

No writer on liberal education has had more of an influence on the discourse and the justifications presented to support the idea than John Henry Newman. Newman's enormous impact on the discussion of a liberal education is due in part to the skillful manner in which he articulates his idealization, his language being ornate and persuasive.[1] The concepts Newman uses and the themes he elaborates still resonate today[2] as we attempt to cope with the challenges that arise in planning and implementing programs of liberal or general education in schools and colleges. This is so whether one is debating the nature and structure of knowledge, the requirements of the core curriculum, the social and personal needs of students, or the crucial roles of professors and teachers. The ideas and theories introduced and elaborated by Newman and the effortless and compelling manner in which he expresses them are intuitive and commonsensical.[3] There are those today, as has always been the case with Newman, who forcefully question his stance.[4] It is not surprising, nonetheless, that it has been said that *Idea of a University* "remains the singlemost influential book on the meaning of a university in the English language."[5] Newman's ideas, as if embedded in our consciousness, continue to shape both our conceptualization of the issues and the language and content of the debate around liberal education as the central purpose of education.[6] Yet, I shall argue that, in the final analysis, Newman's position on liberal education has been misrepresented even by him.

Before getting to this, I shall first present overlapping accounts of Newman's theory of knowledge and his theory of liberal education. I shall then turn to his treatment of issues related to teaching and learning, with particular reference to discipline of mind, the personal influence of the teacher, character formation, and moral and religious education. All of these occupy an important place in Newman's educational thought. Particular attention will be given to an aspect of Newman's work that has largely gone unnoticed. This I once termed "Newman's Retreat from a Liberal Education,"[7] and it has profound implications for any theory of liberal education, not least Newman's own.

LIBERAL EDUCATION AND THE NATURE OF KNOWLEDGE

Newman writes about liberal education in the university setting. This is understandable. Much of his life was spent at Oxford, first as an undergraduate student and later as a fellow and tutor of Oriel College and as a member of the Anglican ministry. Deeply involved in the intellectual life of his times, Newman took a particular interest in religious matters and wrote widely on religious subjects.[8] A leading member of the Oxford movement critical of aspects of the teachings and practices of the Church of England, he converted to Catholicism in 1845. This led to his departure from Oxford in his mid-forties. Following this he moved to Birmingham, where he lived most of the rest of his life as a member of a small community of priests at the Oratory. A major disruption to this pattern was the six years or so in the mid-1850s during which Newman served as the first Rector of the new Catholic University of Ireland in Dublin.[9] It was to prove a turbulent time in Newman's life,[10] and while the venture was personally painful and less productive than he would have wished for, it was also the occasion for his writing of the classic *Idea of a University* and the lesser-known *University Sketches*.

Once described as the perfect handling of a theory,[11] *Idea of a University* is perhaps best known and most widely sought out today for its powerful statement of the nature and value of a liberal education as a core element in a university education. This being so, the reader might be surprised to find that much of the work is devoted to a defense of the place of religion in a university course of studies.[12] In support of his argument for the inclusion of religion, Newman sets out at some length his theory of the nature and structure of knowledge. In addition to supporting his argument for the study of religion in the university, it is this theory that also lays the basis for many of the claims Newman makes on behalf of a liberal education. This is not to suggest that his defense of liberal education was a casual addition. On the contrary, the argument was fashioned at least in part in response to practical developments. These include the rise of the University of London and its elective curriculum offerings and the hotly contested debate in the *Edinburgh Review* regarding the relevance of an Oxford University education. Newman's *Idea of a University* then, in much the same way as Matthew

Arnold's *Culture and Anarchy*, was not formed in isolation from an ongoing debate or merely in response to the new responsibilities cast upon Newman in undertaking his duties for the Catholic University of Ireland.

For Newman, liberal education consists in the ability to think analytically and critically and in the possession of broad knowledge and deep understanding. The intellectual formation such education provides, he claimed, enables one to see things in perspective, to relate them to one another, and to gauge their value. Once the intellect has been trained to "have a connected view of things," moreover, it "makes itself felt in the good sense, sobriety of thought, reasonableness, candour, self-command, and steadiness of view which characterizes it."[13] Those who have no such view are possessed with a single object and take an exaggerated view of it, making it a standard measure of all things. Some, lacking any measure at all, are blown hither and thither, unable to decide in the face of choice and dependent on others for their every course of action. Never, thankfully, is the cultivated intellect that comes with a liberal education at such a loss.

The connatural qualities of a liberal education to which Newman refers take the form of a delicate taste; a candid, equitable dispassionate mind; and a noble and courteous bearing.[14] Nowhere are these more memorably described than in Newman's celebrated portrait of the gentleman, of whom it is almost a definition to say that "he is one who never inflicts pain."[15] Careful not to offend, the gentleman is considerate toward friends and adversaries alike and ever so modest and unassuming about his achievements. His outlook is philosophical and mature, and he is always "patient, forbearing, and resigned."[16] Toward the weak-minded and dull he is indulgent; too wise to be a dogmatist or fanatic, he is ever tolerant of religious convictions.[17] He is up to the mark in literature and the arts, in history, and in public affairs.[18] Even if the characterization may seem a little quaint, the gentleman is no mere relic of an age gone by. He exhibits in many ways the virtues of mind and spirit, of understanding and equanimity, that James Freedman idealizes and wishes to preserve in liberal education in our own day.[19]

While Newman clearly understands liberal education as a "process of training, by which the intellect . . . is disciplined for its own sake," he also talks of it in terms of its outcome or product. "Liberal Education," he writes, "viewed in itself, is simply the cultivation of the intellect, as such, and its object is nothing more or less than intellectual excellence." Somewhat at a loss to explain readily what he means by "cultivation of the intellect" or "intellectual excellence," Newman considers the terms 'genius,' 'wisdom,' and 'knowledge' as unsuitable for one reason or another. Genius is rejected because it belongs more to "raw material" than to excellence, which is the result of exercise and training. Wisdom is rejected because of its direct relation to human conduct. And knowledge, even though it expresses purely intellectual ideas, is not a state or quality of intellect.[20]

Rejecting these words as inappropriate, Newman has recourse to a usage more customary in his day to express the idea of intellectual excellence, and he calls into use such terms as philosophy, philosophical knowledge, enlargement of mind, and illumination.[21] Even then, he uses these terms individually infrequently, fearing perhaps that the one carries a nuance lacking in another.[22] Furthermore, he specifically states that he uses them to convey with regard to intellectual proficiency or perfection an idea corresponding to health as it is used in connection with physical nature or virtue as used with reference to moral nature. Especially important to Newman's terminology here is a number of distinctions he draws when speaking of knowledge, philosophical knowledge, and enlargement of mind.

The term 'knowledge' does not speak to a state or quality of intellect when it is understood in its "ordinary" or "vague" sense to denote factual knowledge or mere learning.[23] So Newman turns to a richer concept with which the word may also be associated, one that suggests reflection and one with which the idea of liberal education is widely associated. In its richer meaning, knowledge means "Philosophy or, in an extended sense of the word, Science."[24] Here science—or the sciences—is understood as the forms of understanding that "serve to transfer our knowledge from the custody of memory to the surer and more abiding protection of philosophy."[25] The intellect of man, Newman writes, "perceives in sights and sounds something beyond them. . . . It assigns phenomena to a general law, qualities to a subject, acts to a principle, and effects to a cause." In a word, he continues, it philosophizes. For that is what is meant by science or philosophy: it is "this habit of *viewing*, as it may be called, the objects which sense conveys to the mind."[26]

The implications of the reflective or active connotations associated with Newman's richer concept of knowledge or the sciences on which he draws in elaborating his idea of liberal education are considerable. But before examining them more fully, it may be helpful to look at Newman's general theory of the nature and structure of knowledge and the relationship he envisages between knowledge and truth. Even before Newman began writing *Idea of a University*, he took issue with the views of education and religion espoused by the University of London as it began to make its mark on higher education from the 1820s onward.[27] In departing from the idea of a set course of studies and a close relationship between religion and education, London was not merely defining higher education anew in an age of useful knowledge forged by science and the Industrial Revolution. It was threatening the *status quo* in higher education on both sides of the Atlantic. It was also challenging core beliefs held by Newman, not least his beliefs surrounding the place of religion in the university. Dealing with the religious challenge posed by the University of London was therefore central to Newman's response to London. His argument would be straightforward: no one subject could be omitted from a course of studies without disrupting the circle of the sciences and undermining the integrity of the university.[28]

In Newman's notion of the unity and structure of knowledge, the various branches of knowledge, which for him chiefly include theology, literature, and science,[29] are viewed as interrelated. This is essential to his idea of liberal education, and it requires the student not only to possess factual knowledge but to have knowledge of the relations among the various branches of knowledge. Knowledge is knowledge of things and since all knowledge is interrelated, the greater our knowledge, Newman argues, the greater our knowledge of the relative value of things. In order to arrive at a knowledge of the relative value of things as a basis for good judgment, moreover, knowledge must be certain and incontrovertible. Fortunately, in the sciences or academic disciplines we possess such knowledge and so, as he treats of it in *Idea of a University*, the sciences are an essential component of liberal education.[30] Other things being equal, the greater one's knowledge of the different sciences the closer one approaches the ideal of liberal education.[31]

Closely allied to his concept of the unity of knowledge is Newman's view of truth, and it plays an important role in justifying for Newman the pursuit of knowledge itself. Truth serves both as the measure of knowledge and the proper object of the intellect.[32] The object of knowledge, Newman writes, is truth, by which he means facts and their relations. All that exists forms one complex fact comprised of a number of particular facts which, as portions of a whole, are interrelated with one another. Knowledge is the apprehension of these facts in themselves and in their interrelations. Taken together they form one subject, with no real limits between one part and any other.[33]

For Newman, the unity of the sciences or academic disciplines does not derive from shared concepts or any commonality in their methods of investigation and proof. In fact, the various sciences can and do differ from each other in their methods, and such variance sets them off from each other as distinct disciplines. Theology, whose method of inquiry is deductive, for example, differs both in its content and in its method of investigation from physics, which proceeds inductively.[34] It is from their common object of investigation—the truth, that one large system or complex fact, which in turn owes its unity to God, its creator—that the unity of the sciences is derived.

The concern of the sciences is with arranging and classifying facts, reducing separate phenomena under common laws, and tracing effect to cause. This being so, knowledge drawn from the sciences, Newman maintains in *Idea of a University*—striking a chord that will come to haunt him—is never brought home to one quite so forcefully as that gained by the senses. Yet scientific knowledge goes beyond sense knowledge by imparting order and system to a collection of unrelated facts. At the same time, the sciences facilitate the communication of knowledge to others. However, for the very reason that the sciences assist in the search for knowledge, by presenting to the mind but one aspect of the truth at a time, they are also subject to a severe limitation. Each science may possess a piece of the truth insofar as its disciplinary boundaries extend but that piece is not the whole truth. If the sciences are to present the whole truth, they need to complement one another for "they all belong to one and the same circle of objects." They are all interconnected and, as mere aspects of things, they are incomplete in themselves and for their own purposes. On both accounts, therefore, they both need and serve each other. Conversely, the omission of any one science or any one view of a thing makes the attainment of the entire truth impossible.[35]

This central fact points to the problem with the University of London: because it omitted the study of religion from its curriculum, it could not present the whole truth to its students. On this ground alone, the very integrity of the university is brought into question. Insofar as liberal education is dependent upon the exposure of the student to the full circle of the sciences, both the liberal education ideal itself and the educational formation of the student are jeopardized by any such omission.

We have seen that for Newman scientific or philosophical knowledge is possible because of our capacity to go beyond what is presented in sense knowledge and construct laws and generalizations from particulars. When we do this with the factual or particular knowledge we receive from the senses, we are being philosophical. We are enlarging the mind by transforming factual knowledge into scientific, organized, or philosophical knowledge. But this is not Newman's full account. By way of elaboration, he asserts that, while mere knowledge is a condition of enlargement of mind, it is not the only condition.[36] In order for enlargement to follow there must also be a "digestion of what we receive, into the substance of our previous state of thought." But "when this analytical, distributive, harmonizing process is away, the mind experiences no enlargement"; it is not enlightened or illuminated.[37]

Not only is this point consistently maintained by proponents of a liberal education but, Ian Ker emphasizes, for Newman the ability to think is the core element in his idea of a liberal education.[38] The notion of digestion or analysis is central to Newman's concept of intelligence and his understanding of how the mind grows and develops, and it remains so as he elaborates on his concept of philosophy as it relates to philosophical knowledge or a philosophical habit of mind. In doing so, Newman introduces yet another concept: the idea of philosophy as the architectonic science or the science of sciences,[39] referred to in Idea of a University as "the arbiter of all truth."[40] Here we find the "comprehension of the bearings of one science on another, and the use of each to each, and the location and limitation and adjustment and due appreciation of them all, one with another."[41] In A. Dwight Culler's account of Newman's idea of the architectonic science, it is the "recombination" of all the sciences, which "is not the same as all the sciences taken together but is a science distinct from them and yet in some sense embodying the materials of them all." It is a sort of *"tertium quid* of the intellectual world."[42] With philosophy and the philosophical habit of mind understood as an architectonic science, then, the task of liberal or philosophical education becomes in part to impart the architectonic science to the student or to have it develop within the student. This done, students may be said to possess that universal form of knowledge by which they come to form the connected view of things. It is a connected view of things, as Ker points out, that is as cognizant of their normative dimensions as of their strictly factual or scientific ones.[43]

It is one thing to possess knowledge in the form of the architectonic science; it is another to employ such knowledge, however. And the idea of a liberal education involves both elements. So the question arises, how can one both possess the architectonic science and also use it? Newman's answer is that knowledge can be considered from two points of view, epistemological and psychological. The one is knowledge conceived in static form, the other is knowledge considered in its living, dynamic form— knowledge become conscious of itself, as it were. With knowledge understood in this dynamic way, through the mind's active engagement with factual knowledge, one can develop the philosophical habit of mind and come to have "a connected view of the old with the new; an insight into the bearing and influence of each part upon every other; without which there is no whole, and could be no centre. It is the knowledge, not only of things, but of their mutual relations. It is organized, and therefore *living knowledge*."[44] (Italics added.) Thus, can Newman maintain that a liberal education consists in possessing a great store of knowledge and being able to use it analytically and interpretively.

Up to now the kind of knowledge gained in a liberal education has been said by Newman to be philosophical or scientific. An attempt was made by Newman to show in what way such knowledge may be said to be philosophical. As yet it has not been shown what it means for Newman to say that knowledge is liberal, although he does use the terms 'liberal knowledge' and 'philosophical knowledge' somewhat interchangeably. Even so, for Newman the word 'liberal' when used in this connection does carry an added connotation. "That alone is liberal knowledge," he writes, "which stands on its own pretensions, which is independent of sequel, expects no complement, refuses to be *informed* (as it is called) by any end, or absorbed into any art, in order duly to present itself to our contemplation."[45] As can be seen from this, liberal as Newman uses it is not uniquely a quality of intellectual labors. It can also be considered a quality of bodily labors. Study for professional purposes is an instance of the former. Bodily activities, such as participation in the Olympic Games, are or may be an instance of the latter, that is, of physical labors that are liberal in character.[46]

Nor are non-liberal pursuits inferior; they simply belong to the distinct class of the useful. Aristotle conveyed the meaning of the word liberal, Newman maintains, when he said, of possessions "'those rather are useful, which bear fruit; those *liberal, which tend to enjoyment.* By fruitful, I mean, which yield revenue; by enjoyable, where *nothing accrues of consequence beyond the using.'*"[47] Applying this meaning to the word liberal, a liberal education for Newman brings to mind Michael Oakeshott's characterization of education as an intellectual conversation.[48] It is an education in which knowledge ranging across various disciplines is engaged and discussed by students for its own sake and not for any extrinsic benefits. It thereby enables the idea of liberal education, Frank Turner suggests, to transcend religious as well as geographical and cultural boundaries.[49] Knowledge is considered by Newman to be especially liberal, that is to say, sufficient for itself, when and insofar as it is philosophical. The principle of real dignity in knowledge, writes Newman, is its scientific or philosophical quality. It is this that enables it to be an end in itself and to be considered liberal. Newman's own usage of the term reflects this understanding throughout.[50] Moreover, for Newman, knowledge "is an object, in its own nature so really and undeniably good, as to be the compensation of a great deal of thought in the compassing, and a great deal of trouble in the attaining."[51]

The argument by Newman that the person of a cultivated intellect who has a comprehensive knowledge and understanding of the world in which we live and has learned how to think and reason well can successfully turn to a career in the professions with a facility lacking in those who possess no such cultivation has long been accepted by defenders of a liberal education against the charge that it is useless. Persuasive as Newman's argument on this point may be, and the same may also be said on behalf of "the potential of the study of the classics to empower and liberate,"[52] not everyone agrees. This was made very clear in the *Edinburgh Review* even before Newman entered the debate.

When it comes to combating the many objections that arise regarding the usefulness of liberal education, Newman puts forward a twofold defense of his position. Knowledge, he writes, further revealing his Aristotelian leanings,[53] is valuable because of what its very presence in us does for us after the manner of a habit, "even though it be turned to no further account, nor subserve any direct end."[54] Since the object of the intellect is knowledge or truth,[55] its perfection consists in possessing knowledge, that is, in being "philosophical" or "illuminated." With knowledge understood especially as a philosophical habit of mind, as the perfection of the intellect, therefore, it can be said to be a good in itself.[56]

Taking on a challenge that appears to have become more pronounced with the passage of time—namely, justifying a liberal arts education when the demands of the economy and personal advancement seem to call for a more useful form of education—Newman claims to have met the objection that a liberal education is useless. He does so by arguing that the cultivation of the intellect is its own end, and "what has its *end* in itself, has its *use* in itself also." Maintaining a general line of reasoning often dismissed in present-day appeals to quantified proofs, Newman carries the argument still further, stating as a principle that "though the useful is not always good, the good is always useful." Consequently, "if a liberal education be good, it must necessarily be useful too."[57] Since this is necessarily so, Newman is unwilling to deny that a liberal education can be useful. All he wants to deny is that one must be able to indicate its specific vocational or professional applicability to claim that an education is useful, a theme that persists in the debate about the relevance of liberal education into the present. Similarly, Newman does not wish to deny that the kind of education he is advocating has any vocational or professional value. On the contrary, such an education equips a person intellectually to pursue any subject or a range of callings "with an ease, a grace, a versatility, and a success to which another is a stranger. In this sense then, . . . mental culture is emphatically *useful*."[58]

To bolster his position, Newman makes reference throughout his exposition of the mental qualities of the liberally educated person to what he deems analogous physical states.[59] Although nothing may come of it, health of body is good in itself and worth pursuing for itself, but so great are the advantages that accompany good health that one never thinks of it as good alone but as useful also, Newman suggests. Health is prized for what it does as well as for what it is, even though it may be impossible to point out anything specific that it can be said to bring about. As the body may be exercised "with a simple view to its general health," Newman writes, "so may the intellect also be generally exercised in order to its perfect state; and this *is* its cultivation."[60] Again, as health should precede bodily labor, for a person in good health can work as a sick person cannot, so also is general culture of mind the best aid to professional and scientific study. The educated can do what the uneducated are not up to. The person of cultivated intellect, who has learned how to think and reason well, can turn to a professional career in medicine or law with a facility lacking in those who do not have the advantage of such cultivation.[61] Within the confines of the Church, it may be added, as Wulstan Peterburs has pointed out, that Newman also envisioned a special role for an educated laity in contributing on doctrinal matters.[62]

THE ROLE OF THE TEACHER

We have seen that Newman's theory of the unity and structure of knowledge and what might be termed his concept of mind or intelligence are fundamental to his theory of liberal education. Fundamental to his theory of knowledge, in turn, is the Aristotelian view that knowledge is knowledge of the real world, from which Newman concludes it contains objective truth about the world in which we live and the multitude of issues about which we make judgments affecting the course of everyday events. When a program of studies reflects the basic unity and structure of knowledge, it becomes possible for the student to acquire a comprehensive view of reality and knowledge of the relative value of things, essential attributes of the person of a liberal education.[63] The existence of a vast body of knowledge and the mind's capacity to analyze, abstract, and generalize, however, are not sufficient in themselves to ensure a liberal education. As a matter of practical or pedagogical necessity, a liberal education calls for the personal intermediacy of a teacher between the body of knowledge and the student.[64] This personal intermediacy is necessary for two reasons: for presenting the universe of knowledge to the student and for imparting a discipline of mind.

The theory of knowledge presented in *Idea of a University*, emphasizing as it does the interdependency of all branches of knowledge, could be construed to imply that if students are ever to achieve a liberal education they would have to study all of the academic disciplines.[65] While Newman is willing to accept that it is impossible to study all of the disciplines in depth, and even to grant that a liberal education is strictly speaking an ideal to aspire to, he still believes it possible to approximate the ideal.[66] It is to the personal intermediacy of the teacher that Newman turns to ensure that this can be accomplished. In doing so, he highlights the centrality of the teacher to his idea of a university and of a liberal education. As a consequence, aspects of Newman's educational thought that throw important light on how his educational ideal is to be attained show a profound insight into the teacher's role and a view of education that ranges well beyond academic dimensions, embracing personal, emotional, moral, and spiritual aspects as well. Newman's writings in regard to the centrality of the teacher express an attitude that stands in contrast to the adherence to sometimes rigid principles associated with formulaic academic programs and bureaucratic requirements surrounding general education in schools and colleges. They reveal the university and the college associated with it—the disciplines and the teacher—as interdependent and at the same time, when taken together, as fountain of knowledge and tutor, counselor, moral guardian, and spiritual guide.[67]

In a passage in *Idea of a University,* Newman depicts the teacher, both as an individual and as a member of a team of teachers, as a kind of living embodiment of the universe of knowledge. A student may be able to study only a few subjects, yet he or she can profit "by an intellectual tradition, which is independent of particular teachers, which guides him in his choice of subjects, and duly interprets for him those which he chooses." It may be impossible for anyone to study all of the disciplines. But by living and learning in the midst of those who represent them, one can apprehend "the great outlines of knowledge, the principles on which it rests, the scale of its parts, its lights and its shades, its great points and its little."[68]

Elsewhere in *Idea of a University* and in *University Sketches* Newman visualizes the teacher as a necessary intermediary in presenting the world of knowledge to the student. Valuable as books and self-education may be, there is still a need for the teacher.[69] Personal factors such as the bodily communication of knowledge from one person to another are important.[70] Here Newman displays an appreciation for the role of the teacher or professor that sets him apart from others in the tradition of liberal education. It is to such factors as the teacher's accent and intonation, manner and gestures, genius, and virtue—even the teacher's very name—that Newman looks for the seat of the teacher's influence. It is in the presence of the teacher that one imbibes the invisible atmosphere of genius. Just to gaze on Plato, Newman surmises, must have been an education in itself.[71] In a passage in *University Sketches* that is reminiscent of the *Grammar of Assent* and the *Oxford University Sermons,* Newman dwells on the personal element in knowledge in a similar vein. University education and religious teaching have at least this much in common: their great instrument or organ has ever been that which nature prescribes in all education, the personal presence of a teacher, or, in theological language, oral tradition. "It is the living voice, the breathing form, the expressive countenance," Newman writes, "which preaches, which catechises. Truth, a subtle, invisible, manifold spirit, is poured into the mind of the scholar by his eyes and ears, through his affections, imagination, and reason."[72]

The personal intermediacy of the teacher between the students and the body of knowledge contained in the various sciences, and the notion of the various disciplines being represented by the university teachers is, for practical purposes, fundamental to Newman's idea of a university and his theory of liberal education. Students cannot study all of the subjects, yet they are in need of an understanding and a broad overview of the various branches of knowledge and their interrelations if they are to develop the philosophical habit of mind. Only through interaction with teachers who represent the various sciences and appreciate both their extent and their limitations can students develop a sense of the whole. Furthermore, knowledge is presented more forcefully and in more living form and detail through the personal presence of the teacher than in books or through self-study alone.[73]

Speaking in this way of the personal influence of the teacher and of the teacher's place in the educational process in *University Sketches* and other writings, Newman brings out more clearly than he does in *Idea of a University* the crucial role of the teacher as both the living embodiment and the medium of the universe of knowledge. Yet in spite of the indispensable role he assigns to the teacher, Newman is also mindful of the limitations. For him two great principles are at work in human affairs: influence and system or law. The cultural and educational ideal of Athens, Newman suggests, was hardly realized in practice. It was system or law or discipline, lacking in Athens, that achieved so much in Rome.[74] Attempting to sketch the conditions under which both principles can best operate in the university,[75] Newman introduces a further core element in his theory of liberal education, namely, discipline of mind.[76] As he does so, it is necessary to recognize that when Newman refers to the university and the college or the university professor and the college tutor, the nomenclature he employs is not generally that of the American university of today, although a close approximation of the idea is to be found at Yale.[77] In Newman's usage, 'the college' does not refer to a school or organizational unit such as a college of arts and sciences or a college of agriculture. The college for Newman has a strong residential component, and it combines elements of the domestic with the tutorial and academic, the spiritual and religious. Based on contemporary practice at Oxford, Newman also acknowledges an important distinction between the university and the college, between the professorial system and the collegiate as he knew them.

Although a university consists in the communication of knowledge, in teachers and students, in the "professorial system," as Newman calls it, this is not sufficient for its well-being. Suggesting wherein he sees the critical element in the relationship between the university and the college, Newman continues that while the professorial system constitutes the essence of the university, "for its sure and comfortable existence we must look to law, rule, order; to religion, from which law proceeds; to the collegiate system in which it is embodied."[78] Stressing the interdependence of influence and law, of the professor and the college, Newman sees each as having its own distinctive roles. What these distinctive roles are he sets forth in a key passage in *University Sketches*. The university is for the professor, and the college for the tutor; the university is for the philosophical discourse, the eloquent sermon, or the well-contested disputation; and the college for the catechetical lecture. The university is for theology, law, and medicine, for natural history, for physical science, and for the sciences generally and their promulgation. The college is for the formation of character, intellectual and moral, for the cultivation of the mind, for the improvement of the individual, for the study of literature, for the classics, and for those rudimental sciences that strengthen and sharpen the intellect. The university, being the element of advance, will fail to make good its ground as it goes; the college, from conservative tendencies, will be sure to go back, because it does not go forward.[79]

At first one might be surprised to see Newman speak of the college and the university as being dependent upon one another, with each having its own particular function. Neither of them, he points out is "complete without the other."[80] As he writes in *University Sketches*, "The Professorial system fulfils the strict idea of a University, and is sufficient for its *being*, but it is not sufficient for its *well being*. Colleges constitute the *integrity* of a University."[81] For Newman to say that the college constitutes the integrity or well-being of the university is tantamount to his saying that for practical purposes the university cannot function satisfactorily in isolation from the college.[82] One must ask, therefore, in what respects the college is necessary for the satisfactory functioning or integrity of the university as Newman envisages it.

There are a number of ways in which, for Newman, the college is necessary to the well-being of the university. Already we have seen Newman speak of the university and the college as complementary institutions, each possessing excellences of opposite kinds, the one a seat of influence, the other a source of discipline.[83] This is a general theme that runs throughout *University Sketches*. More specifically, the college is concerned with both the moral and religious welfare of students, as well as with their intellectual growth. Thus it is distinguishable from the university, which in its strict idea has no concern for moral or religious welfare. His critics notwithstanding, Timothy Corcoran, an articulate critic of Newman, did have a point—with which W. B. Carnochan agrees—in arguing that Newman's theory of liberal education as distinct from his broader view of a university education was not concerned with moral development.[84]

What Corcoran's critics failed to acknowledge is that his contention that Newman failed to address the moral dimension in education was not inaccurate as an assessment of Newman's theory of liberal education. Liberal education, Newman made very clear, is simply "the cultivation of the intellect" or "intellectual excellence."[85] It was as a criticism of Newman's more broadly conceived theory of a university education that Corcoran's analysis is inadequate, a point that the critics did little to highlight. In *University Sketches*, for instance, Newman leaves no doubt that one of the functions of the college, one of the ways in which the college completes or ensures the integrity of the university—and the full university education of the student beyond liberal education—is through attending to this very omission. Thus did Newman envisage the college as a sort of home away from home. When a boy leaves his home, says Newman, his faith and morals are in great danger both because he is in the world and because he is among strangers. The remedy of the perils that a university presents to the student is to create homes within the university. Reflecting a theme that becomes pronounced in the thought of Jane Roland Martin, such is the college for Newman: it "is all, and does all, which is implied in the name of home."[86] The established practice at Yale of housing students in small residencies reflects a similar concern to Newman's, a concern shared by those who recognize the importance of community as well as the need to address the social and other challenges facing students in today's university settings.[87] It is a theme overlooked by some who have turned to Newman in support of liberal education.

As has been pointed out already, the college also has an intellectual role, and it is arguable that it is in its intellectual role that the college plays the most fundamental part in contributing to the well-being and integrity of the university. This is so because the intellectual role of the college can be seen as attending to one of the necessary conditions of a liberal education to which reference has been made already, namely, discipline of mind. A liberal education, which for Newman is the main purpose of a university "in its treatment of its students,"[88] calls for knowledge and understanding of the broad outlines of knowledge as well as a discipline of mind. It is the function of the university professors to provide the former; the latter, it seems, is to be nurtured in the college.

In considering the relationship between the university and the college and the distinctive features of each, it is therefore helpful to examine more fully what Newman has to say regarding discipline of mind and its place in his idea of a university and his theory of liberal education. The active, digestive approach of the mind to new knowledge, it has been seen already, is a prerequisite for the enlargement of mind of which Newman speaks. But this active involvement of the mind with new knowledge is, for Newman, a matter of training,[89] for while the mind has a natural tendency to analyze, to abstract, to generalize, it also is wont to generalize, to enunciate principles, to formulate a view hurriedly and on the basis of insufficient evidence. Until such time as the mind is cultivated, disciplined, practiced, it is liable to be carried off by fancies, instead of making the effort to acquire sound knowledge.[90] This training or cultivation is to be carried out largely in the college.

In a lecture entitled "Elementary Studies" that appears in the second part of *Idea of a University*, Newman gives examples of the kind of intellectual activities he considers essential training for developing discipline of mind. From studies such as grammar and composition, the students learn to analyze the meaning of words and phrases. They learn how to state clearly what they want to say. They rid themselves of inconsistencies and develop a steadiness and perseverance in all that they do.[91] When it comes to the cultivation or discipline of mind, as in the case of learning the outlines of knowledge, there is a need for a teacher, for tutoring, and for catechetical instruction. In a lecture on "Discipline of Mind," Newman similarly makes the point as he spells out what he means by catechetical instruction. Addressing the students themselves, he tells them, "you have come to make what you hear your own, by putting out your hand, as it were, to grasp it and appropriate it." As students, they do not come just to attend a lecture but for instruction, specifically "catechetical instruction," consisting in a conversation between lecturer and student, where the lecturer examines the student and "will not let you go till he has proof, not only that you have heard, but that you know."[92]

Discipline of mind, then, which is essential to the idea of a liberal education, just as is an understanding of the great outlines of knowledge and its principles, is the product of certain elementary studies, of tutoring, of catechetical instruction—and of the college. Broad knowledge and discipline of mind work hand in hand in developing the philosophical habit of mind. The one provides the basis for an informed mind; the other enables the student to make knowledge his or her own and develop analytical, methodical, and systematic habits of thought. There are occasions, admittedly, when Newman does appear not to exclude some role for the university in the matter of discipline of mind.[93] There can be no doubt, however, that for the most part it is to the college that one goes for the elementary studies, the classics, the catechetical lecture, and the tutor, all of which Newman associates with discipline of mind. It is equally clear from what Newman has to say in the key passage from *University Sketches* quoted earlier, in which he delineates the distinctive roles of the college and the university, that it is to the college that Newman looks for the strengthening and sharpening of the intellect, as he puts it.[94]

THE RETREAT FROM A LIBERAL EDUCATION

Although there are exceptions,[95] much of the literature on Newman's educational thought does not take into consideration his writings beyond *Idea of a University*. Yet, *Idea of a University* and *University Sketches*, Newman's major educational writings, comprise only a small portion of his total output, and they were composed in about an eight-year time period. I have drawn on writings of Newman beyond *Idea of a University*, notably *University Sketches*, to paint a more comprehensive picture of Newman's educational thought than that represented by his theory of liberal education strictly interpreted as the cultivation of the intellect. But there are other works beyond *University Sketches* that have even more far-reaching implications for his theory of liberal education as presented in *Idea of a University*. When this other work is taken into account, new interpretations of Newman's educational thought become possible—even mandatory—and new questions arise. These questions, which have largely gone unanswered, have serious implications for all who espouse the idea of a liberal education.

As first Rector of the newly founded Catholic University of Ireland, Newman was concerned with getting the university established, but he also had to deal with the sometimes conflicting expectations of the Irish hierarchy,[96] expectations that influenced the formulation of his ideas.[97] Yet it is not the historical circumstances surrounding Newman's educational writings that I wish to draw upon in presenting a reinterpretation of his educational thought. Neither is it the implicit critique of the metaphysical underpinnings of Newman's theory contained in Paul Hirst's theory of liberal education to which I turn.[98] The reinterpretation of Newman's theory of liberal education that I suggest is based largely on writings in which Newman seriously undermines the ideal of liberal education so ably portrayed in *Idea of a University*. These are primarily Newman's more philosophical writings, including *Oxford University Sermons* and the *Grammar of Assent*. In both these works, Newman presents a mental philosophy and a theory of knowing that may startle the serious reader of *Idea of a University*. Specifically, I refer to his theory of apprehension and assent, including his celebrated distinction between notional and real apprehension, his concept of reasoning in concrete affairs, and his contested notion of the illative sense.[99] The implications that these hold for Newman's educational thought, and for the theory of liberal education in general, are far reaching.

At first, Newman's theory of apprehension seems to contain little that is novel: knowledge of the external world is ultimately dependent upon the senses and from knowledge so gained; the mind can formulate knowledge of an abstract or theoretical kind. Then Newman introduces an important distinction between knowledge received directly through the senses and knowledge derived from abstraction. In the *Grammar of Assent*, he describes apprehension as "an intelligent acceptance of the idea or of the fact which a proposition enunciates,"[100] or an interpretation of the terms of which it is composed.[101] As such it constitutes knowledge.[102] But propositions are of two kinds. When they describe what is abstract or general, such as 'man is an animal,' they are notional propositions. They are notional for being concerned not with real things, e.g., 'a man,' but with notions, e.g., 'man,' the idea of man. Propositions in which the terms are singular and in which they stand for real individual things, such as 'Philip was the father of Alexander,' are real propositions, and the apprehension of these is termed real apprehension.[103]

Real apprehension, by which one gains knowledge of particulars, and notional apprehension, in which one arrives at knowledge of universals, are also distinguishable by a noticeable contrast in their effects. Since abstractions are not nearly as immediate as concrete reality, notional apprehension is not as impressive as real; real apprehension is more arresting, more vivid and forceful. As a consequence, real apprehension gives rise to a tendency to action in a way that notional apprehension does not.[104] The distinction between the two modes of apprehension is further accentuated by the inability of notions of things consistently and accurately to represent those things. Notions are simply aspects, more or less exact, of what they purport to represent. Sometimes, even, they are mistakes from the beginning.[105]

Each mode of apprehension has its merits and its limitations. To have notional apprehension is to have breadth of mind but to be shallow; to have real apprehension is to be deep but narrow-minded. The former is the principle of advancement of knowledge; the latter is its conservative principle. Without the apprehension of notions one would be confined to a limited amount of knowledge; yet without a firm grasp of things, one would waste time in vague speculations. Real apprehension has priority, however, in that it is the measure of the notional. The more complete the mind's grasp of things, the more accurate its notions of them.[106] Assent, defined by Newman as "the absolute acceptance of a proposition without any condition,"[107] is also affected differently by notional and real apprehension. In each case, the mind absolutely adheres to the proposition assented to. But even though all assents are unreserved and unconditional, they can and do differ in strength. Thus, while assent can be given to a proposition regardless of whether the proposition is notionally or really apprehended, the assent is elicited more heartily and with more fervor when it is made upon real apprehension, having things for its object, than when made upon notional apprehension, having mere ideas for its object.[108] Accepting Newman's distinction between notional and real assent, then, it is possible to visualize a scale of assents ranging from casually accepted up to tenaciously held. Typically, notional assents would be found on the lower reaches of the scale while real assents would be located near its upper reaches.[109]

With this theory of apprehension Newman has laid the basis for his concept of reasoning in concrete affairs. According to Newman, one reasons when one holds this in virtue of that (or a because of b). In reasoning, knowledge based on some previous knowledge is arrived at indirectly, as distinct from the direct way in which knowledge is gained through the senses. Usually reasoning constitutes a simple act, though for purposes of analysis it is portrayed as a series of acts. Proceeding by a "sort of instinctive perception, from premiss to conclusion," one first apprehends the antecedent and then the consequent, without any awareness of the medium connecting the two. Ordinarily reasoning is spontaneous, carried on without one's knowing how and without any effort or intention on one's part.[110] Such is the nature of reasoning, or "ratiocination" as Newman sometimes

calls it, in its ordinary or natural state and as it is typically found in the uneducated. Not that it is any the less reliable for that. Indeed, it is compara-
ble to the memory or the senses. Like these, it deceives one occasionally, but
there is no reason in principle why it should not be correct in the knowledge it supplies. Occasional inaccuracies can be overcome by a method in
which the reasoning process is analyzed and which can serve as an intellectual standard and common measure between minds. This is the method of
logical inference. Inference need not be expressed as technically as it is in
the Aristotelian syllogism, however. Verbal reasoning, as distinct from mental reasoning, qualifies as inference and differs from logic only in that logic
is the scientific form.[111]

Inference is described by Newman as the conditional acceptance of a
proposition. Assent, he has said, is the unconditional acceptance of a
proposition. Whereas the truth serves as the object of assent, the object of
inference is the "truth-like."[112] Consequently, Newman adds, inference is
primarily concerned with labels or words and does not reach as far as facts.
It is employed in formulae and deals with real objects only insofar as they
constitute the materials of argument.[113] The normal state of inference is to
apprehend propositions as notions. When it is exercised on things, it tends
to be little more than conjecture with little or no logical force.[114]

In so far as logical inference proposes to provide both a test and a common measure of reasoning, Newman finds it to be only partly successful.
The fact that it can and does fail is attributable to the relation between
words and the thoughts they stand for, as in a somewhat similar way the
weakness of notions lies in their failure to represent things properly. Words,
Newman maintains, cannot satisfactorily attain an accurate representation
of thoughts. The symbols employed in mathematics, to which definite and
unchanging values are assigned, may perfectly represent those values. As
such, mathematics is extremely suited to the method of logical inference,
but the same is not true of words.[115]

On this point, Newman's approach is similar to that of both Freidrich
Schiller and Henri Bergson. In *Studies in Humanism*, Schiller wrote that "the
'logical' context never recovers its full concreteness, and so can never guarantee to 'Logic' a knowledge of the actual meaning." He continues, a little
later, "In abstracting from the assertor's actual meaning, 'Logic' always runs
the risk of excluding the real point. For this may lie in some of the 'irrele-
vant' psychical details of the actual meaning, whose essence may not lie in
its plain surface meaning, but in some subtle innuendo."[116] Bergson, too,
writes in this vein: *"fixed concepts can be extracted by our thought from the mobile reality; but there is no means whatever of reconstituting with the fixity of concepts the mobility of the real."* But, he continues, this is not so with intuitive
knowledge, which *"establishes itself in the moving reality and adopts the life itself of things."*[117] (All italics in original.) In this way, intuition attains the ab-

solute—the real, for Newman. Similarly, Newman explains, whereas mathematical symbols lose nothing when placed in the syllogism, words when so placed are stripped of much of their living meaning. Eventually they represent no more than an aspect of the thing or thought they purported to represent. Thus, are rivers, "full, winding, and beautiful," transformed into "navigable canals," for not without doing violence to the real living world, which is as little a logical world as it is a poetical one, can it be attenuated into a logical formula. When inference converts real things into notions so as to manipulate them according to its own method, Newman adds, it misrepresents them. When employed upon questions of fact, inference can conclude only in the abstract and only to probabilities, not to truths.[118]

The limitations of inference, then, are attributed to the inadequacy of notional knowledge or apprehension. Dealing in abstractions and generalities, inference can neither fully capture the real nor conclude to anything more than a probability in concrete affairs. But when real knowledge replaces notional as the content of arguments, conclusions with regard to concrete matters are both insightful and more reliable. It is in this insistence on the greater insight into concrete affairs and the higher degree of reliability that one can attribute to conclusions afforded by real knowledge that Newman's presumably inadvertent disavowal of some of the central theses of his theory of liberal education becomes apparent.

Commenting on Newman's views on the question of concrete reasoning, J. F. Cronin observes that according to Newman—where he once again addresses a theme that reemerges in Martin—life is for action: "if we insist on proofs for everything, we shall never come to action." Scholarly argument and debate might well be a part of "liberal curiosity" for those who can afford it but it is not suited to the multitude.[119] By nature, says Newman, "we are so constituted that faith, not knowledge or argument, is our principle of action."[120] In fact, argument and debate very often lead to skepticism. But when people's emotions and interests are involved, action is not far behind. Related to this also, according to Cronin, is the fact that for Newman it is not the intellect alone but the whole of a person that reasons.[121] To the majority of people, argument can make a point more doubtful and much less impressive. A human being is not merely a rational animal but one who also feels and acts.[122]

That we live in a world of sense, in a world where we are much more concerned and involved with real things than with notions or abstractions, Newman believes, is evident even in our most abstract kinds of argument. Thought is greatly influenced by the human and environmental conditions surrounding it.[123] Often it is those very factors that prove decisive, unaware as one may be of them in making up one's mind. It is not to the syllogism nor to inferential proofs that one looks for the formative cause of opinions but to those preexisting beliefs and views "in which men either already agree with each other or hopelessly differ, before they begin to dispute, and which are hidden deep in our nature, or, it may be, in our personal peculiarities."[124] So logic does not really convert or convince one of the truth of anything. To have certitude in concrete matters, "we require an *organon* more delicate, versatile, and elastic than verbal argumentation."[125]

Newman is confident that we do possess such an alternative means of proof. The inadequacy of logic, he maintains, can be compensated for by one's "own living personal reasoning," by one's "good sense." Such good sense is the healthy condition of such personal reasoning, though it cannot properly express itself in words. It is, for instance, the means by which one is "possessed with the most precise, absolute, masterful certitude" of his dying sometime, a conclusion to which logic alone could never bring one. Many of one's most strenuously held yet "reasonable" convictions or certitudes are similarly dependent upon proofs of such an informal and personal nature that they simply cannot be brought under logical rule.[126] Indeed, in concrete reasoning, one often has to start again from those predicaments from which it was thought logic would relieve us. In such cases, Newman goes on, "We judge for ourselves, by our own lights, and on our own principles."[127] Such processes of reasoning, by which one is led to assent, to action, and to certitude, are far too varied, subtle, and implicit to permit of being formalized. For Newman, our reasoning, as Basil Mitchell puts it, can be "tacit and informal."[128] Human thought is too keen and varied; its sources too remote and hidden; its path too personal, delicate, and circuitous; and its subject matter too varied and intricate to be encompassed by any language, however subtle. The ways of reasoning in concrete affairs are deeply personal, and inference or verbal argument is useful only in subordination to their higher logic.[129] Accordingly, it is to the subtle actions of the mind, and not to science, that one must turn to determine the limit of converging probabilities and the reasons sufficient for proof. It is here in the living mind that one locates the ability to employ correctly principles, facts, doctrines, and experiences, true or probable, and to discern to what conclusions they lead once accepted.[130]

At this point, Newman's emphasis on the necessity of real knowledge and concrete reasoning for an understanding of practical matters becomes central to my argument. The next step for Newman, while inevitable, is of the greatest significance. Thus, he asks, heralding his unheeded retreat from the theory of liberal education, how is "an exercise of mind, which is for the most part occupied with notions, not things, competent to deal with things, except partially and indirectly?"[131] Here Newman, more forcefully than any critic, begins to offer the most incisive critique of his own theory. For what he is now questioning is how a person, in virtue of the training imparted in a liberal education, is equipped to address the very real and persistent problems of life when, "arguments about the abstract cannot handle and determine the concrete."[132] This is a rejection of claims made by Newman while idealizing his theory of liberal education in *Idea of a University*. There, it will be recalled, he said of liberal education itself that, if it be good, it must necessarily be useful.[133] In a similar vein, he claimed that once the intellect has been trained to "have a connected view of things" through force of a liberal education, it makes itself felt in a "good sense."[134] This is now being brought into question. Writing of this very point as somewhat of an aside, Jay Newman (no relation) has remarked that "this reminds us of a strange tension in Newman's thought." He continues, "The author of the *Grammar* exalts the common man's judgment at the expense of that of philosophers, intellectuals, and rationalists; but as the author of *The Idea of a University*, he offered an eloquent and much admired defense of liberal education."[135]

As was seen earlier, for Newman a liberal education is such that its subject matter is almost entirely composed of theoretical or scientific knowledge, that is, of notional knowledge. It also involves training in abstract reasoning and, to use a Piagetian phrase, a development of the formal operations. Altogether, it consists in a breadth of knowledge and a logical facility. But is it not just such knowledge and intellectual dexterity that Newman has now brought into question? Newman's continual emphasis on the need for concrete reasoning when it comes to real life problems, notably in the *Grammar of Assent* and the *Oxford University Sermons*, leaves no question about this.

As if this were not sufficient grounds for concern, it is in respect to the kind of knowledge it furnishes, scientific or notional knowledge, that a liberal education is now open to the most serious criticism by Newman himself. Scientific knowledge, which is held in such high regard in Newman's writings on liberal education, has now been shorn of much of its appeal. Now it is incomplete knowledge, for it can reach truth only in the abstract. Arguments in the abstract cannot determine the concrete. Unable as they are to reach to particulars, they can conclude only to probabilities. Inference, no matter how fully worded, can never reach facts. Indicative of Newman's almost total reversal of his position is his view that inference can come to "no definite conclusions about matters of fact, except as they are made effectual for their purpose by the living intelligence which uses them."[136]

The universals of which theoretical knowledge is made up are now found to be unreliable in practice. What is called a universal is only a general, and what is general does not lead to a necessary conclusion. One can infer only to a probability.[137] And herein lies the weakness of formal inference—and of liberal education to the extent that it shares the exclusive concern of such inference with notional knowledge. All of its processes as expressed in language require general notions if they are to reach conclusions. But the appeal to a general principle or law, made to prove a particular case, never attains sufficient force to warrant anything more than a probable conclusion.[138]

Admittedly, formal inference is still of some value. It is the great principle of order in thinking. It enables "the independent intellects of many, acting and re-acting on each other, to bring their collective force to bear upon one and the same subject-matter, or the same question."[139] Though it does not actually ascertain the truth, it indicates the direction in which truth lies. The value of inference as a tool for the advancement of scientific knowledge cannot either be discounted easily. Besides, inference does have some value even for living in the real world of concrete realities, for a guide to the probable in life has its value. Furthermore, reasoning by rule is plainly natural to humans. We think in logic just as we talk in prose, without aiming to do so. We put our conclusions in objective shape, and this tangible record is so associated with our beliefs and so fortifies and illustrates them as to constitute a force that can even bear upon action.[140] To the extent that all of this is true, it follows that a liberal education retains some value.

Nevertheless, both scientific knowledge and logical inference fall short of providing an understanding of the concrete realities of life. And with their fate goes very largely that of liberal education. Scientific knowledge is too abstract and too simple to be the measure of fact or reality, unable as it is to capture the shades and nuances of real things. Logic is inconclusive, ultimately, by virtue of its starting on the one hand from assumed premises and concluding on the other hand short of the concrete.[141] Real knowledge and concrete reasoning are the only means of gaining insight into the real and important affairs of life.

With this, Newman has achieved an almost complete reversal from his position on liberal education, and he has done so in a manner that is somewhat paralleled by Hirst's retraction of his own theory of liberal education on the basis of a similar kind of reasoning.[142] From the position taken in his educational writings, where scientific or notional knowledge and abstract reasoning were held in high regard, Newman moves to a position where the primacy of both is replaced by the primacy of real knowledge and concrete reasoning. Moreover, Newman has not only seriously—perhaps fatally—undermined his own theory of liberal education; he has also raised correspondingly grave doubts regarding that proud European educational tradition reaching back to Plato and Aristotle and forward to our own day, a tradition in which theoretical knowledge and abstract reasoning are held in the highest esteem and one from which Newman's own theory of liberal education draws so much. If Newman is now correct in his emphasis on the primacy of the real and the need for concrete reasoning, then the traditional ideal of a liberal education, to which Newman himself contributed so much, is in need of serious rethinking.

IMPLICATIONS

At the outset of this book, I asked in what ways—if any—and why the ideal of a liberal education still speaks helpfully to the educational challenges we face today. One way to address that question is to consider the implications of the ideas of those whose work is under consideration here. The first of three main implications of Newman's thought flows from his theory of liberal education; the second flows from his more broadly based idea of a university education, including the attention he gives to the moral, religious, and pedagogical dimensions; the third flows from his theory of reasoning in concrete affairs and, in particular, its implicit retreat from the idea of liberal education.

Based on Newman's theory of liberal education, the main implications to be drawn are not very different from what is normally associated with the mainstream tradition of liberal education. In terms of curriculum, they are that subject matter ought to be drawn from the academic disciplines and that there ought to be a compulsory core of studies to ensure all students learn the main outlines of knowledge. This is so whether it is to promote the growth of understanding, or preparation for citizenship, or work, or all three. In Newman's view, this would be aided by a cadre of teachers representing the full range of the academic disciples who together carefully present their subject matter to students in such a way as to promote a breadth of knowledge and a development of intellectual skills. These teachers would insist that students—to use a phrase employed by the Sizers—would grapple with the content in a manner designed to have them struggle with meaning and grow in thinking as they acquired information.[143] For in addition to the acquisition of organized knowledge to be derived from such a common curriculum, there would be an emphasis on developing intellectual skills.

The curriculum, or more broadly today's school or college, would not be bound by a merely intellectual formation as described by Newman. This is an aspect of Newman's thought not highlighted by those whose interest lies in the more narrowly focused theory of liberal education. It is also a point on which we begin to see a divergence between Newman and twentieth-century theorists of general or liberal education who otherwise are largely in agreement with him. Clearly, for Newman liberal education does not constitute the whole of education, nor would the school or college be seen as a place restricted to academic formation. A full education calls for more than this. It calls for, at the least, a moral and perhaps a religious formation along with the cultivation of those connatural qualities of a liberal education admired by Newman. Embracing a theme that receives extensive treatment from a number of contemporary feminist theorists, the school or college would be a home as well as a school or college. Being a home, it would contribute to the social and emotional growth of students by providing a caring and loving environment. Being for Newman a spiritual home, it would also have a pronounced religious dimension. This aspect of the college flows not from Newman's theory of liberal education, which aims at intellectual excellence, but rather from his more broadly conceived theory of university education in which the college plays a major role in the moral, religious, and character formation of the student. This role the college plays even as it also has a role to play in intellectual formation.

It is the focus on intellectual formation central to Newman's theory of liberal education that many who invoke Newman have been drawn to and that they have highlighted and celebrated. For the most part, this has been done in reference to higher education.[144] Less attention has been given to what Newman has to say regarding religious and moral formation and to the image of school or college as home. Yet these are inescapable aspects of Newman's broader educational thought, aspects that both schools and colleges are continually and increasingly called upon to deal with. And they are aspects of Newman's thought that, reaching beyond the strict boundaries of liberal education as envisaged by him, suggest a point of departure from it. Newman's theory of liberal education glorifies the value of theoretical knowledge and the academic disciplines in developing an understanding of the world and the capacity for reflective thought—the philosophical habit of mind, to use Newman's term. Newman's theory of concrete reasoning, by contrast, suggests that theoretical knowledge is inadequate as a guide in life, incapable as it is of reaching beyond probabilities.

So, where does all of this leave one in drawing out possible implications of Newman's thought for today? Shortly I shall turn to a consideration of the implications of the powerful contradiction inherent in Newman's overall thought between advancing an ideal of academic learning, on the one hand, and highlighting both the importance and the primacy of experiential knowledge on the other. Before doing that, however, one can still draw out some possible implications of his emphasis on the role of personal influence and experiential knowledge and his advocacy of moral and spiritual formation. In the past, these may have attracted less notice than his focus on intellectual formation; in the future, they may well be the elements in his thought that earn the greater attention.

Newman's theory of reasoning in concrete affairs runs counter to the theory of a liberal education at several crucial points. As revealed in the *University Sketches* and the theory of concrete reasoning elaborated in *Grammar of Assent* and the *Oxford University Sermons*, Newman's thinking does support many aspects of his more broadly based educational thought, such as his recognition of the importance of the personal influence of the teacher in the academic formation of students. It is especially so when the concern is with social, spiritual, and moral formation, lending support in turn to those who argue that education needs to go beyond liberal or academic education and prepare students for active participation in the world. The concern with moral education and, in particular, education for action is not emphasized in *Idea of a University*, where the preoccupation is with characterizing liberal education as concerned with cultivation of the intellect.

In the *University Sketches*, Newman is very attentive to the role of the teacher and the moral formation of students. In dealing with these matters there, he shows an appreciation of the role of personal experience and experiential knowledge of the kind found in the *Grammar of Assent* and the *Oxford University Sermons*. It is these aspects of his thinking that led Newman himself beyond the theory of liberal education conceived specifically as mere cultivation of the intellect to a broader view of education and of human cognition and volition. So also today these ideas have the potential to support an argument for a theory of education that, at the least, goes beyond liberal education to embrace social, moral, practical, and possibly religious formation.

If Newman's stance on these matters puts him in the company of those such as Jacques Rousseau and John Dewey, writers not normally associated with the tradition of liberal education, it also sets him apart from many who are usually considered part of this tradition. In his recognition of the place of experiential or non-academic dimensions of education, Newman is at odds with the mainstream figures of the twentieth century, who pay little attention to the matter and who are decidedly reluctant to recognize a place for non-academic studies in the school curriculum. These include Philip H. Phenix, who was at particular pains to exclude nondisciplinary studies from the school curriculum and others, such as Harry S. Broudy, B. O. Smith, and Joe R. Burnett, who, while perhaps less exclusionary, said little to the contrary.[145] Hirst's theory of liberal education, although later disavowed by him,[146] is especially interesting. Having argued that only the seven disciplinary forms of knowledge he identified should be included in the curriculum, Hirst subsequently accepted that his original theory of liberal education did not include the entirety of what a total education would include, excluding as it did character education and a concern for moral commitment.[147] He did not advocate for such additional forms of education, as Newman did, however. And unlike such a strong advocate of liberal education as Mortimer Adler, Newman did envisage a powerful role for moral formation in the broader education—if not the strictly liberal education—of the young.

The moral dimension of Newman's educational thought might be unexpected from him as a proponent of liberal education understood strictly as intellectual cultivation. This dimension is clearly evident, however, in the moral and parental roles he attaches to the college through its residential character and tutorial system and in the spiritual role he expected to be provided by the religious dimension of a broader university education. So pronounced are these elements in Newman that it is of writers more closely associated with progressive and feminist lines of educational thought, writers whose commitment to traditional conceptions of liberal education is in many ways muted, that one is reminded. These include Maria Montessori, Jane Roland Martin, and Nel Noddings, all strong advocates for what Martin calls the three Cs, namely, care, concern, and connection, and for preparing the young for interacting with and serving others and for being respectful toward others and nature itself. Both schools and colleges have come to recognize that not only may such formation of the young be morally and socially desirable, schools and colleges have also come to recognize the importance of caring in their dealings with students. So we have in schools and colleges and, notably on university and college campuses, attempts at strengthening familial bonds between colleges and students, between university faculty and students, and among students themselves. These efforts are seen as crucial elements in learning. This is not to suggest that these roles never existed before, as in the traditional role of the residence hall director, but they are gaining a new prominence in programs devoted to enhancing transition years and the first-year experience in college and in the attention now given to such matters as collaborative learning and the formation of so-called learning communities on university and college campuses.[148]

While such positive ideas emerging from Newman's recognition of the experiential and the practical could be expanded upon, there is, thirdly, the matter of the conflict between his theory of liberal education and his theory of reasoning in concrete affairs or, as I have termed it, his retreat from liberal education. It is a matter that needs to be addressed here, as do its possible implications for the continuing viability of the liberal education construct itself. If there is a contradiction between the two positions adopted by Newman, as I have argued there is, what are the implications for education? Is there room for compromise? Is there any common ground? These questions are a challenge especially for colleges and universities.

Notwithstanding the high regard in which Newman holds real apprehension and assent and experiential knowledge, he also acknowledges limitations of experiential knowledge in the *Grammar of Assent*, such as the fact that while the real apprehension with which it is associated is deep, it is also narrow-minded and slowly accumulated. Recognition of these limitations may open the way to accepting one of the contradictory benefits of theoretical knowledge of the kind associated with liberal education: it enables one to see the big picture. As was already noted, for Newman formal inference associated with notional apprehension and assent is of some value. It is the great principle of order in thinking and in science, enabling us to go beyond sense knowledge and bring order and system to what we perceive through the senses. To the extent that this is true, even though both scientific knowledge and logical inference may still fall short, liberal education would appear to retain some value.

If this is so, theoretical knowledge and personal knowledge may serve to complement one another. It further suggests that there may be scope for both kinds of knowledge to be included in the curriculum. This may not be accepted by Newman in his theory of liberal education—or by others such as Phenix, Hirst, and Adler—but it is accepted in his broader theory of a university education. In this broader theory of education, as we have seen, Newman requires the student to have a moral, spiritual, and social education, grounded it would appear in direct experience and personal knowledge.

Whether one agrees with him or not, it can hardly be doubted that Newman has given us the basic vocabulary and the guiding rationale that serves and sustains the general theory of liberal education up to the present day. He has highlighted the central focus of liberal education on the cultivation of the intellect, its reliance upon a broadly based knowledge, its independence of moral and religious stipulations, its being its own end, and notwithstanding this, its being the best preparation for further studies and vocation. But there are further possibilities in Newman than those enumerated in his celebrated theory of liberal education.

These possibilities lie in Newman's broader educational thought as reflected in his theory of university education, which incorporates social, moral, and spiritual formation along with intellectual or liberal education. They are also rooted in his broader philosophical thought, in which he develops a more wide-ranging theory of knowledge and of knowing than is laid out in his educational writings. As applied to the challenges we face today, these theories would appear to bring Newman close to theorists such as Richard Pring, Martin, and Noddings. In varying degrees, these theorists accept the merits of academic education but they also insist that that education may be in need of careful adjustment and supplemented by forms of experiential and practical knowledge, practical skills of different kinds, and a strong orientation to social formation.

NOTES

1. Ian Ker, *The Achievement of John Henry Newman* (Notre Dame, IN: University of Notre Dame Press, 1990), ix, and John Henry Newman, *The Idea of a University*, ed. Frank M. Turner (New Haven: Yale University Press, 1996), 283.

2. Newman, *The Idea of a University*, ed. Turner, 259.

3. In this connection, see Jaroslav Pelikan, *The Idea of a University: A Reexamination* (New Haven: Yale University Press, 1992), 1–10.

4. See, for example, J. M. Roberts, "*The Idea of a University* Revisited," in *Newman after a Hundred Years*, ed. Ian Ker and Alan G. Hill (Oxford: Clarendon Press, 1990), 193–222, and Martha McMackin Garland, "Newman in His Own Day," in *The Idea of a University*, ed. Turner, 265–281. Of particular relevance here is the important critical work of Jay Newman, *The Mental Philosophy of John Henry Newman* (Waterloo: Wilfrid Laurier University Press, 1986).

5. Sheldon Rothblatt, *The Modern University and Its Discontents: The Fate of Newman's Legacies in Britain and America* (Cambridge: Cambridge University Press, 1997), 7.

6. For a balanced and very summary account of Newman's central educational ideas, see P. J. Fitzpatrick, "John Henry Newman," in *Fifty Major Thinkers on Education*, ed. Joy A. Palmer (London: Routledge, 2001), 100–104.

7. D. G. Mulcahy, "Newman's Retreat from a Liberal Education," *Irish Journal of Education* 7, no. 1 (Summer 1973), 11–22.

8. In a little-known undertaking, Newman was involved in establishing a school connected to the Oratory in Birmingham. See V. A. McClelland, "A Catholic Eton: By Hook or by Crook? John Henry Newman and the Establishment of the Oratory School," *Aspects of Education* 22 (1980): 3–17.

9. See V. A. McClelland, *English Roman Catholics and Higher Education, 1830–1903* (Oxford: The Clarendon Press, 1973), 87–172, and Fergal McGrath, *Newman's University: Idea and Reality* (London: Longmans, Green and Co., 1951).

10. See Louis Bouyer, *Newman: His Life and Spirituality* (Cleveland, OH: The World Publishing Company, 1960), 300–315, and Ker, *The Achievement of John Henry Newman*, 2. See also McGrath, *Newman's University*.

11. George N. Shuster, "Introduction," in John Henry Cardinal Newman, *The Idea of a University* (Garden City, NY: Doubleday and Company, Inc., 1959), 21.

12. See also George M. Marsden, "Theology and the University: Newman's Idea and Current Realities," in *The Idea of a University*, ed. Turner, 302–305.

13. John Henry Cardinal Newman, *The Idea of a University Defined and Illustrated*, ed. Charles Frederick Harrold (New York: Longmans, Green and Co., 1947), xxxiv–xxxv.

14. Newman, *Idea of a University*, 107.

15. Newman, *Idea of a University*, 185–187; see also John Triffin, "In Defense of Newman's 'Gentleman'," *Dublin Review* 239 (Autumn 1965): 245–254.

16. Newman, *Idea of a University*, 186.

17. Newman, *Idea of a University*, 186.

18. John Henry Cardinal Newman, *An Essay in Aid of a Grammar of Assent*, ed. Charles Frederick Harrold (New York: Longmans, Green and Co., 1947), 42.

19. James O. Freedman, *Liberal Education and the Public Interest* (Iowa City: University of Iowa Press, 2003), 54–70.

20. Newman, *Idea of a University*, 107–110; see also John Henry Cardinal Newman, *Fifteen Sermons Preached before the University of Oxford* (London: Rivingtons, 1887), 278–287, where Newman tends to equate "wisdom" and "enlargement" with "philosophy" as here understood. Future references to this work will be abbreviated to *Oxford University Sermons*.

21. On this usage of the term 'philosophy,' see W. B. Carnochan, *The Battleground of the Curriculum: Liberal Education and American Experience* (Stanford: Stanford University Press, 1993), 31–34.

22. John Henry Newman, *Idea of a University* (Longmans Green, and Co., 1898), 125. It should be noted that here the text reads "... terms which are not *uncommonly* given to it. . . ." (italics added) as opposed to the Harrold edition, 111, which reads "... terms which are not *commonly* given to it" (italics added). I have chosen the 1898 edition in this case because it fits the context better and also corresponds with what Newman had earlier written in the *Oxford University Sermons*, 282. On this point, see also David J. DeLaura, *Hebrew and Hellene in Victorian England: Newman, Arnold, and Pater* (Austin, TX: University of Texas Press, 1969), 62–66. See also how reminiscent of Newman is the language used in referring to the mission of Yale College in the Yale NEASC Self-Study of 1999, at http://www.yale.edu/accred/standards/s1.html (accessed July 25, 2007): "To these ends, the College emphasizes the training of the discipline of the mind, the enlargement of knowledge, and the cultivation of sympathy of spirit through its curriculum, its special form of residential life, and its extracurricular opportunities."

23. Newman, *Idea of a University*, 98, 112–113, 119.

24. Newman, *Idea of a University*, 98.

25. Newman, *Idea of a University*, 42.

26. Newman, *Idea of a University*, 66.

27. In this connection, see McClelland, *English Roman Catholics*, passim.

28. See Ker, *The Achievement of John Henry Newman*, 22–33, and *The Idea of a University*, ed. Turner, 286.

29. Newman's understanding of literature, in particular, is different from ours. For him, literature would have had a broader meaning and would be more akin to what we understand by literature, history, philosophy, and the social sciences. See Newman, *Idea of a University*, 201–286.

30. Newman views science both as a study of the natural sciences and as a systematic or disciplinary study in any subject.

31. To today's reader, Newman's philosophical and epistemological stance might be considered outdated. But even if the metaphysical scaffolding of the Aristotelian philosophy he relies upon is removed, his curriculum stance could still be supported by an alternative philosophical stance. In this connection, see P. H. Hirst, *Knowledge and the Curriculum* (London: Routledge and Kegan Paul, 1974), especially 30–53.

32. See C. John McCloskey, "Newman's University in Today's American Culture," in *Newman's Idea of a University: The American Response*, ed. Peter M. J. Stravinskas and Patrick J. Reilly (Mt. Pocono, PA: Newman House Press, 2002), 55–56.

33. Newman, *Idea of a University*, 40–41.

34. Newman, *Idea of a University*, 319–320.

35. Newman, *Idea of a University*, 42–47, 66–67. Roberts is well aware of the subtlety of Newman's prose. Yet on this point, Roberts' plainspoken objections to Newman's apparent insistence on comprehensive knowledge as fundamental to the idea of an educated person are surely challenging. See Roberts, *"The Idea of a University Revisited,"* 204–206.

36. Newman, *Idea of a University*, 114–115, 118; see also Newman, *Oxford University Sermons*, 287–289.

37. Newman, *Idea of a University*, 118–119. This is at odds with Culler's view that for Newman enlargement of mind signifies the mind's merely passive acceptance and storing of facts. See A. Dwight Culler, *The Imperial Intellect: A Study of Newman's Educational Ideal* (New Haven: Yale University Press, 1955), 206, and D. G. Mulcahy, "Cardinal Newman's Concept of a Liberal Education," *Educational Theory* 22, no. 1 (Winter 1972), especially 89–92.

38. Ker, *The Achievement of John Henry Newman*, 4–10.

39. Newman was not alone in using the term 'science of sciences' in relation to philosophy as the object of liberal education. See, for example, Carnochan, *The Battleground of the Curriculum*, 32–33.

40. Newman, *Idea of a University*, 80.

41. Newman, *Idea of a University*, 46.

42. Culler, *The Imperial Intellect*, 182. On this point, see also Ker, *The Achievement of John Henry Newman*, 3–8, where, in part, Ker takes issue with Culler.

43. Ker, *The Achievement of John Henry Newman*, 17–18.

44. Newman, *Oxford University Sermons*, 287.

45. Newman, *Idea of a University*, 95–96.

46. Newman, *Idea of a University*, 94–95.

47. Newman, *Idea of a University*, 97–101, quoting Aristotle, *Rhetoric* I. 5.

48. Michael Oakeshott, *The Voice of Liberal Learning: Michael Oakeshott on Education*, ed. Timothy Fuller (New Haven: Yale University Press, 1989).

49. *The Idea of a University*, ed. Turner, 290–291.

50. Newman, *Idea of a University*, 98–101. On the point of Newman's treatment of knowledge as its own end, see DeLaura, *Hebrew and Hellene*, 68–70, and Pelikan, *The Idea of a University*, 32–43.

51. Newman, *Idea of a University*, 91. In this connection, see the pertinent if inconclusive essay by R. S. Peters, "Ambiguities in Liberal Education and the Problem of Its Content," in *Ethics and Educational* Policy, ed. Kenneth A. Strike and Kieran Egan (London: Routledge and Kegan Paul, 1978), 3–21.

52. Timothy G. Reagan, "Paideia Redux," *Journal of Thought* 38, no. 3 (Fall 2003): 22. Even the endnotes in this article merit close attention.

53. Newman's Aristotelian leanings are well brought out in Joseph Dunne, *Back to the Rough Ground* (Notre Dame, IN: University of Notre Dame Press, 1993), 31–54, and Laurence Richardson, *Newman's Approach to Knowledge* (Leominster, Herefordshire: Gracewing, 2007).

54. Newman, *Idea of a University*, 92.

55. Newman, *Idea of a University*, 134, 159–160; Newman, *Grammar of Assent*, 130.

56. Newman, *Idea of a University*, 143–147.

57. Newman, *Idea of a University*, 143–145.

58. Newman, *Idea of a University*, 147.

59. The notion of the mind as a muscle associated with the doctrine of mental discipline was also commonplace in American educational thought in the nineteenth century. See, for example, Herbert M. Kliebard, *The Struggle for the American Curriculum, 1893–1958* (New York: Routledge, 1995), 4–8.

60. Newman, *Idea of a University*, 146.

61. Newman, *Idea of a University*, 143–147.

62. Wulstan Peterburs, "Newman's *Idea of a University*, 'the Circle of the Sciences,' and the Constitution of the Church," in *Victorian Churches and Churchmen: Essays Presented to Vincent Alan McClelland*, ed. Sheridan Gilley (Woodbridge, Suffolk: The Boydell Press, 2005), 200–233.

63. Newman, *Idea of a University*, 61–62, 88–90.

64. Newman does imagine circumstances where students getting together themselves may grow more intellectually than when faced with a teacher who simply imposes factual information to be absorbed. See Newman, *Idea of a University*, 129–132.

65. Newman, *Idea of a University*, 147: the university "teaches *all* knowledge by teaching all *branches* of knowledge, and in no other way."

66. Newman, *Idea of a University*, 135.

67. On the place of the college and its relationship to the university in Newman's thought, their respective roles in advancing the mission of teaching universal knowledge, and their historical antecedents in Oxford and Cambridge, see Rothblatt, *The Modern University and Its Discontents*, 12–21.

68. Newman, *Idea of a University*, 89–90.

69. Newman, *Idea of a University*, 129–132, 371–372.

70. John Henry Newman, *University Sketches*, ed. Michael Tierney (Dublin: Browne and Nolan Limited, 1961), 12–13, 7–9, 47.

71. Newman, *University Sketches*, 8–9, 39–41.

72. Newman, *University Sketches*, 14.

73. See, for example, Newman, *University Sketches*, 6–16.

74. Whereas Newman stresses the importance of the personal influence and presence of the teacher, and while he himself had once been a champion of the university against the colleges that he believed had come to dominate it, he also recognized a need for system and discipline. For this, he turns to the college as opposed to the university.

75. Newman, *University Sketches*, 66–88.

76. Ker is emphatic on this point. See *The Achievement of John Henry Newman*, 1–34.

77. This is how the situation that obtains today at Yale is described in a Yale document: Beginning in the 1930s, residential colleges modeled on Oxford and Cambridge were established at Yale. Undergraduate students were housed in twelve separate communities of about 450 members so as to facilitate "both the intimacy of a small college environment and the vast resources of a major research university." In this way, the college is seen as "providing a congenial community where residents live, eat, socialize, and pursue a variety of academic and extracurricular activities. Each college has a master and dean, as well as a number of resident faculty members known as fellows, and each has its own dining hall, library, seminar rooms, recreation lounges, and other facilities." at http://www.yale.edu/about/history.html (accessed July 25, 2007).

78. Newman, *University Sketches*, 70.

79. Newman, *University Sketches*, 220–221.

80. Newman, *University Sketches*, 175, 69.

81. Newman, *University Sketches*, 175.

82. Newman, *University Sketches*, 173–176. See also Newman, *Idea of a University*, xxvii, where Newman speaks in similar terms of the relationship between the university and the church.

83. Newman, *University Sketches*, 220–221.

84. Timothy Corcoran, "Liberal Studies and Moral Aims: A Critical Survey of Newman's Position," *Thought* 1, no. 1 (June 1926): 54–71. See also Carnochan, *The Battleground of the Curriculum*, 41–47. For criticisms of Corcoran's position see, for example, Fernande Tardivel, *J. H. Newman Educateur* (Paris: Les Presses Modernes, 1937), 86–105; Michael Tierney, "Catholic University," in *A Tribute to Newman*, ed. Michael Tierney (Dublin: Browne and Nolan Limited, 1945), 172–206; John E. Wise, "Newman and the Liberal Arts," in *American Essays for the Newman Centennial*, ed. John K. Ryan and Edmond Darvil Benard (Washington, DC: The Catholic University of America Press, 1947), 133–150; Edmond Darvil Benard, "Newman's Idea of a *Catholic* University," *American Ecclesiastical Review* 121 (December, 1949): 447–468; and Alfred O'Rahilly, "The Irish University Question: V Newman on Education," *Studies* 50 (Winter 1961): 363–370.

85. Newman, *Idea of a University*, 107.

86. Newman, *University Sketches*, 207, 182.

87. Of particular note here is the work of John Gardner and his associates at the National Resource Center for the First-Year Experience and Students in Transition in developing programs to enhance college learning, retention, and graduation. See, for example, John N. Gardner, A. Jerome Jewler, and Betsy Barefoot, *Your College Experience* (Boston: Thomson Wadsworth, 2007).

88. Newman, *Idea of a University*, 90.

89. Newman, *Idea of a University*, 134–135.

90. Newman, *Idea of a University*, 369, 134–135.

91. This lecture is not included in the Harrold edition of the *Idea of a University*. It can be found in *The Idea of a University*, intro. Shuster, 312–351.

92. Newman, *Idea of a University*, 362. See also Newman, *University Sketches*, 14. Though Newman, as Rector in Dublin, combined this tutorial or catechetical function with that of the professor, it would appear from Newman's writings generally that he envisaged two main types of teachers, namely, the university professor and the college tutor. Both were to exercise a necessary personal influence. The professor was to present and represent the broad outlines of knowledge; the tutor was to discipline the mind in the way indicated in the passage quoted and to cater to the moral welfare of the student.

93. See, for example, Newman, *Idea of a University*, 128–131, 362.

94. Newman, *University Sketches*, 220–221; see also Newman, *Idea of a University*, 372–373. To elaborate, according to Newman in *University Sketches*, in the college the student's diligence will be steadily stimulated, "he will be kept up to his aim; his progress will be ascertained, and his week's work, like a labourer's measured." It is not easy for a young man, Newman continues, to determine for himself whether he has mastered what he has been taught. Accordingly, "a careful catechetical training, and a jealous scrutiny into his power of expressing himself and of turning his knowledge to account, will be necessary, if he is really to profit from the able Professors whom he is attending; and all this he will gain from the College Tutor" (182–183).

95. Culler, *The Imperial Intellect*, and McGrath, *Newman's University*. See also Peter M. Collins, "Newman and Contemporary Education," *Educational Theory* 26, no. 4 (Fall 1976): 366–371, and Richardson, *Newman's Approach to Knowledge*, 133–139, both of which devote attention to connections between the *Grammar of Assent* and Newman's educational ideas.

96. See Bouyer, *Newman*, 300–315, and McGrath, *Newman's University*.

97. Bouyer, *Newman*, 304.

98. Briefly stated, this critique undermines one of the key claims made by Newman on behalf of liberal education, namely, that possessing knowledge of the sciences or academic disciplines provides one with knowledge of the world that can be drawn upon in making judgments in and about it. This claim by Newman is possible only so long as one can rely on an Aristotelian metaphysics in which knowledge is understood to be a true account of reality. But this position is now rejected by many, including Hirst, who seeks an alternative metaphysical basis on which to construct his own theory of liberal education. Applied to Newman, it is a rejection that denies crucial underpinnings of the claims he makes for liberal education. See Hirst, *Knowledge and the Curriculum*, especially pp. 30–53.

99. Though the clarity of Newman's notion of the illative sense has been seriously questioned in Jay Newman, *The Mental Philosophy of John Henry Newman*, 164–193 and elsewhere, here and in what immediately follows, one can see clearly Newman's reliance on Aristotle's notion of *phronesis*, which appears to have elements in common with the illative sense in Newman. See Dunne, *Back to the Rough Ground*, especially 33–38.

100. Newman, *Grammar of Assent*, 16–17.

101. Newman, *Grammar of Assent*, 11.

102. Newman, *Grammar of Assent*, 11–12; Newman, *Idea of a University*, 41.

103. Newman, *Grammar of Assent*, 7–8.

104. Newman, *Grammar of Assent*, 9–10, 29–31.

105. Newman, *Grammar of Assent*, 38.

106. Newman, *Grammar of Assent*, 27–28, 8.

107. Newman, *Grammar of Assent*, 11.

108. Newman, *Grammar of Assent*, 13–14; Newman, *Idea of a University*, 29–30.

109. Newman, *Grammar of Assent*, 28.

110. Newman, *Grammar of Assent*, 197–198; Newman, *Oxford University Sermons*, 206–207, 256–260.

111. Newman, *Grammar of Assent*, 198–200; Newman, *Oxford University Sermons*, 257–259.

112. Newman, *Grammar of Assent*, 119.

113. Newman, *Grammar of Assent*, 69.

114. Newman, *Grammar of Assent*, 32.

115. Newman, *Grammar of Assent*, 36–40.

116. F. C. S. Schiller, *Studies in Humanism* (London: Macmillan, 1912), 87.

117. Henri Bergson, *The Creative Mind*, trans. M. L. Andison (New York: Citadel Press, 1992), 189, 192.

118. Newman, *Grammar of Assent*, 200–204.

119. Newman, *Discussions and Arguments on Various Subjects* (London: Longmans, Green, 1924), 295.

120. Newman, *Oxford University Sermons*, 188.

121. On this and related points, see Ker, *The Achievement of John Henry Newman*, 46–50.

122. J. F. Cronin, *Cardinal Newman: His Theory of Knowledge* (Washington, DC: Catholic University of America Press, 1935), 33– 39; Newman, *Grammar of Assent*, 72–82, 120–124; Newman, *Discussions and Arguments on Various Subjects*, 292–297; Newman, *Oxford University Sermons*, 256.

123. Newman, *Grammar of Assent*, 205–206.

124. Newman, *Grammar of Assent*, 210.

125. Newman, *Grammar of Assent*, 206.

126. Newman, *Grammar of Assent*, 228–229; Newman, *Oxford University Sermons*, 256–257.

127. Newman, *Grammar of Assent*, 230.

128. Basil Mitchell, "Newman as a Philosopher," *Newman after a Hundred Years*, ed. Ian Ker and Alan G. Hill (Oxford: The Clarendon Press, 1990), 227.

129. Newman, *Grammar of Assent*, 216, 229–230; Newman, *Oxford University Sermons*, 256–257.

130. Newman, *Grammar of Assent*, 273–274. It should be said that these are areas in Newman's thought of which Jay Newman, *The Mental Philosophy of John Henry Newman*, is particularly skeptical.

131. Newman, *Grammar of Assent*, 211.

132. Newman, *Grammar of Assent*, 211.

133. Newman, *Idea of a University*, 143–145.

134. Newman, *Idea of a University*, xxxiv–xxxv.

135. Jay Newman, *The Mental Philosophy of John Henry Newman*, 171. If one accepts Jay Newman's criticisms of Newman's mental philosophy, this may excuse theories of liberal education other than Newman's from the same kind of criticism. It does not undo the contradictions or ease the tensions that surround Newman's theory.

136. Newman, *Grammar of Assent*, 211–212.

137. Newman, *Grammar of Assent*, 212.

138. Newman, *Grammar of Assent*, 215–218.

139. Newman, *Grammar of Assent*, 217.

140. Newman, *Grammar of Assent*, 217–218.

141. Newman, *Grammar of Assent*, 215–218.

142. This is borne out in Hirst's discussion of the philosophy of education as an exercise in practical reason in "A Response to Wilfred Carr's 'Philosophy and Education'," *Journal of Philosophy of Education* 39, no. 4 (November 2005): 615–620 and in "Education, Knowledge and Practices," in *Beyond Liberal Education: Essays in Honour of Paul H. Hirst*, ed. Robin Barrow and Patricia White (London: Routledge, 1993), 184–199.

143. Theodore R. Sizer and Nancy Faust Sizer, "Grappling," *Phi Delta Kappan* 81, no. 3 (November 1999), 184–190.

144. A notable exception is to be found in a report that reflected influential educational opinion in Ireland in the mid-twentieth century, namely *The Report of the Council of Education: The Curriculum of the Secondary School* (Dublin: The Stationary Office, 1960). The strain of Newman's thought discernible in the report probably owes much to the fact that the acknowledged Newman scholar Fergal McGrath was a member of the Council.

145. Philip H. Phenix, *Realms of Meaning* (New York: McGraw Hill, 1964), and Harry S. Broudy, B. Othanel Smith, and Joe R. Burnett, *Democracy and Excellence in American Secondary Education: A Study in Curriculum Theory* (Chicago: Rand McNally & Company, 1964).

146. Hirst, "Education, Knowledge and Practices."

147. Hirst, *Knowledge and the Curriculum*, 96, and Paul H. Hirst and R. S. Peters, *The Logic of Education* (London: Routledge and Kegan Paul, 1970), 17–41, 66–67. See also D. G. Mulcahy, "Jane Roland Martin and Paul Hirst on Liberal Education: A Reassessment," *Journal of Thought* 38, no. 1 (Spring 2003): 25–29.

148. Gardner, Jewler, and Barefoot, *Your College Experience.*

3

Adler: Liberal Education for All

The range of progressive tendencies in Newman's thinking does not reach into the civic or political realm, and the call to extend educational opportunity to all that became a hallmark of the twentieth century is foreign to him. Not so Mortimer Adler, for whom the quest for equality is a mark of his educational thought.

Mortimer Adler's advocacy of liberal education caught the attention of the public in ways not commonly achieved by educational theorists. *Encyclopedia Britannica*, for example, is a household name in part because of Adler's association with it and the educational ideas that he brought to it. Presented in different forms and a variety of publications throughout Adler's long career, these ideas were expressed with great effect in his 1982 book *The Paideia Proposal*.[1] There he proclaimed, consistent with his work of a lifetime, that to achieve its major objectives, basic schooling must be "general and liberal" and "nonspecialized and nonvocational,"[2] to which he later added, "humanistic, not technical."[3]

In writing of liberal education as he did, Adler was tapping into an age-old European tradition of which Newman was an exemplary exponent in the nineteenth century. Adler was also attempting to enrich that tradition. As he did so, he was by and large true to its historical roots and evolutionary adaptations, and in his curriculum theorizing he may be said to represent its core principles faithfully. He was also suggesting that this tradition provides the most important underlying philosophy for the conduct of basic schooling in America, and schooling everywhere for that matter. For Adler, therefore, the viability of liberal education as a guiding ideal for contemporary schooling is entirely beyond question. The focus of attention here, accordingly, is on inquiring into how Adler's view of liberal education may contribute to developing an improved vision of education in schools and colleges for the future

As a young man Adler asserted his strong commitment to the academic ideal of education by not taking a course in physical education as an undergraduate at Columbia University, even though it was a requirement for graduation. As a consequence, he did not earn his BA, but following the publication of *The Paideia Proposal* Columbia relented, and Adler was awarded the degree in 1983. Following graduate studies, also at Columbia, he was awarded the PhD in 1928. He was appointed as a professor at the University of Chicago in 1930, and along with the president and later chancellor of the University of Chicago, Robert Hutchins, entered into a number of often contentious but highly successful educational and business ventures. The most notable of these included serving in a number of editorial capacities for *Encyclopaedia Britannica* and the *Great Books of the Western World*. The ideas underlying these two projects and expressed in his many writings are central to Adler's philosophy of education and his lifelong devotion to the idea of liberal education in both schools and colleges.

THE CONTEXT OF *THE PAIDEIA PROPOSAL*

The Paideia Proposal is a short but compelling statement of the idea of a liberal or general education as the remedy for a widely perceived decline in American public schools toward the end of the twentieth century. It was a remedy for which Adler and like-minded educators had long advocated. A growth in the influence of progressive educational thought and practice in the United States during the 1920s and 1930s led many to believe that education was departing from the values and principles to which it ought to be committed. Those such as Adler and Hutchins, who were especially concerned with what they perceived to be a move away from the intellectual purposes of education, formulated a view of education whose roots and defining characteristics may be traced to Plato and Aristotle in ancient times, Thomas Aquinas in the Middle Ages, and John Henry Newman in the nineteenth century. Contemporaries of Adler and Hutchins commonly associated with this view, some of whom expanded its scope to accommodate religious thinking, included Mark Van Doren, Scott Buchanan, and the eminent neo-Thomist philosopher, Jacques Maritain. As we moved through mid-century and witnessed the expansion of school and college education on both sides of the Atlantic in the years following World War II, a new breed of philosopher of education in this general tradition introduced additional forms of analysis to the debate. While maintaining much common ground with Adler, Hutchins, and Maritain, these new thinkers departed from them on important details and in the process developed new and influential justifications for academic studies as the core of a liberal or general education. Prominent among these were Paul Hirst and R. S. Peters in England and Philip H. Phenix, Harry S. Broudy, B. O. Smith, and Joe R. Burnett in the United States.

The end of the twentieth century saw a renewed concern on both sides of the Atlantic regarding the quality of schooling. With the publication of *The Paideia Proposal* in 1982, Adler highlighted the cause of educational standards in the United States. The issue gained further attention with the appearance of the highly publicized government report *A Nation at Risk* in 1983. Popular interest in the subject was maintained by books from Allan Bloom and E. D. Hirsch. Contributions from Ernest Boyer and Ted Sizer presented additional perspectives of note.[4] Much as Arthur Bestor and Admiral Hyman Rickover had weighed in on the education debate a generation earlier, many of these writers took a generally conservative stand on the issues. Within the same broad time frame, the issue of educational standards had also attracted the attention of conservative critics in England.[5] An effort aimed at ensuring that any educational reforms would be true to the logical character of education itself was taken up by Hirst and Peters, the two most influential philosophers of education of the day. A hallmark of the positions of philosophers such as Adler, Hirst, and Peters is the manner in which they equate liberal education with general education, and even with the idea of education itself.[6]

Along with their rejection of what they saw as a departure from the intellectual emphasis in education, Adler, Hutchins, and Maritain condemned the denial of eternal truths and absolute principles and values in education. This they considered to be implicit in progressive education, which had gained a strong footing in the early decades of the twentieth century, and explicit in the philosophy of pragmatism that came to be associated with it. They were often referred to as perennialists for their acceptance of the belief that truth is eternal and everywhere the same, that certain principles are absolute and unchanging, and that all human beings are equal and essentially the same. While the emphasis on absolute truth would lead otherwise like-minded philosophers to divergent formulations of the ideal of liberal education, principles enunciated by Adler, Hutchins, and Maritain nonetheless remained central to this general way of thinking. Not least among these was the view that education should be everywhere and always essentially the same and may be defined as the development of the person.

The primary aim of education according to Maritain is to "form a man."[7] In setting forth what they considered to be the aims or objectives of education, however, Maritain and others sometimes made a distinction between the primary purpose of education, elaborated in terms of the full development or realization of the potential of the individual person, and secondary purposes, those pertaining to the social sphere, such as the passing on of the culture from one generation to the next, education for citizenship, and education for work.[8] Other characterizations of education included the view that it is directed at a preparation for adulthood and that it is a means of drawing out the common element in our human nature. Those of a religious persuasion, such as William McGucken[9] and Maritain, characterized education, in addition, as a means of religious formation. Generally speaking, vocational education, that is, education focused on preparation for particular jobs, is not considered liberal education, and all forms of training in which the emphasis is upon the perfection of skills rather than the acquisition of knowledge and the deepening of understanding are suspect.

A distinctive feature of Hutchins' treatment of general education in *The Higher Learning in America*[10] is the commitment to a curriculum made up of what he calls the permanent studies. For these thinkers, many of whom drew on the philosophy of realism, knowledge is the truth; it is knowledge of what is real, and it is permanent and unchanging in much the same way as it is for Newman. Contrary to the view of Richard Rorty, for example, knowledge may be compared to holding a mirror up to nature.[11] As such, its implications for education are considerable: knowledge is the most precious aspect of the culture, enabling us to understand the world in which we live. The academic disciplines are the storehouses of this knowledge, the great books of mankind its most noble expression. If we wish to know and understand the world in which we live, if we are to adapt and to control it to our advantage, then it behooves us to make a study of the academic disciplines the centerpiece and the mainstay of the curriculum.

There is yet more to be gained from a study of the academic disciplines; for many in the tradition of liberal education not only do the disciplines provide us with knowledge of reality, but the study of the academic disciplines is the best way to develop the mind and promote the capacity to reason. The study of the *trivium*—logic, grammar, and rhetoric—was historically understood to aid in this process and was held in such high regard by Hutchins that it was reflected in the general education program based on a study of the great books that he encouraged at the University of Chicago.[12] In an earlier, nineteenth-century application, Newman had wanted students to translate from Greek and Latin to English because it promoted so-called intellectual gymnastics and the intellectual discipline he regarded so highly as a means of training students to think. Similarly, the *Yale Report* of 1828 emphasizes the primacy of discipline of mind. Having indicated that the *"discipline"* and the *"furniture"* of the mind are two great points to be gained in intellectual culture, the report adds that "the former of these is, perhaps, the more important of the two."[13] While the interests and capacities of the student may be borne in mind in matters of method and approach, in this view, contrary to that espoused by theorists such as John Dewey and constructivist theorists in general, the content of education is seen as a matter to be determined by the educator. Like knowledge and truth, therefore, the content of education is always and everywhere essentially the same, and abandoning the curricular canon to meet the practical exigencies of time and place or conform to the interests, capacities, and experience of students is misguided.

Those in the tradition of liberal education take the view that great social change understandably leads to change in education. Change in education is even welcome if it ensures that a better job of educating the young can be accomplished. Such change may reflect advances in science and may result in more effective educational methods and organization or ways of conducting schooling. But it does not warrant the rejection of the perennial truths regarding the nature of mankind and of reality and hence the content of education. Indeed, it is erroneous and dangerous when change leads to the elimination of the true content of education by false appeals to relevance to the needs of contemporary society or the interests of the child. It is such thinking, proponents of this tradition maintain, that led to the decline in educational standards against which philosophers of liberal education fought throughout the twentieth century.

THE SCOPE OF *THE PAIDEIA PROPOSAL*

For over fifty years, Adler was an outspoken and energetic exponent of views that make him a highly recognized twentieth-century representative of curriculum theorizing in the rationalist mold of liberal education. *The Paideia Proposal* was written by him on behalf of the Paideia Group which, like Adler, believed that the way forward in American education was through the reinstatement of traditional educational values of the kind associated with the idea of liberal education. While the publication received widespread attention, it met with a mixed reaction. It was deemed worthy of serious-minded consideration and was seen as potentially contributing to the debate on American public schooling, yet lacking in a sharp focus on the issues.[14] Following closely upon the publication of *The Paideia Proposal*, Adler produced two supporting books that between them restated and elaborated upon the essential position of *The Paideia Proposal* itself. These were *Paideia Problems and Possibilities* in 1983 and *The Paideia Program: An Educational Syllabus* in 1984.[15] There were also a number of shorter follow-up pieces by Adler published in *Reforming Education* and elsewhere.[16]

It is a fundamental premise of Adler's position in *The Paideia Proposal* and its related publications that all citizens are equal, that democracy is dependent upon an educated citizenry, and that it calls for the same quality of education for all. True education is a lifelong process, but schooling has an important role to play. Echoing the earlier words of Maritain, Adler writes that schooling "forms the habit of learning and provides the means for continuing to learn after all schooling is completed."[17] Accordingly, if schooling is considered the preparatory stage of education, and if democracy calls for the same quality of education for all, schooling must have the same educational objectives for all children without exception.

In the importance he attaches to the principles of democracy, Adler, like Hutchins, attempts to depart from some elitist notions that may have been built into the tradition of liberal education from its inception. He also appears, at least on the surface, to make another departure when he sets out the basis for determining the three main objectives of schooling. Appealing to as wide an audience as possible with his educational reform proposals, Adler declares that the objectives of schooling are determined by the callings or vocations common to all children when they grow up as citizens. While such an apparently utilitarian justification is anathema to many in the liberal education tradition, it does resonate with the approach of Broudy, Smith, and Burnett in their reliance on the uses of knowledge as a basis for the selection of curriculum content.[18]

The first objective of basic schooling, according to Adler, is to prepare all children "to take advantage of every opportunity for personal development that our society offers"[19]—mental, moral, and spiritual. The second objective relates to the individual's role as an enfranchised citizen: "an adequate preparation for discharging the duties and responsibilities of citizenship."[20] The third objective derives from our need to earn a living in some occupation: basic schooling must give all children "the basic skills that are common to all work in a society such as ours."[21]

To achieve the three objectives, basic schooling must be "general and liberal" and it must be "nonspecialized and nonvocational."[22] In addition, it should conform to the principle that "the best education for the best is the best education for all."[23] The program of study, furthermore, must be compulsory and must be "in several, crucial, overarching respects, one and the same for every child. All sidetracks, specialized courses, or elective choices must be eliminated."[24] The course of study is to be made up of three major components along with a small group of auxiliary subjects. Reference is also made to extracurricular activities, but it seems these are not part of the course of studies set forth.[25] The three major components correspond to three different ways in which the mind can be improved: by the acquisition of organized knowledge, by the development of intellectual skills, and by the enlargement of understanding. The program required to achieve these purposes may be demanding, but Adler does not doubt that students will rise to the challenge. In fact, it is the very absence of challenge and intellectual stimulation that leads to boredom and delinquency.

Corresponding to the ways in which the mind can be improved, the major components of the course of studies to be followed in Adler's plan are depicted in terms of three columns.[26] The three columns are interconnected, yet each column emphasizes its own particular goals, subject areas and activities, and methods of teaching. In column one, the goal is that of acquiring organized knowledge. This is to be achieved largely by means of didactic instruction, lectures, and the use of textbooks and other teaching aids in the three areas of subject matter indispensable to basic schooling: language, literature and fine arts; mathematics and natural sciences; and history, geography, and social studies.

In column two, the goal to be achieved is the development of intellectual skills, the skills of learning, including competence in the use of language and in dealing with a wide range of symbolic devices, such as calculators, computers, and scientific instruments. Since skills cannot be acquired in a vacuum, they are to be learned in the study of the three basic areas of subject matter found in column one. At the same time, instruction in the basic areas cannot proceed unless students develop and use the basic skills of learning. Columns one and two are therefore interdependent. Because the emphasis in column two is on the development of skills, in learning *how to do* something ('knowledge how'), as opposed to learning *about* something ('knowledge about'), which was the concern of column one, a different kind of teaching is called for. A form of teaching "akin to the coaching that is done to impart athletic skills"[27] engages students in the performance of the skills to be perfected under the supervision of a teacher.

The goal in column three is the enlargement of understanding of ideas and values. The materials of learning are books other than textbooks and other works of art, including music, visual art, plays, dance, film, and television. The appropriate mode of instruction in column three is the socratic method, "a mode of teaching called 'maieutic' because it helps the student bring ideas to birth. It is teaching by asking questions, by leading discussions, by helping students to raise their minds up from a state of understanding or appreciating less to a state of understanding or appreciating more."[28] In line with the objective of creating an educated citizenry, Adler believes that particular attention ought to be given by students to reading and discussing such works as the Declaration of Independence and the Constitution, as well as works that "deal with the ideas operative in the life of their time and place."[29] In a word, column three extends and reinforces the learnings of columns one and two by engaging the mind in active thought and critical consideration of ideas, events, and works of art.[30]

The learnings of columns one, two, and three are supplemented by auxiliary studies. These consist of twelve years of physical education accompanied by instruction about health; a number of years of manual activities such as typing, sewing, cooking, woodwork and metal work, driving, household maintenance, and the like; and some instruction to prepare students for choosing and finding a career. In preparation for work, the emphasis is not upon a particular job but upon introducing students to the wide range of work and its rewards and opportunities.

Adler calls for a twelve-year program of basic schooling, but he recognizes that some students may be at a disadvantage due to defective nurturing in the years before schooling. Some people erroneously conclude from this, he maintains, that such children are not educable and hence ought not to be afforded the same quality of education. In fact, Adler believes, all people share a common nature and, as students, children differ from one another only in their capacity for learning. Where deficiencies exist due to inadequacies in the home environment, one or two years of preschool tutelage must be provided; if the school is to succeed in basic schooling, all must be prepared in roughly equal measure.

The basic sameness of human nature common to us all has other implications, according to Adler. One may object to Adler's insistence on the same educational objectives and the same course of study for all on the grounds that it overlooks the importance of individual differences among students. What these objectors overlook, Adler tells us, is "the sameness in the context of which these differences exist."[31] Individual differences are always and only differences in degree, not in kind; children are all the same in their human nature. In a democracy, furthermore, children share a future that is the same in many essential respects. And it is these "facts of sameness that justify the sameness of the objectives at which our program for basic schooling aims. These are the facts of sameness that justify requiring the same course of study for all."[32]

When it becomes necessary to take individual differences into account, this should be done not by retreating from the proposed program, but by "adjusting that program to individual differences by administering it sensitively and flexibly in ways that accord with whatever differences must be taken into account."[33] Children with deficiencies must be given remedial teaching in the form of more time and more help from teachers and parents alike. It may be that a considerable number of children will need such teaching and, perhaps, in the earlier rather than the later years of the program. One way or another, it must be available whenever it is needed.

Important as is the proclamation of principles, the setting of objectives and course structures, and the maintenance of standards of achievement, the heart of the educational experience lies in the quality of learning that occurs. This, in turn, depends upon the quality of teaching. According to Adler, on a point of apparent agreement with progressive education, all genuine learning is active, not passive, but the vast majority of students need good teachers as "aids in the process of learning by discovery."[34] Students must also be required to behave in a manner that is conducive to learning. Important as good teaching is, many factors, including the low status of the profession, an overload of non-teaching duties, and unsuitable classroom conditions, contribute to a shortage of good teachers.

But what makes a good teacher in the first place? A proper course of university preparation, in which the main elements would be a continuation of general education of the kind proposed in *The Paideia Proposal*, and, following that, teaching practice under supervision constitute the preparatory stages of teacher education; thereafter, teachers should continue to grow intellectually throughout their careers. The quality of leadership in a school also has a huge bearing on the quality of teaching and learning. For this reason, school principals must first and foremost be teachers, and they must be empowered to execute their educational decisions, including those of hiring, firing, and enforcing proper conduct.

Among the benefits expected by Adler to accrue from the program of basic education he advocates is an improvement in the preparation of young people to go on to college, thereby enabling colleges and universities to concentrate on providing a higher education. The main concern of *The Paideia Proposal*, of course, is with the reform of basic schooling so as to raise the standard of living and the quality of living for all and "to preserve our free institutions."[35] To achieve the stated objectives, however, there must be an enlightenment of parents that the goal of basic schooling is to enable their children not just to earn a living, but to live well. There must also be a commitment to a policy of full employment, a point on which Adler and those in the reconstructionist and critical pedagogy traditions of American educational thought would likely share some rare common ground.

THE AIMS OF EDUCATION: CULTIVATION OF THE INTELLECT

In *The Paideia Proposal*, Adler sets forth a view of the objectives of schooling that attempts to point a way forward for the school. The objectives are in need of elaboration and clarification, however. As they stand, they are open to different interpretations.

Few will object to Adler's first objective of personal development, that is, the idea of the school enabling students to grow and to develop as fully as possible. In fact, one can hardly imagine schools surviving or justifying their existence if they sought otherwise. Growth or personal development may take many forms, however, and people hold different views of what desirable growth consists in; different kinds of growth or development may even be considered desirable for different persons, a point of view espoused by Nel Noddings, for example.[36] It is true that Adler sees growth as encompassing mental, moral, and spiritual development, but even this leaves one asking what kind of mental, moral, or spiritual development, and what kind of emphasis for each.

According to Adler, drawing on the idea of a person in which intellect is preeminent, there are three different ways in which the mind can be improved.

These are through the acquisition of organized knowledge, the development of intellectual skills, and the enlargement of understanding. A fuller idea of how the mind can be improved in each of these ways can be gained by referring to the subject matter that makes up organized knowledge and to the operations and activities entailed in the development of intellectual skills and the growth of understanding. This improvement will be brought about by a knowledge of language and literature, the fine arts, mathematics, and the sciences; by learning the skills of learning; and by an increase in understanding resulting from a study of the great works, ideas, and creations that represent the highest achievements of the human race throughout the ages.

Elaborating on what is meant by the development of mind—the three ways in which the mind can be improved—helps us to see a connection between the overall educational objectives of personal development and the sub-objectives or goals of the three columns of learning identified by Adler, the methods of teaching and learning in each column, and the content of each. That is to say, it is helpful in understanding what is meant by development in the mental or cognitive aspects of personal growth. But what of moral development? And what of the other two main objectives of schooling identified by Adler: preparation for citizenship and preparation for work?

Adler pays little attention to the question of moral development, apparently satisfied with the observation that the "moral sense develops under the discipline and examples that define desirable behavior . . . supported by stern measures to check or prevent misconduct."[37] This may well be the case, but does Adler have any exemplars in mind? If so, are they to be found in the study of great works of mankind, and which models are to represent desirable and which undesirable behavior? In fact, what is intended is unclear and quite unlike what is said of the concept of mental or intellectual development. Yet this lack of attention reflects Adler's long-held view that the primary role of the school is intellectual, not moral. "Educational institutions cannot be primarily responsible for moral education," he once wrote. The primary responsibility for that, he suggested, lies in the home, the church, and the broader community, though he did accept that intellectual education "is auxiliary to the formation of moral virtues."[38]

Adler is no more forthcoming regarding the objectives of preparation for citizenship and for work. It leaves us to wonder what he has in mind, and it contrasts with the kind of general analysis offered by Joel Westheimer and Joseph Kahne, for example, who have recently identified three conceptions of the good citizen.[39] Having identified the personally responsible, the participatory, and the justice oriented, they then indicated some of the qualities of each. It can be said, of course, that many of the learnings and skills that are envisaged in the three columns are likely to be applicable in the workplace and in carrying out the responsibilities of citizenship. Lack of competence in writing and simple computational skills, for example, is a concern of many employers, and a certain level of literacy in the electorate is surely a precondition of a democratic society.[40] But are competence in the three Rs and other general knowledge laid out in column one sufficient as a preparation for citizenship and for work? In the workplace, considerable importance attaches to the ability of people to work together, and sometimes to be able to exercise initiative and to take responsibility. To these may be added other skills required of workers and citizens alike. These include the ability to appreciate and accommodate the views of others, the ability to arrive at compromise as the most reasonable way forward in many cases, and the ability to appreciate the complex nature of group decision making. His commitment to democracy notwithstanding, there is need for a greater exploration of how Adler's proposals will contribute to specific civic goals, be they the advancement of critical literacy, social justice, or public service through the study of the great books or other elements of his program. Though Adler's program may educate one for these diverse attainments and activities, he does not demonstrate in any way that it does. And aside from listing different learning skills as objectives, he has little to say about the objectives of education for citizenship or for work, how they relate to that of personal development, or how they might be promoted other than through the three columns.

Undoubtedly Adler intended that students, or at least citizens, should achieve moral growth and should be prepared for citizenship and for work. But no analysis of what moral development, preparation for citizenship, or preparation for work might mean in terms of personal attributes or personal development or of the implications of these requirements for the curriculum of basic schooling is undertaken. This is unfortunate because, as a consequence, we do not know from *The Paideia Proposal* what it means for Adler to be moral, to be a citizen, or to be a worker.[41] Neither, as a consequence, can we know what will constitute a suitable curriculum for such purposes. In the absence of a clear indication of what is meant by such notions or how the proposed overall course of study will bring about moral development or develop the capacity of students for work or for citizenship, and in the absence of a general characterization of the attributes of persons so prepared, it is difficult to believe, moreover, that the three objectives of schooling that Adler identifies are taken equally seriously by him.

This interpretation gains further support from *Paideia Proposals and Possibilities*, one of the two follow-up books to *The Paideia Proposal*. Here the objective of preparation for self-development is explicitly recognized as being more important than the other two main objectives.[42] This is a point on which Maritain was largely in agreement with Adler when he distinguished between the primary aim of education, to "form a man," and the secondary aims, which included passing on the culture, preparation for life in society and for good citizenship, and preparation for family responsibilities and for making a living.[43] In regard to the objective of preparation for self-development, moreover, the emphasis in Adler is clearly upon the development of mind or, as Jane Roland Martin has said of Hirst's theory, a particular view of mind in which cognition is the focus of attention.[44] The overall view taken—namely, that a schooling that prepares one for personal growth and development also provides, as a sort of happy by-product, the best general preparation for work and for citizenship—is a standard belief associated with theories of liberal education of all varieties.

The centrality of Adler's concept of personal development to his idea of education and its implications for the curriculum bear reflection. Of special importance is the highly rationalistic character of the concept, in which human personality is conceived almost entirely in terms of cognition. There is no reference to feelings or emotions, none to goals and aspirations or a wide range of social and practical endeavors in the life of a person, or at least none that fall outside the realms of work and citizenship. Speaking of the concept of person implied in the theory of liberal education espoused by Hirst, one heavily determined by a particular concept of mind, Martin holds that the kind of person envisaged was severely limited in important ways. Such a concept of a person, and the theory of curriculum it implies, have important social consequences. "So long as the rest of education is slighted, Hirst's or any curriculum theory that singles out mind as the sole focus of liberal education," she writes, "implicitly sanctions a world inhabited by lopsided, apathetic people and, in so doing, a social, economic, and political order that will accommodate them."[45] Recognizing that Hirst's concept of liberal education as the development of mind is not peculiar to him alone, Martin's critique of Hirst could be similarly applied to positions of Adler and others in the tradition of liberal education. It would be based on Martin's broader concept of the educated person than that found in Adler and other proponents of liberal education, one that accepts that "a person consists in reason and emotion," and that "a person is a thinker and an actor." More importantly, for Martin, as for Newman, "reason and emotion are inextricably bound together in persons and so are thought and action."[46]

By such accounts, Adler's concept of human personality or personal development is a restricted one as is, consequently, his theory of liberal education. In other respects, too, Adler's concept is not well developed, although it may be elaborated upon by interpreting it in terms of the three goals that he posits for the three columns of learning. As such, given the kind of critique suggested by Martin's analysis of Hirst's theory of liberal education, and given Adler's failure to elaborate upon what he means by a citizen and a worker, Adler's presentation suggests that his views of and proposals regarding the curriculum are also restricted. Before turning to a closer consideration of Adler's curriculum stance and its implications for curriculum theorizing in general, a final word is necessary regarding what he has to say of a fourth objective of schooling.

In addition to the three objectives identified in *The Paideia Proposal* and discussed already, Adler spoke of another result or objective that also finds widespread approval in the public debate on schooling, what President Clinton once referred to as preparing students to "keep on learning for a lifetime."[47] We are told little by Adler about how this result is to be achieved, though presumably he expects that the course he proposes will provide students with basic skills, such as the three Rs, that enable them to go on learning. But people have always gone on learning throughout their lives, with or without knowledge of the three Rs. More challenging than providing the skills of learning is a preparation that motivates students to want to go on learning. Unfortunately, while the motivation of students in academic matters remains a matter of concern, Adler has not thrown very much light on how that objective might be attained.

THE BEST EDUCATION FOR ALL

From Aristotle to Adler, those in the liberal education tradition have often called for essentially the same education for all. Their reasons are not always the same, however. According to Aristotle, all should have the same education because "the state as a whole has a single end."[48] For Hutchins, all should have the same education because to do otherwise is to deny that there is any particular content to education.[49] The argument put forward by Adler in support of the same educational objectives and the same course of study for all students "regardless of native ability, temperamental bent, or conscious preferences"[50] in summary is this: the sameness of human nature that is shared by all people is of greater significance than the accidental differences between individuals. This view is bolstered by an educational argument of sorts contained in the dictum attributed by Adler and others to Hutchins, namely, that "the best education for the best is the best education for all."[51]

It is difficult to find fault with Adler's sense of justice here or his commitment to the principles of equality and democracy, which leads him to want to treat everyone equally, and there is widespread agreement with his view that all people share a common human nature. That this common human nature makes all people equal as human beings and worthy of equal respect and recognition is also widely accepted. But does this equality in what Adler calls the essence of our being mean that differences in the accidentals of our being are of little or no consequence educationally? Does it mean that despite the existence of individual differences—differences that Adler agrees do exist but which he considers to be merely accidental—the course of study must still be the same for all?

In short, for Adler, it does. Central to the belief that the best education for the best is the best education for all is the view that it is possible to know, in advance of teaching and without reference to any particular student, what is the best form of education for each student. To be sure there is a common human nature. There is also a common culture that all members of a society must share if both the individual and the society are to survive and prosper. But can we really know in advance of teaching what form of education is best for any particular student, without knowing anything of how an individual student or group of students will respond, and regardless of their talents, experience, interests, and cultural background? Dewey and Ira Shor view this matter very differently from Adler. So does Richard Pring, among others.[52] For these and for constructivist theorists in general, this stance of Adler and of the liberal tradition as a whole fails to recognize a core pedagogical dimension of education or, as Madeleine Grumet put it, "fails to grasp the reciprocity between knowledge and the knower."[53] This means that progress in learning requires the educator to take cognizance of the existing experience of the learner—even engage the learner in the decision-making process—before deciding on the content to be taught. Added to this are additional arguments advanced by Noddings, who pays particular attention to Adler in several of her writings. For Noddings, a major problem with Adler's thought is that by construing equal to mean identical he fails to recognize that individual students may respond to the same curriculum differently and he proceeds to propose a course of studies that is monolithic, culturally insensitive, and static.[54]

As we can see, serious doubt persists about whether commonalities of the kind Adler has in mind dictate the same course of study for all. These doubts gain added force if such a course overlooks differences or neglects the unique educational needs—or talents—of individual students throughout their course of basic schooling in the way that *The Paideia Proposal* appears to do. Nor does allowing for differences of approach, which Adler is willing to accept, necessarily solve the problem. We may all be equal as human beings, but our faith in such equality will not enable the blind to see or the deaf to hear. The fact that these, like other differences of this kind mentioned by Adler, are merely differences in the accidentals of our human nature does not make them any less concrete or determining factors in how we behave and in what we can know, appreciate, and perceive as individual people. It is a point that seems to be acknowledged in one chapter in *The Paideia Program*.[55] Yet for Adler, the blind and the deaf, for example, are human beings whose essential sameness as all other human beings mandates that they must have not simply the same quality of education but the same course of study. That is the only way to provide for the same quality: if we are to treat students as equals, we must ensure that they follow the same program, irrespective of differences in individual capacity or interests or personal circumstances.

Adler's concept of equality, in which we all share a common or essential nature but may differ from one another in the accidentals of that nature, is but one interpretation of equality, however. It could be argued that to disregard what Adler calls the accidentals of different people's nature, such as their capacities and their particular strengths and weaknesses, for example, is to treat people unequally. It is to proceed as if there is but one form of excellence.[56] This would be especially true if it meant providing for some students, such as those of low IQ or who are deaf or blind, only what is considered (rightly or wrongly) the best for others, such as those with a high IQ or the hearing and seeing. Not only may students respond very differently to the same course of study, for some students the response may also be markedly deleterious. And if the difference of response is attributable to the content, the adaptations of methodology, approach, and organization that Adler advocates may not address the matter.

In addition to overlooking interpretations of equality other than his own, Adler also confuses the reader. This is clearly the case in his reliance on the view that the best education for the best is the best education for all. This he introduces to support the idea of providing the same course of study for all as a way of ensuring equality for all. Far from being an argument, the claim that the best education for the best is the best education for all is nothing but a slogan. It might have the appearance of a self-evident principle, but in fact it depends upon an empirical truth claim that needs to be proven if it is to be accepted. To say that everyone is to be treated as an equal is to take a philosophical stance; to say that there ought to be the same objectives for all is to make a related logical point, that is, a point that can be argued without reference to quantitative or empirical data or proof. To claim that the best education for one person is the best education for another, however, is not to make a philosophical or logical point at all. It is to make an empirical truth claim, one that requires proof. It is like claiming, for example, that a person with an IQ of 90 can benefit most from a course of study from which a person with an IQ of 130 can also benefit most. Despite its appeal at a superficial level, the claim that the best education for the best is the best education for all is therefore nothing less than a claim in support of which Adler provides neither evidence nor proof. To say nothing of the experience of teachers who dispute Adler's contentions in *The Paideia Proposal*,[57] it is a shaky foundation upon which to base his controversial claim that all should follow the same course of study.

There is a further difficulty with the idea that the best education for the best is the best education for all.[58] We can reasonably take it that what Adler considers to be the best education is that which he himself advocates. We can also reasonably take it that by "the best"—for whom the best education is considered to be best—he means the best people. But who are the best people? Is it those in whom the intellectual life has been brought to its highest perfection and is given free reign? Would Plato's philosopher-king fit the bill, or Newman's gentleman? How about Rousseau's Emile? What of those whose lives are devoted to caring for others, such as Mother Teresa? Where would Rousseau's Sophie stand? And where would all of this leave even someone so close to Adler as Maritain and others who have argued that we reach our highest perfection through a life of religious belief and practice in which we come to know and love God and deny self? These are questions that can and will be answered differently depending on philosophical and religious beliefs. Yet even if Adler could satisfy us on these grounds he is still not out of the woods. If, as he has stated, everyone is to be considered essentially the same, and if, moreover, all citizens are equal, how can one person be better than anyone else? How could there ever be a best?

HEADWORK

If Adler's justification for requiring the same course of studies for all is unsound, this does not invalidate his curriculum; other justifications could, and as we shall see, have been provided to support this or similar claims. Underlying Adler's particular proposals, moreover, is a framework that ensures a balance and structure in the curriculum of basic schooling, one that respects recognized standards of curriculum design and development. Following such a model of curriculum design and development, a crucial task in drawing up a curriculum or school program is that of selecting and organizing appropriate curriculum content.

Not just any content will do. In the first place, the content selected must be appropriate for attaining the educational aims or objectives that have been decided upon. It is in these that the chosen content serves its purpose and finds its ultimate justification. Likewise, the organization of the curriculum for purposes of teaching and learning must lead to attaining the objectives that have been decided upon. In the second place, if the intended educational goals or objectives are to be achieved, one must take account of a range of practical and pedagogical principles in the selection and organization of curriculum content. While there are points at which Adler's framework is deficient, it sets out clearly the relationship among the various curriculum or program elements. Whatever limitations exist in and among these elements, the relationships between them and the objectives of schooling, and the relationships between them and the methods of teaching, are brought out. For example, when the objective is the attainment of organized knowledge, as is the goal of Adler's column one, the content of various school subjects is chosen and a particular kind of teaching—didactic instruction—is prescribed. It is the same with column two and column three. The curriculum content and the methods of teaching suggested by Adler are chosen in the belief that they are suitable for attaining the goals of developing the intellectual skills and the enlargement of understanding, the goals of columns two and three, respectively.

Martin has recently made the point that education can be an unpredictable and unruly affair that confounds those who seek to control and manage it.[59] Yet the search for order, coherence, and at least a modicum of predictability is a common feature of advocates of liberal education, where the purpose, content, and justification of the school curriculum is determined by a view of the nature and structure of organized knowledge. Such a view has long been associated with liberal education, and it enjoyed a special prominence in the school curriculum reform movement of the 1960s. In his work, Phenix saw the structure of knowledge in terms of six realms of meaning,[60] each representing a distinctive kind of systematic knowledge. These realms he identified as symbolics, empirics, esthetics, synnoetics, ethics, and synoptics. These being the only systematic or scientific and reliable kinds of knowledge that existed, it is only they that should be included in the school curriculum, he argued. This being the nature and structure of knowledge, he further argued, it ought to be reflected in the school curriculum by requiring every student to study in each of the six realms.

Broudy, Smith, and Burnett envisioned the nature and structure of school subjects somewhat differently. They argued that four different uses of school knowledge may be identified, namely, the replicative, the associative, the interpretive, and the applicative. As they envisioned the subject matter of general education, they believed it ought to be focused largely upon enabling students to become adept in the interpretive uses of knowledge. These uses, they believed, could best be presented to students by organizing them into five areas of school knowledge that incorporate the key ideas and criteria and the necessary symbolic and logical operations necessary for interpretation. These areas included the symbolics of information including language and mathematics; basic sciences including general science, chemistry, physics, and biology; developmental studies including history, geography, politics, economics, and technology; exemplars including art appreciation and value education; and the consideration of molar problems aimed at instruction in the art of collective deliberation.[61]

Perhaps the most widely cited example in the closing decades of the twentieth century of a theory of the nature and structure of knowledge being brought to bear on determining the content of the school curriculum is found in the work of Hirst.[62] Hirst has argued that there are different kinds of organized knowledge, and each must be represented in the school curriculum. According to Hirst, it is possible to identify some seven distinct forms of knowledge, each of which corresponds to a way in which people, over time, have attempted to understand the world. Accordingly, in the theory of liberal education he once propounded, education was to be centered, of necessity, on the study of these different forms. For Hirst, as for Newman, who insisted on students being exposed to the full circle of the sciences, to have omitted the study of any form would have left an education less than complete and rendered seriously deficient.

Adler's position regarding the nature and structure of the school curriculum is not well supported or fully justified. Yet a broad justification is presented on the grounds that the three areas of organized knowledge considered by Adler to be compulsory "comprise the most fundamental branches of learning. No one can claim to be educated who is not reasonably well acquainted with all three."[63] In the program for basic schooling set forth by Adler, those educational goals of personal development—as distinct from the three objectives of basic schooling—that he identifies are the normally accepted goals of liberal education. These goals are acquaintance with the broad areas of systematic knowledge known to us, understanding and appreciation of the value dimensions of the human situation, and development of the intellectual skills necessary for the further pursuit of knowledge and the critical consideration of the variety of social, moral, and political issues with which we are all inevitably faced. Insofar as these are the goals of personal development that Adler's curriculum proposals are aimed at attaining, theorists of liberal education would consider his plan acceptable as a program of basic schooling. These goals presume if not include the study of the three Rs and basic computer skills; practice in order to develop skills, including the skills of analytical and critical thinking; exposure to a broad range of scientific, cultural, and esthetic experiences, including music and literature; and the discussion of value questions. It is not made immediately clear by Adler or others how teachable or even how suitable all of this would be at the elementary-school level, but it has long been believed that there is much to be gained from such a course of study in secondary education.

Highly prized as the distinctive intellectual attributes of the person of liberal education may be, however, there are other attributes of mind and personality demanded of the individual in his or her life as a citizen, as a worker, and even in the ordinary activities of everyday living for which liberal education is popularly considered to be inadequate. The point is explicitly accepted by Hirst. In a follow-up piece to his original article setting forth his forms of knowledge theory of liberal education, he wrote that liberal education:[64]

can not be regarded as providing a total education. It explicitly excludes all objectives other than intellectual ones, thereby ignoring many of the central concerns of, say physical education and the education of character. . . . The lack of concern for moral commitment, as distinct from moral understanding, that it seems to imply, is a particularly significant limitation to this concept's usefulness.

To a degree this point is taken by Adler as shown by his adoption, alongside the objective of general personal development, of the objectives of preparing students both for work and for citizenship as well as by his proposals for auxilliary studies. But the point remains very much underdeveloped in Adler's theory of liberal education. This is true both in his failure to elaborate upon the objectives of preparation for work and for citizenship and what they imply in terms of growth, as I have already suggested, and in the inadequacy of the provision made by Adler in the area of the auxiliary studies, as I shall argue presently. What is said of Adler's positon there will be broadly true of curriculum theorists who favor liberal education, for Adler is not alone among them in refusing to accommodate nontraditional or nondisciplinary forms of curriculum content in his educational thought.[65]

It is largely within the space of one page of *The Paideia Proposal* devoted to a treatment of physical education, manual activities, and education for work that the nature and place of the auxiliary studies is dealt with. Given the view taken there, it is not surprising that auxiliary studies are excluded, both in their presentation and in their conceptualization, from the columns of learning around which the essential substance of Adler's position on goals, methods of teaching, and curriculum take shape. They are placed well beyond the bounds of legitimacy.

In regard to physical education, Adler tells us that young people need physical exercise—as distinct from physical education—for the sake of their health—as distinct from their education. They also need it "as an outlet for their abundant energy." A program of "physical education and participation in various intramural sports and athletic exercises," to last a full twelve years and to be accompanied by instruction about health is mandated for all. To twelve years of physical education in the sense described is to be added a number of years in which all students, boys and girls alike, are to be required to "participate in a wide variety of manual activities" such as sewing, cooking, typing, household maintenance, automobile driving and maintenance, and craftwork, including woodwork and metalwork.[66] We are never told why these activities are required. Neither is any attempt made to indicate or explore what their educative value might be.[67] Career education is reserved for the later years. And here the objective is not to prepare students for a particular job but rather to ensure that young persons may be "introduced to the wide range of human work—the kinds of occupations and careers, their significance and requirements, their rewards and opportunities."[68] Aside from these and the activities associated with the three columns, all other school-related activities are considered to be extracurricular and seemingly even farther beyond the pale.

The fact that Adler saw fit to augment the studies in the three columns of learning with the more directly useful and practical auxiliary studies suggests that the three columns were considered incomplete in some way, although no elaboration as to reasons is provided. Not surprisingly, Adler's concept of auxiliary studies and practical education is also underdeveloped. In equating physical education with exercise and education for work with a description of jobs, their salaries and relative status, Adler fails to distinguish between the external manifestations of what education in these areas can enable students to do and the understandings, insights, appreciations, attitudes, values, and skills that constitute their fuller educational significance. It is a failure, moreover, that provides no grounds for Adler's response to Steven M. Cahn's criticism of his stance on vocational education[69] with the assertion that he sees practical activities as having the educational potential that Dewey does. It is also disingenuous of Adler to claim in response to Cahn that "what Dewey said of gardening as a liberal and leisure pursuit, we say of carpentry, machine and household repairs, cooking and so forth."[70] Nothing of the kind was said in *The Paideia Proposal* nor was any basis provided to warrant saying so.

Neither is any awareness shown by Adler that physical education, as opposed to physical exercise, promotes coordination of movement, the development of interests and skills, the learning and development of healthful living habits, an understanding of the body and its capabilities, the development of social skills, and an understanding of discipline, loyalty, and commitment to goals and ideals. Physical education in conjunction with sporting and athletic activities, of course, can also have a motivational significance in the school, and it has enormous potential for leisure and recreation and esthetic education. Yet one sees little in *The Paideia Proposal* or in any of the follow-up works by Adler to suggest awareness of these possibilities. Much the same can be said of the areas of education for work and the various other practical studies included in auxiliary studies, where their educative potential is largely disregarded.

Related to Adler's underestimation of the educative potential of auxiliary studies is his hesitancy to harness approaches to teaching and learning that would appear to be appropriate to growth and development in these areas. This failure is due, at least in part, to his underestimation of the educative potential of practical knowledge in physical education, education for work, and education for citizenship. But it arises also out of a failure to consider with the same commitment as in the case of the three columns of learning what may be the most appropriate and beneficial ways of dealing with various forms of practical education such as those represented by auxiliary studies.

It may be helpful to consider some examples. Didactic instruction, as opposed to coaching or socratic questioning, and information or mere 'knowledge about,' we are told by Adler, are inadequate for advancing skill development or understanding, the goals of columns two and three. In the brief account given of auxiliary studies, we are told that students will be instructed about health and, it would appear, about work, too. From what he has to say of instruction by contrast with teaching for skill development or understanding, it is clear that Adler sees instruction as concerned merely with passing on information.[71] This suggests, therefore, that health education and education for work are concerned merely with the facts, and that skill and understanding are dispensable in the case of education for health and work. If so, some important questions arise. Is health education not concerned with developing skills and habits and ways of understanding the health of individuals and communities? Are the facts alone sufficient as a basis for education for work if skills and understandings are dispensable here also? It would appear not.

In health education and in work education we are not concerned merely with the facts—facts that in themselves are as useless as the facts contained in column one without the additional skills and understandings promoted in columns two and three. In matters of health and work, we are concerned with values, understandings, and attitudes as much as with facts, and education in such matters requires as sympathetic a hearing and treatment as does education in the matter of literature or science. The same is true of education for citizenship and the many other auxiliary or practical studies given cursory treatment by Adler. In such areas of education, facts alone are not adequate. There is no reason to believe that, as a minimum, they need not be supplemented by teaching of a kind envisaged for columns two and three, teaching aimed at developing skills through supervised practice and a heightening of understanding through discussion.

Adler is not alone among liberal education theorists in failing to recognize the educational potential represented by the areas of experience associated with auxiliary studies and their relevance to the lives of students, a criticism that Martin has also directed toward advocates of the academic disciplines.[72] If, as I have suggested, health education is one area where this is evident, it may be asked how Adler fares when it comes to his advocacy of education for work and for citizenship, areas that would appear to share the practical orientation of auxiliary studies. Adler, and highly rationalist theorists of liberal education in general, may be correct in maintaining that school is not a place to train students for particular jobs. This does not mean, however, that education for work will be adequately catered to by the proposals set forward by Adler when he claims such preparation to be a general outcome of his overall curriculum proposals or in what he has to say of career education. Preparation for work is not confined to information about jobs or training for specific jobs. General knowledge, skills, and understandings of work itself are also necessary. This being so, the opportunity to have experience of work and of the workplace may have much to commend it as a way of achieving certain insights and understandings, a point that appears to earn limited acceptance in *The Paideia Program*[73] and finds some support in the school-to-career movement.[74] Such experience cannot be exhaustive or comprehensive, but it is a mode of learning in regard to work akin, for example, to acting and performing, held up in *The Paideia Proposal* as ways of gaining fuller understanding of dramatic works or musical compositions. If it provides such understanding, to deem it illiberal is highly questionable, even if it falls outside the ambit of the academic disciplines or is labeled vocational by some.

Much the same kind of case can be made in regard to education for citizenship, a point recognized by others since Adler.[75] Even as early as *High School*, the Report of the Carnegie Foundation published shortly after *The Paideia Proposal*, Boyer called for the introduction of a new Carnegie unit devoted to community service.[76] Yet, this is an area where Adler fails to see possibilities for practical forms of educational experience. Given what we know of service-learning and of civic education, for example, Adler's proposals for an exclusively literary approach to education for citizenship may actually be counterproductive. A somewhat similar criticism has been leveled by Martin against Martha Nussbaum, in whose classical defense of liberal education special attention is given to the role of liberal education as a preparation for citizenship.[77] Reflecting Martin's own commitment to education for participation, Martin's criticism of Nussbaum is directed at her failure to recognize a place for such education in her proposals for a new form of liberal education aimed at cultivation for the functions of life generally.[78] For Martin, the weakness of Nussbaum's position, admirable as it is in many respects, is that Nussbaum "wants the products of liberal education to be intelligent participants in *debates about* the world's pressing problems but says nothing about their learning to participate in activities that might actually solve the problems."[79]

In the final analysis, it is difficult to know what to make of Adler's inclusion of auxiliary studies in part because we are given no explanation or justification for their place in his proposal. Perhaps they are included as an attempt to address the question of practical education, though they do little to moderate the emphasis on theoretical or academic education at the expense of the practical. Neither is there any attempt to address the issue of the purpose of such education, either from the point of its content or for its potential pedagogical or motivational value. What can be said, however, is that the recognition of a place for practical or useful knowledge in the school curriculum, for whatever reason, does mark a modest departure in the mainstream of liberal education.[80]

Adler's failure to explore the educative potential of preparation for work and preparation for citizenship and the dismissive attitude that excludes auxiliary studies from his core curriculum of general or liberal education is a hallmark of his curriculum stance. It is also symptomatic of the entire tradition of liberal education that he wishes to extend to the public school. In this view, certain subjects are deemed appropriate subject matter not only for the education of mind, but more broadly for the education of "man as man." Examples include those subjects on the upper half of Plato's divided line of knowledge; the seven liberal arts and sciences comprising the *trivium* and the *quadrivium*; literature, science, and theology as advocated by Newman; and those represented in Hirst's seven forms. Knowledge pertaining to action, to making objects, to practical endeavors, is considered not only mechanical or merely useful. It is inferior and inessential.

To suggest this much is not to say that theoretical studies are less important than practical knowledge. Neither is it to say that the practical or technical studies are without serious merit, so lacking in value that they do not earn a place in the education of the young. Practical endeavors too are essential to living and even to the growth of understanding. Besides, for many students, practical studies are the ones from which they most readily grow in knowledge and understanding and gain self-respect. For others, there may be greater safety, security, and even growth in book learning.

While preferential status has historically been accorded to academic studies in theories of liberal education, less attention has been given to articulating what it is that academic studies contribute to the well-being of the community at large beyond the growth of the individual. Considerably less attention has been given to articulating not only what it means to be a worker and a citizen—in terms of knowledge, attitude, and skills—than to examining how the subjects of liberal education contribute to personal development or the formation of self. Similarly, little attention has been given to inquiring into what kinds of studies, including experiential and practical studies, are best suited to the formation of workers and citizens. What discussion there has been around these matters, moreover, makes it clear that some antagonism exists toward them and little appreciation is shown regarding their educative potential. This lack of appreciation of the educative potential of practical studies is clearly evident in Adler's own consideration of auxiliary studies, as I have attempted to show. And this is to say nothing of subjects that might be aimed more at the formation of the young in the knowledge, skills, and attitudes of the home and of personal relations. A special hostility seems to be reserved for these subjects.[81]

This said, the curriculum proposals of *The Paideia Proposal* have their merits. This is particularly true of its proposals in regard to the three columns of learning, the framework of coherence in the curriculum that they provide, and their justification in terms of a theory of liberal education. There will be many students, however, for whom the three columns will pose huge, possibly insurmountable difficulties. Valuable as are the three columns as a basis for drawing up a program of basic schooling, they do not provide for all of the requirements of general schooling, even by Adler's own criteria. The idea of auxiliary studies to complement the core curriculum laid out in the three columns has merit, but it is an idea whose full potential has not been explored. This is true of both the subject matter and the teaching methodologies envisaged.

TEACHING AND PEDAGOGY

The Paideia Proposal does reach beyond a consideration of the content of the curriculum, as when it treats of different methods of teaching. The treatment—or the lack of it—given to auxiliary studies alone, however, raises many questions regarding the pedagogical stance of *The Paideia Proposal*. In particular, there is the question of what account is taken of features of the educational situation other than the purpose and formal content of the school curriculum. These features include teaching, evaluation of learning, and school organization, all of which can have a direct or indirect bearing upon learning. The three main methods of teaching advocated in *The Paideia Proposal*—namely, didactic teaching, coaching, and maieutic or socratic teaching—have long been recognized as important, and each is assigned a distinctive role by Adler. True as this may be, however, Adler's stance demonstrates a general lack of pedagogical awareness and, unlike Newman's, perpetuates a serious underestimation of the importance of the pedagogical dimensions of education and schooling, be it for the purpose of liberal education or any other.

Of the several issues that could be raised to bear out this judgment, two are of special interest. The first is the attention given to the assessment of student learning. Special importance attaches to the assessment of learning in part because it has become so prominent a consideration in public schooling today. This prominence is also a result of Adler's insistence that the same objectives and the same course of study should apply to all by virtue of the sameness of our human nature. This sameness, he further insists, requires that there be "a satisfactory standard of accomplishment for all" or what is referred to on another occasion as all "achieving the requisite standard of performance."[82] With the attachment to standards in governmental policies on education in the closing decades of the twentieth century, the widespread acceptance of standards by many subject organizations, and their enshrinement in the United States in *Goals 2000* in the wake of *A Nation at Risk*, Adler's invoking of standards was prescient.

The establishment of standards, however they may be framed, does appear to be a necessary step in determining whether students have attained the desired level of learning that, presumably, the standards attempt to articulate. As in the debates surrounding the assessment of learning, however, there is no unanimity regarding the need for or even the helpfulness of standards in the educational sphere. In addition, while federal legislation, for example, *Goals 2000*, has made a valiant attempt, achieving such articulation—and the necessary political will—has not been easy, it should be said.[83] Failure to articulate assessable standards for learning, moreover, would appear to render standards of any kind not merely redundant but probably harmful to teaching and learning.

Despite its prescience and the high-sounding rhetoric around the demand for standards, *The Paideia Proposal* does not tell us what represents a satisfactory standard of achievement. Neither does Adler tell us how we are to ascertain whether the requisite standard has been achieved. This being so, it comes as no great surprise that, aside from one or two passing references to the teacher as an examiner, Adler has little or nothing to say on the subject of assessment or examination. To speak so demandingly and insistently of standards and yet to offer no clear explanation of what he means by standards is irresponsible.[84] To gloss over the question in *Paideia Problems and Possibilities* with a rhetorical flourish, asserting that "evaluation is a complicated process"[85] and follow a few years later with some off-the-cuff advice does not reflect well on the range of solutions that Adler proposes, and it leaves huge questions unanswered.[86]

Some form of assessment of learning is necessary to determine if and what students are learning. In the past, assessment frequently took the form of paper-and-pencil tests along with oral examinations. The advent of mass schooling in the nineteenth century was accompanied by the introduction of external public examinations as selection procedures for admission to various occupations, including the civil service. Later, so-called objective testing, which engaged machines in the assessment process and in the calculation of results, entered the scene. On a smaller scale, examinations of practical performance once reserved for special purposes began to become more commonplace. And most recently we have seen the advent of authentic assessment, portfolios, including electronic portfolios, and other technologically based means of assessment. These innovations notwithstanding, satisfactory approaches to the assessment of various forms of learning, such as emotional development and moral formation—including the old chestnut of character education—remain elusive. Despite the huge investment in more formal approaches to assessment and the widespread use of standardized testing in particular, some remain highly skeptical of the reliability of these kinds of assessment and outspoken in the condemnation of them as seriously counterproductive to good teaching and learning.[87]

Like it or not, however, assessment remains essential as a means of feedback to guide the further work of learners and is an important element in any comprehensive theory of schooling. Because of the importance Adler attaches to students attaining a satisfactory standard of achievement as well as the joy in learning he wishes to promote,[88] a joy often difficult to nurture in the face of tests and examinations, it is especially important that Adler should have addressed this question carefully. The failure in *The Paideia Proposal* to do so, or even to address aspects of the questions that have come into the picture in more recent times is a serious deficiency in Adler's manifesto. Given the grave concerns raised by many regarding the deficiencies of standardized assessment in general, moreover, it is unlikely that these can be readily turned to in order to fill in the blanks in his position.[89]

The second issue to be discussed regarding pedagogy and teaching is more general in nature and arises from Adler's apparent unwillingness to consider pedagogical matters seriously or to appreciate adequately their significance. *The Paideia Proposal* shows little awareness of what has been said of the hidden curriculum and its implications for schooling, of the effects of bureaucracy and the institutionalization of schooling on teaching and learning, of the isolation of the school, and through the school, of young people from the community and in particular from adults. In addition, it shows little awareness of changes that have taken place in youth culture and in the patterns of family living and work. There is a pronounced emphasis on education based on a study of texts, but little consideration is given to the life circumstances of students, the unique challenges of childhood and adolescence, or the unrelenting and dehumanizing deprivations of violence, poverty, neglect, and abuse. Nor is it considered how these varied circumstances might be interwoven with, or at least acknowledged in, the curriculum. Of particular importance, no attention has been given to the impact of these everyday realities on the curriculum and little to its impact on teaching and learning. Yet the effects on student learning can be decidedly adverse and the measures taken to deal with it unfair and chilling.[90] As a consequence, while the effectiveness of the school curriculum is hugely affected by these realities, *The Paideia Proposal* sheds little or no light on how liberal or general schooling might respond to them or even take cognizance of them, now or in the future.

The failure to take account of considerations such as these deprives Adler and his rendition of liberal education for today's world of a necessary set of perspectives from which to view the question of the curriculum of basic schooling. Not only does his version of liberal education fail to recognize the existence of these issues, proposals set forth in *The Paideia Proposal* are at odds with recommendations of others. A case in point is the question of the influence of the school as an agent for the isolation of youth. Even before the appearance of *The Paideia Proposal*, a number of commentators, including the Panel on Youth of the President's Science Advisory Committee in its Report *Youth: Transition to Adulthood*,[91] drew attention to the influence of the school as an agent for the isolation of youth from other children and from adults in particular. Through the almost exclusively school-based programs it proposes, its preoccupation with literary and academic studies, the lack of opportunities for encounter with the community outside of the school, Adler's vision fails to address these realities. Adler's proposal keeps students out of places of work, for example, where their predecessors of not too many years earlier learned to mix and to work with adults and to undertake many of the responsibilities of adults. These proposals, while allegedly aiming to prepare students for life, may in fact be denying students experiences necessary for such preparation.

Since the appearance of *The Paideia Proposal*, there have also been additional developments in this area. One is the case of the school-to-career movement supported by both federal and state initiatives. Here schools attempt to prepare students for work by placing them in actual places of work as part of their school programs. Such programs are not without their weaknesses, but they do address the matter of preparing students for the world of work in a manner that Adler was unprepared to consider. Until such approaches are at least considered, however, we cannot evaluate their actual inadequacies; besides, there are benefits, too, as the research shows.[92] How best or to what extent the school can respond to challenges of this kind, and whether it will be necessary to carve out new patterns for the school in its interrelations with other potentially educative agents in society, also needs to be considered.

The Paideia Proposal, for its part, shows no willingness to consider such possibilities and neither does the historical tradition to which it belongs. If anything, Adler's position—with its insistence on compulsory education for all up to the age of eighteen with no out-of-school experiences of note, no significant choices to be made by students or initiatives to be undertaken, no significant opportunity to interact with other educative influences such as places of work, and little or no opportunity for service or any significant individualized projects—would seem to exacerbate the situation. It is difficult to imagine how one could have devised school programs more unsympathetic to addressing the present-day problems of transition from youth to adulthood than those proposed in *The Paideia Proposal*.

ADLER'S DEMOCRACY AND EDUCATION

It is on the questions of the aims or purposes and the curriculum or content of education that the theory of liberal education has made its most significant contribution. Its most widely recognized philosophical, contemporary formulation was the statement by Hirst.[93] One of its more novel formulations is that set forth by Hutchins, in which the focus of study is upon the great books of mankind, aided by a study of grammar, rhetoric, logic and mathematics.[94] Its formulation by Adler in *The Paideia Proposal*, as three columns of learning, each with its own goals, curriculum areas, and methods of teaching, is one of the most clearcut. It is also the formulation that has most explicitly addressed the role of liberal education in the public schools and most clearly laid out a coherent proposal for its implementation therein.

Adler and *The Paideia Proposal* have had their share of critics, of course, and more recently a strong defender in Burton Weltman.[95] None of his critics is more severe than Noddings in the devastating cumulative assessment she offers of Adler, elements of which have already been intimated: for Noddings, Adler is arrogant, given to platitude, the purveyor of half truths, distortions, and misleading statements in the arguments he offers and stances he advocates.[96] For all of this, *The Paideia Proposal* is a notable contemporary formulation of the theory of liberal education and a classic statement of a conservative philosophy of basic schooling that has been characterized as "essentially an Aristotelian or classicist blueprint for educational reform."[97] No single author or text can be said to represent accurately an entire school of educational thought, but a close study of *The Paideia Proposal*, in conjunction with other works, however, does give us the opportunity to assess how a celebrated American exponent of the theory of liberal education perceived and responded to perennial questions and difficulties facing education in the closing decades of the twentieth century. It enables us to ask what contribution this theorizing makes to resolving these difficulties and in what respects this position may be inadequate, possibly misleading, and in need of modification as it attempts to address issues arising in the rapidly changing contexts of education and schooling today.

While the philosophy of education promoted by Adler is clearly inspired by the traditional European ideal of liberal education and interpreted by him in highly rationalist terms, there are aspects of Adler's thought that are characteristically American. An example is his view that the objectives of schooling are to be determined by the vocations or callings common to all people. Central to liberal education has been the notion of education as an end in itself, something worth pursuing for its own sake. While this may be a somewhat ambiguous concept,[98] liberal education has not historically sought justification by an appeal to its utility. This is why it is surprising to see Adler waver from the accepted stance, as when suggesting that the objectives of schooling should be determined by considerations having to do with preparation for citizenship and for work. This is a line of argument that appears to have more in common with the *Cardinal Principles of Secondary Education*, which was anathema to those in the mainstream of liberal education.

Having expressed this point of view, however, rather than pursuing it to its conclusion, Adler ultimately reverts to the academic view of curriculum long accepted in the liberal education tradition. Hence his failure to analyze closely or establish a prominent place for civic and work education in his curriculum proposals. Hence too his acceptance of the classical view of liberal education: not only is education of the kind represented by the three columns of learning the most suitable for the purpose of self-development, it is also the most suitable as a basic preparation for citizenship and for work. This is Adler's version of education as a preparation for life.

If there is the suggestion of an American influence in regard to how the objectives of education are to be determined, namely, if "the three objectives are determined by the vocations or callings common to all children,"[99] this influence is pronounced when it comes to Adler's commitment to democracy. It is this commitment to democracy that is the main basis of his insistence on the same quality and the same course of study for all. Echoing the egalitarian sentiments of Thomas Jefferson, Horace Mann, and Dewey before him, Adler maintains that if democracy requires that all be treated as equals, it is also dependent upon an educated citizenry: "The two—universal suffrage and universal schooling—are inextricably bound together. The one without the other is a perilous delusion. Suffrage without schooling produces mobocracy, not democracy—not rule of law, not constitutional government by the people as well as for them."[100]

While *The Paideia Proposal* invokes Dewey in general, and specifically in its commitment to democracy, it would be incorrect to see *The Paideia Proposal* as in any substantial way Deweyan. While there is some attention to the student as an active learner, there is nothing in Adler that even approximates Dewey's notion of relating the curriculum to the stage of growth or experience of the learner. While sharing a modicum of common ground with reconstructionist theory on socioeconomic issues, Adler does not either belong to this school in American educational theory, and he is clearly out of step with the activist themes characteristic of critical pedagogy and those advocating social justice. Preparation for democracy, for Adler, is a largely cerebral affair with little opportunity or encouragement given to the development of skills of group deliberation and decision making or with education for participation as envisioned by Joseph L. DeVitis, Robert W. Johns, and Douglas J. Simpson[101] and by Shor and Martin. Schooling is undoubtedly seen in *The Paideia Proposal* as being linked to the maintenance of free institutions and promoting the democratic way of life, as well as contributing to the economic well-being of the individual and society. In no sense is the school seen as having a mission to reconstruct society or reshape it radically for future generations. Rather, the emphasis is upon conservation of what is good and upon the full realization of the true meaning of democracy in action, by means of equality of education for all leading to a higher quality of life for all. It is in these general ways that Adler hopes to improve the quality of life for future citizens and not through any specific structural changes in society or in the distribution of wealth or power in the community.

Adler's general stance on the issues facing public schooling in the United States today might then be broadly described as distinctively and conservatively American. This is particularly true of its blending of major elements of the honored European approach to secondary education with the American emphasis on preparation for democracy, along with the suggestion of a need to prepare students for the major activities or callings of everyday living. While Adler is short on detail and supporting arguments for the generally conservative position he adopts in *The Paideia Proposal*, and while this might account in part for the shortcomings of his position, his reform plan is nonetheless comprehensive in its range. He addresses himself to questions of guiding principles, aims, and objectives; to questions of curriculum content and structure; to questions of teaching and learning; and to questions of administration and policy. In addition, he pursues the implications of his proposals in the important area of the preparation of teachers. Accordingly, it is fair to say that Adler deals with many of the central issues that any educational reform program ought to address—with the notable exception of the crucial interrelated issues of standards and assessment—and he does so by drawing on a rich and complex tradition. In the strong stance he has taken on these issues, moreover, there lies a challenge to those of different viewpoints to articulate them.

NOTES

1. Mortimer J. Adler, *The Paideia Proposal: An Educational Manifesto* (New York: Macmillan Publishing Co., Inc., 1982). See also Mortimer J. Adler, *Paideia Problems and Possibilities* (New York: Macmillan Publishing Co., Inc., 1983); Mortimer J. Adler, *The Paideia Program: An Educational Syllabus* (New York: Macmillan Publishing Co., Inc., 1984); and Mortimer J. Adler, *Reforming Education: The Opening of the American Mind*, ed. Geraldine Van Doren (New York: Macmillan Publishing Co., Inc., 1988). It's not out of the way here to cite Adler's own classic *How to Read a Book*, first published in 1940, which contains an early list of the 'great books.' The revised and updated edition is Mortimer J. Adler and Charles Van Doren, *How to Read a Book* (New York: Simon and Schuster, 1972). See also Mortimer J. Adler and Robert Wolff, *A General Introduction to the Great Books and to a Liberal Education* (Chicago: Encyclopaedia Britannica, 1959). The chief writings of Adler that are made use of here are those relating to the Paideia project.

2. Adler, *The Paideia Proposal*, 18.

3. Adler, *Reforming Education*, 282.

4. National Commission on Excellence in Education, *A Nation at Risk* (Washington, DC: U.S. Department of Education, 1983); Allan Bloom, *The Closing of the*

American Mind (New York: Simon and Schuster, 1987); E. D. Hirsch, *Cultural Literacy* (New York: Vintage Books, 1988); Ernest L. Boyer, *High School: A Report on Secondary Education in America* (New York: Harper and Row, 1983); and Theodore Sizer, *Horace's Compromise* (Boston: Houghton Mifflin, 1984).

5. Especially influential among these were those associated with a series of publications of the late 1960s and 1970s known as the black papers.

6. In this connection, see D. G. Mulcahy, "Jane Roland Martin and Paul Hirst on Liberal Education: A Reassessment," *Journal of Thought* 38, no. 1 (Spring 2003), 25–29 and J. Mark Halstead, "Liberal Values and Liberal Education" in *The RoutledgeFalmer Reader in the Philosophy of Education,* ed. Wilfred Carr (London: RoutledgeFalmer, 2005), 115–116.

7. Jacques Maritain, "Thomist Views on Education," in *Modern Philosophies and Education.* 54th Yearbook of the National Society for the Study of Education, Part I, ed. Nelson B. Henry (Chicago: The University of Chicago Press, 1955), 62. The term "the educated man," while once commonly employed, became the object of critique in Jane Roland Martin's analysis of R. S. Peters's idea of the educated man and is rarely used anymore. See Jane Roland Martin, *Changing the Educational Landscape: Philosophy, Women, and Curriculum* (New York: Routledge, 1994), 70–87.

8. Jacques Maritain, *Education at the Crossroads* (New Haven: Yale University Press, 1943), 14–15, and Maritain, "Thomist Views on Education," 62–65.

9. William McGucken, "The Philosophy of Catholic Education," in *Philosophies of Education,* 41st Yearbook of the National Society for the Study of Education, Part I, ed. Nelson B. Henry (Bloomington, IL: Public School Publishing Company, 1942), 251–288.

10. Robert M. Hutchins, *The Higher Learning in America* (New Haven: Yale University Press, 1936), 59–87. See also Robert M. Hutchins, *The Great Conversation: The Substance of a Liberal Education,* vol. 1 of Robert M. Hutchins, ed., *Great Books of the Western World* (Chicago: Encyclopedia Britannica, 1952).

11. See Richard Rorty, *Philosophy and the Mirror of Nature* (Princeton, NJ: Princeton University Press, 1979).

12. See Hutchins, *The Higher Learning in America,* 59–87, and Adler, *Reforming Education,* xix–xxiii.

13. *The Yale Report of 1828,* Part I, at http://collegiateway.org/reading/yale-report-1828/ (accessed July 25, 2007). Also in G. H. Willis, W. H. Schubert, R. Bullough, C. Kridel, and J. Holton, eds., *The American Curriculum: A Documentary History* (Westport, CT: Greenwood Press, 1993), 28.

14. Christopher Lucas, "The Paideia Proposal: An Educational Manifesto," *Educational Studies* 14, no. 3 (Fall 1983): 285, and Marshall Gregory, "A Response to Mortimer Adler's Paideia Proposal," *Journal of General Education* 36, no. 2 (1984): 70–78.

15. Adler, *Paideia Problems and Possibilities,* and Adler, *The Paideia Program.*

16. Adler, *Reforming Education,* 277–317, and Mortimer J. Adler, "The Paideia Proposal: Rediscovering the Essence of Education," *The American School Board Journal* 169, no. 7 (July 1982): 17–20.

17. Adler, *The Paideia Proposal,* 10.

18. Harry S. Broudy, B. Othanel Smith, and Joe R. Burnett, *Democracy and Excellence in American Secondary Education* (Chicago: Rand McNally, 1964). See also Harry S. Broudy, *The Uses of Schooling* (New York: Routledge, 1988).

19. Adler, *The Paideia Proposal*, 16.
20. Adler, *The Paideia Proposal*, 17.
21. Adler, *The Paideia Proposal*, 17.
22. Adler, *The Paideia Proposal*, 18.
23. Adler, *The Paideia Proposal*, 6, 7.
24. Adler, *The Paideia Proposal*, 21.
25. Adler, *The Paideia Proposal*, 34.
26. Adler, *The Paideia Proposal*, 23.
27. Adler, *The Paideia Proposal*, 27.
28. Adler, *The Paideia Proposal*, 29.
29. Adler, *The Paideia Proposal*, 30.
30. In 1987, Adler elaborated on what he understood by socratic teaching as employed in relation to column three by clarifying what he meant by seminar teaching. See Adler, *Reforming Education*, 298–308.
31. Adler, *The Paideia Proposal*, 42.
32. Adler, *The Paideia Proposal*, 43.
33. Adler, *The Paideia Proposal*, 44.
34. Adler, *The Paideia Proposal*, 50.
35. Adler, *The Paideia Proposal*, 77.
36. See Nel Noddings, *The Challenge to Care in Schools* (New York: Teachers College Press, 1992); Nel Noddings, *Happiness and Education* (Cambridge: Cambridge University Press, 2003); and Nel Noddings, *Critical Lessons: What our Schools Should Teach* (Cambridge: Cambridge University Press, 2006). A version of this general view advocated some years ago by the English writer G. H. Bantock generated a good deal of controversy; Bantock proposed two quite different programs for different students, urging a traditional academic program of the kind associated with the British grammar school for the minority of students who are academically minded. A second program, intended for the majority of students not considered to be in a position to benefit from traditional academic fare, would be based more on folk culture. See G. H. Bantock, "Towards a Theory of Popular Education," in *The Curriculum: Context, Design and Development*, ed. Richard Hooper (Edinburgh: Oliver and Boyd, 1971), 251–264.
37. Adler, *The Paideia Proposal*, 56.
38. Mortimer J. Adler, "In Defense of the Philosophy of Education," in *Philosophies of Education*, 41st Yearbook of the National Society for the Study of Education, Part I, ed. Nelson B. Henry (Bloomington, IL: Public School Publishing Company, 1942), 220.
39. See Joel Westheimer and Joseph Kahne, "What Kind of Citizen? The Politics of Educating for Democracy," *American Educational Research Journal* 41, no. 2 (Summer 2004): 237–269, especially 239–244.
40. Steven E. Tozer, Guy Senese, and Paul C. Violas, *School and Society: Historical and Contemporary Perspectives* (Boston: McGraw-Hill, 2006), 256–291. Here four levels of literacy—namely, conventional, functional, cultural, and critical—are examined along with their implications for living in a democratic society. Others have created different classifications of literacy types. On this point, see Cara M. Mulcahy, *Marginalized Literacies* (Information Age Publishing, forthcoming).

41. For an excellent analysis of differing views of citizenship and citizenship education that indirectly point to the lack of analysis in Adler's portrayal, see Yusef Waghid, "Action as an Educational Virtue: Toward a Different Understanding of Democratic Citizenship Education," *Educational Theory* 55, no. 3 (August 2005): 323–342.

42. Adler, *Paideia Problems and Possibilities*, 8.

43. Maritain, "Thomist Views on Education," 62, and Maritain, *Education at the Crossroads*, 14–15.

44. Martin, *Changing the Educational Landscape*, 173–176.

45. Martin, *Changing the Educational Landscape*, 180.

46. Martin, *Changing the Educational Landscape*, 180.

47. President William J. Clinton, *State of the Union Address*, 1997, at http://clinton2.nara.gov/WH/SOU97/ (accessed July 25, 2007), and Adler, *The Paideia Proposal*, 15.

48. *Aristotle on Education: Extracts from the Ethics and Politics*, trans. and ed. John Burnet (Cambridge: Cambridge University Press, 1903), 106.

49. Hutchins, *The Higher Learning in America*, 70–73.

50. Adler, *The Paideia Proposal*, 41.

51. Adler, *The Paideia Proposal*, 6–7; Adler, *Reforming Education*, xxvi.

52. See, for example, John Dewey, *Experience and Education* (New York: Collier, 1963); John Dewey, *Democracy and Education* (New York: The Free Press, 1966); Richard Pring, *Knowledge and Schooling* (London: Open Books, 1976); and Ira Shor, *Empowering Education: Critical Teaching for Social Change* (Chicago: University of Chicago Press, 1992).

53. Madeleine R. Grumet, "*The Paideia Proposal*: A Thankless Child Replies," *Curriculum Inquiry* 16, no. 3 (Autumn 1986): 338–339. See also 342, where Grumet adds that *The Paideia Proposal* "perpetuates a standard of knowledge that ignores the specificity of the knower and refuses to address the alarms and pleasures of every day life."

54. Nel Noddings, "The False Promise of the Paideia: A Critical Review of the Paideia Proposal," *Journal of Thought* 19, no. 1 (Spring 1984), 81–91; Noddings, *The Challenge to Care in Schools*, especially 28–30, 33–34, 163–166; and Noddings, *Critical Lessons*, 14, 16, 221.

55. Adler, *The Paideia Program*, 148; Adler, *The Paideia Proposal*, 41–42.

56. For a discussion of different forms of excellence, see Noddings, "The False Promise of the Paideia."

57. See, for example, Ronald Gwiazda, "The Peter Pan Proposal," *Harvard Educational Review* 53, no. 4 (November 1983), 386–387, and Floretta Dukes McKenzie, "The Yellow Brick Road of Education," *Harvard Educational Review* 53, no. 4 (November 1983), 390–391.

58. For further discussion of the issue of the best for the best, see also Noddings, *The Challenge to Care in Schools*, 28–38, 163–164.

59. Jane Roland Martin, *Educational Metamorphoses: Philosophical Reflections on Identity and Culture* (Lanham, MD: Rowman and Littlefield, 2007), 20–23.

60. Philip H. Phenix, *Realms of Meaning* (New York: McGraw Hill, 1964).

61. Broudy, Smith, and Burnett, *Democracy and Excellence*, 245–246.

62. P. H. Hirst, *Knowledge and the Curriculum* (London: Routledge and Kegan Paul, 1974), especially 30–53, and P. H. Hirst and R. S. Peters, *The Logic of Education* (London: Routledge and Kegan Paul, 1970), especially 60–73.

63. Adler, *The Paideia Proposal*, 24.

64. Hirst, *Knowledge and the Curriculum*, 96. For a fuller statement of Hirst's original position on liberal education, see Hirst, *Knowledge and the Curriculum*, 30–53 and 84–100. It should be noted that Hirst later retracted his stance on liberal education in P. H. Hirst, "Education, Knowledge and Practices," in *Beyond Liberal Education: Essays in Honour of Paul H. Hirst*, ed. Robin Barrow and Patricia White (London: Routledge, 1993), 184–199.

65. For a pertinent discussion of the relationship between academic disciplines and school subjects as understood by Hirst, see *Knowledge and the Curriculum*, 132–151, and in a rather different setting, P. H. Hirst, "The Foundations of the National Curriculum: Why Subjects?" in *Assessing the National Curriculum*, ed. Philip O'Hear and John White (London: Paul Chapman Publishing, Ltd., 1993), 31–37.

66. Adler, *The Paideia Proposal*, 33.

67. A similar point is made in Steven M. Cahn, "Two Cheers for the Proposal," *Harvard Educational Review* 53, no. 4 (November 1983), 404.

68. Adler, *The Paideia Proposal*, 33.

69. Cahn, "Two Cheers," 404–405.

70. Mortimer J. Adler, "The Paideia Response," *Harvard Educational Review* 53, no. 4 (November 1983), 410.

71. Adler, *The Paideia Proposal*, 26–33. On this point see also D. G. Mulcahy, "Is the Nation at Risk from *The Paideia Proposal*?" *Educational Theory* 35, no. 2 (Spring 1985), 218–220.

72. Martin, *Changing the Educational Landscape*, 133–153.

73. Adler, *The Paideia Program*, 141–164.

74. See, for example, Bonnie-Marie Doughty-Jenkins, "The Connecticut School-to-Career System" (EdD diss., Central Connecticut State University, 2005).

75. See, for example, Joseph L. DeVitis, Robert W. Johns, and Douglas J. Simpson, "Introduction," in *To Serve and Learn: The Spirit of Community in Liberal Education*, ed. Joseph L. DeVitis, Robert W. Johns, and Douglas J. Simpson (New York: Peter Lang, 1998), 6–18. See also Richard Pratte, *The Civic Imperative: Examining the Need for Civic Education* (New York: Teachers College Press, 1988), especially 107–122.

76. Boyer, *High School*, 202–215.

77. Martha C. Nussbaum, *Cultivating Humanity: A Classical Defense of Reform in Liberal Education* (Cambridge, MA: Harvard University Press, 1997), 1–14, 293–301.

78. Jane Roland Martin, *Coming of Age in Academe: Rekindling Women's Hopes and Reforming the Academy* (New York: Routledge, 2000), 139, and Nussbaum, *Cultivating Humanity*.

79. Martin, *Coming of Age in Academe*, 138, and Jane Roland Martin, *The Schoolhome: Rethinking Schools for Changing Families* (Cambridge, MA: Harvard University Press, 1992), 85–87.

80. It could be noted that in the *Politics* Aristotle would appear to have had little difficulty in accepting such an idea given his openness to the view that education ought to include useful subjects as a matter of common sense. See *Aristotle on Education*, 105–111.

81. This allegation is a constant refrain in Martin's work. For an everyday example of the hostility, see George F. Will, "Ed Schools vs Education," *Newsweek*, January 16, 2006, at http://www.msnbc.msn.com/id/10753446/site/newsweek/ (accessed July 25, 2007).

82. Adler, *The Paideia Proposal*, 43–44.

83. For an indication of the difficulties involved in articulating and differentiating among standards, see, for example, Marshall S. Smith, Susan H. Fuhrman, and Jennifer O'Day, "National Curriculum Standards: Are They Desirable and Feasible?" in *The Governance of Curriculum*, ed. Richard F. Elmore and Susan H. Fuhrman, (Alexandria, VA: Association for Supervision and Curriculum Development, 1994), 12–29. Whether for purely political reasons or not, President Clinton's policies as presented in *Goals 2000* ran into huge opposition in Congress when the Republican Party gained control of Congress following the midterm elections in 1994. *Goals 2000* was never formally rescinded, but key provisions were removed.

84. For further discussion, see Mulcahy, "Is the Nation at Risk from *The Paideia Proposal?*" 215–216.

85. Adler, *Paideia Problems and Possibilities*, 53.

86. For Adler's minimal elaboration see Adler, *Paideia Problems and Possibilities*, 50–53, and *The Paideia Program*, 180–183, where there is a consideration of evaluation as scorekeeping. See also Adler, *Reforming Education*, 295 and 297, where there are some further observations and unsubstantiated recommendations, and 312–313, which is perhaps Adler's most sustainable treatment of assessment. Even though it gives rise to still further questions regarding his insistence in *The Paideia Proposal* on all students attaining the "requisite standard," here Adler calls for "an assessment of the student's achievement wholly in terms of that student's capacity without reference to any other individual's achievement."

87. A particular case in point is Alfie Kohn; see *The Case against Standardized Testing: Raising the Scores, Ruining the Schools* (Portsmouth, NH.: Heinemann, 2000) and *What Does It Mean to Be Well Educated?* (Boston: Beacon Press, 2004). Kohn has also written a detailed critique of character education, "How Not to Teach Values: A Critical Look at Character Education," *Phi Delta Kappan* 78, no. 6 (February 1997), 428–439.

88. Adler, *The Paideia Proposal*, 32.

89. For a variety of critiques of standardized testing, see, for example, Deborah Meier and George Wood, eds., *Many Children Left Behind* (Boston: Beacon Press, 2004); Kohn, *The Case against Standardized Testing*; and Peter Sacks, *Standardized Minds: The High Price of America's Testing Culture and What We Can Do to Change It* (Cambridge, MA: Perseus Books, 1999).

90. Some such measures and their effects are presented in the study of zero tolerance policies in Ronnie Casella, *At Zero Tolerance: Punishment, Prevention, and School Violence* (New York: Peter Lang, 2001).

91. Panel on Youth of the President's Science Advisory Committee, *Youth: Transition to Adulthood* (Chicago: University of Chicago Press, 1974), 80–83. Smith and Orlosky wrote in a similar vein in B. Othanel Smith and Donald E. Orlosky, *Socialization and Schooling: Basics of Reform* (Bloomington, IN: Phi Delta Kappa, 1975), iii.

92. See Doughty-Jenkins, "The Connecticut School-to-Career System."

93. Hirst, *Knowledge and the Curriculum*, especially 30–53.

94. Hutchins, *The Higher Learning in America*, 59–87.

95. See *Harvard Educational Review* 53, no. 4 (November 1983), a special issue devoted to a consideration of *The Paideia Proposal*; Nel Noddings, "The False Promise of the Paideia," and Mulcahy, "Is the Nation at Risk from *The Paideia Proposal?*" See also Burton Weltman, "Individualism Versus Socialism in American Education: Rereading Mortimer Adler and *The Paideia Proposal*," *Educational Theory* 52, no. 1 (Winter 2002): 61–79.

96. Noddings, "The False Promise of the Paideia"; Noddings, *The Challenge to Care in Schools*, especially 28–30, 33–34, 163–166; and Noddings, *Critical Lessons*, 14, 16, 221.

97. Tony Johnson, "Classicists Versus Experimentalists: Reexamining the Great Debate," *Journal of General Education* 36, no. 4 (1985): 277.

98. R. S. Peters, "Ambiguities in Liberal Education and the Problem of Its Content," in *Ethics and Educational Policy*, ed. Kenneth A. Strike and Kieran Egan (London: Routledge and Kegan Paul, 1978), 3–21.

99. Adler, *The Paideia Proposal*, 16.

100. Adler, *The Paideia Proposal*, 3.

101. DeVitis, Johns, and Simpson, "Introduction," 6–18.

4

Martin: Gender-Sensitive Liberal Education

Jane Roland Martin rises to the challenge laid down by Mortimer Adler and like-minded proponents of liberal education. It would be a stretch to say that, like Adler, she is a passionate advocate of liberal education or that, like John Henry Newman, she has set forth a traditional statement of the idea. It is closer to the truth to say that, while she has supported the idea of liberal education, she also has exposed it to a compelling contemporary critique and wishes to redefine it substantially within the context of her particular concept of the educated person. It is in this critique and redefinition that she makes her most important contribution to the debate regarding the ongoing viability of the concept of liberal education. To grasp the nature of her redefinition, it is necessary to look at various strands that make up Martin's more wide-ranging educational thought and, in the process, examine how her particular idea of liberal education is shaped by them. Of importance is the emphasis Martin gives to introducing the experience and the voices of women—and the values and priorities they highlight—into any conversation dealing with education. For Martin, it is to our detriment that we have, up to her day at least, largely excluded these voices and the values they articulate, what she terms the three Cs of care, concern, and connection. These are largely the values of the private world of the home, including nurturance of the young, care of the needy, concern for all, and connection to the community. Accordingly, Martin wishes to fashion a view of education that fully reflects this experience. The implications of this view for liberal education and for the question of whether liberal education is still a useful construct in considering educational futures today are fascinating, and they merit careful consideration.

The two aspects of Martin's thought that impact most forcefully the theory of liberal education are her epistemological and gender critiques and her proposal for gender-sensitive education.[1] The critiques are to be found in the collection of articles brought together in *Changing the Educational Landscape* and elsewhere. The idea of gender-sensitive education is well developed in *The Schoolhome* and *Coming of Age in Academe*, among other writings. Martin's more recent works, notably, *Cultural Miseducation* and *Educational Metamorphoses*, do not for the most part address directly issues in liberal education. The cultural wealth thesis set forth in *Cultural Miseducation*, and in particular the position taken on the content of the curriculum, does have implications for liberal education, however, although what these might be is unclear. What is said there regarding a differentiated curriculum, in particular, points to some uncertainties in Martin's overall curriculum stance. Rather than dwelling upon these, I shall focus primarily on the unequivocal positions Martin has adopted in regard to the epistemological and gender critiques and her idea of gender-sensitive education. These have important implications for liberal education and where it should go in the future, regardless of the positions taken in *Cultural Miseducation* and *Educational Metamorphoses*.[2]

Several of the strands woven through Martin's educational thought make it distinctly feminist in character. As these first began to take form in the early to mid 1980s, they can be found in her book *Reclaiming a Conversation*,[3] which is subtitled *The Ideal of the Educated Woman*, and in two important articles from that time period. *Reclaiming a Conversation* takes a close look at five historically important contributors to the ideal notion of the educated woman: Plato, Jean Jacques Rousseau, Mary Wollstonecraft, Catharine Beecher, and Charlotte Perkins Gilman. From each, Martin picks out particular elements that are important, either positively or negatively, for the ideal. Two other writers whose work is not treated in *Reclaiming a Conversation* but who are also the subject of critical analysis by Martin, and in response to whose ideas she further develops her own position, also need to be taken into account. These are Paul Hirst and R. S. Peters. Another such writer to whom Martin later gives close attention and on whom she draws heavily is Maria Montessori.[4]

The main focus of attention in *Reclaiming a Conversation* is on examining the ideal of the educated woman. In a surprising turn toward the end of the book, however, Martin shifts her focus from the ideal of the educated woman and presents an encapsulation of what her reflections on the five thinkers examined suggest as a way forward in dealing with a different and broader but related question. This is the question of the ideal of the educated person, irrespective of gender.[5] Martin's attempt to address that question issues throughout the next twenty years in a range of articles and books that provide a manifold and extensive account of Martin's concept of the educated person.

These writings also enable us to identify the salient features of her particular concept of liberal education as she portrays it, to view that vision within the context of her broader view of education, and to consider the implications.

THE IDEAL OF THE EDUCATED WOMAN

Plato, the first of the influential theorists of education to whom Martin turns her attention in examining the ideal of the educated woman, is a frequent point of reference in her work. Nowhere is this more evident than in regard to Plato's celebrated plan for the education of the philosopher-king. Plato is not the cornerstone in the edifice of Martin's educational thought or her major source of inspiration, however; that comes from feminist theory in general. The interplay between these two influences is a good point of departure for us.

Production and Reproduction

When great minds turn their attention to education, what they say about education, and specifically what they say about the education of women, has largely been overlooked, Martin maintains. Indeed, she holds, to a significant extent discussion of education has been conducted in such a way as to exclude women. This exclusion, she believes, is rooted in a distinction fundamental to her thinking, one drawn between what she terms the productive and reproductive processes in society.[6] As she describes them, the productive processes include economic, political, and social processes such as the production of goods, the exercise of government, and the conduct of military affairs—activities considered to belong to the public world, which is dominated by men and the affairs of governing and economics. Although most frequently associated with men, the productive processes can, in fact, be carried out by men and women. The reproductive processes, by contrast, are normally associated with women even though men can and do sometimes engage in them. These include, for example, caring for and rearing the young, tending to the educational work of the home, and providing health care, activities considered as belonging to the private or domestic sphere.[7]

For Martin, education—by which she has often meant schooling[8]—is shaped by the needs of the public world, the world of production, and of the men who people it. The needs of the private world, the world of reproduction, and of the women who inhabit it, she maintains, somehow do not enter into the education picture. Yet the dispositions and knowledge needed to carry out the reproductive processes may have salutary effects in a public world shaped by violence toward girls and women and disrespect for minorities, the poor, the downtrodden, and even nature itself.

Plato's Philosopher-King

The exclusion of women from educational thought has been exacerbated by historians of education, Martin contends. In the case of Plato, for example, proposals presented by him in Book 5 of the *The Republic* regarding the education of women and their roles have been rejected, she maintains, because they contradict the western tradition on a range of prickly issues. Accepting elements of the widely held interpretation of Plato,[9] Martin understands Plato's view to be as follows. We are born with different natures and talents from one another. Our roles in society and our education will be determined by these differences, of which there are mainly three. Women and men are endowed by nature with the capacity to become artisans, warriors or auxiliaries or, because of special qualities of intellect, guardians or philosopher-kings. Gender plays no part in determining our natures, and therefore none in determining our roles in society or our education. Women receive the same education as men, depending only on their nature or talents. According to Martin, Plato largely ignored the reproductive processes in society, confining attention mostly to the productive ones; yet he did not assume that the reproductive processes belonged by nature to women.[10]

Notwithstanding those views of his that cast women in a favorable light, according to Martin, even Plato was unable to provide for equal treatment for women, in education or in society. He allows for "role opportunity" for males and females, for example, but not for "role occupancy." This is because, for gender reasons and to the extent that there is differential socialization for boys and girls in Plato's idealized just state, his educational model is more suited to males than to females.[11] Plato's identity postulate extends both a male-based pedagogy and subject matter to females. Not only does this make it difficult for women to achieve equal role occupancy; it also makes it almost impossible for women to be seen and treated as equals of males. The curriculum Plato provides, accordingly, favors males and denigrates females. The identity postulate ensures this by requiring the same education for everyone, not an equal (and equally suitable) education for all. Martin's concern, contrary to Adler's, is "that identical education is not in every instance equal education."[12]

What Martin sees as Plato's production model of education raises the issue of equal respect and equal treatment for men and women in education and in society. For Martin, identical education may not be equal because it can lead to trait genderization, in which women are penalized for possessing traits, such as rationality and autonomy, that in men are considered admirable and valuable. Although the traits attributed to guardians are considered masculine, females would have to acquire such traits to be considered guardians. Yet, as women, they would be derided for possessing these masculine attributes. So females will receive different treatment and unequal respect for developing the same traits and receiving the same education as males do.[13]

Rousseau's Sophie

In Plato, gender was a determinant neither of one's nature nor of one's education, yet Plato is called to task by Martin for offering the same education to males and females. One reason for this criticism, presumably, is because of the impact of trait genderization. A second reason is because, for Martin, different people learn differently, not because of different natures but because of differences in upbringing and experiences,[14] suggesting to her that the education of boys and girls ought to differ to some extent.[15] In turning to Rousseau, in whose work one's nature and, accordingly, one's education are determined by gender, one might expect to find different educations for men and women, and an educational philosophy of which Martin may be inclined to approve, at least in some respects. Martin may be glad to learn, in Rousseau's treatment of the education of Emile and his wife, Sophie, that Sophie's education is to be different from Emile's. She is dismayed, however, to discover that Sophie's education is also not equal to Emile's. Through his constant reiteration of a growth model of education, according to which one's education is determined by nothing other than one's nature, Rousseau would have us believe that a woman's different education is tied to her different nature. In having us so believe, Rousseau is misleading us, says Martin, and historians in large numbers have joined in the deception and compounded the problem of gendered education.[16]

Historians of educational thought, Martin writes, "have implicitly defined their subject matter as the education of male human beings, rather than the education of all human beings."[17] In so doing, they have downplayed, if not entirely disregarded, Rousseau's differential treatment of the education of Emile and Sophie—and Emile's dependency on Sophie—as much as they have ignored Plato's inconvenient views on the education of women. They have also allowed to go unchallenged Rousseau's assertion that this differential treatment is rooted in nature and a growth model of education. Having rebuked these historians, Martin offers a reinterpretation, arguing that Rousseau's educational ideas are basically functional in character, employing a production model of education just as Plato's did, and, contrary to the general view perpetuated by historians of education, not based on a growth model. Both Emile and Sophie are, in fact, educated for what Rousseau sees as their particular male and female roles in society, even though this entails severe constraints on their natural growth. The role envisaged for Emile is that of family patriarch and citizen; the role for Sophie is that of pleasing and subservient wife and mother. The education of each will be different based upon their expected roles as much, if not more than, upon their different natures. The manipulation allowed by Rousseau in the education of Emile Martin sees as further evidence that a nature or growth model is abandoned by Rousseau.[18]

Clearly, according to Martin, Rousseau would have both men and women function within gender boundaries. Men and women are different by nature, Rousseau conveys, so their education will be different; it will fit the nature of each and, as with Plato, will bring potential to fruition. But nature needs assistance. Accordingly, only those traits that Rousseau wants to develop will be promoted, and he even shows fear lest other unsuitable ones might emerge. It is societal and political forces or values, according to Martin, that shape Rousseau's image of male and female education, not, as he insinuates, a growth principle. This is the whole point of his production model of education. Both males and females are to be educated—formed or produced—for two very different societal roles, even though in both cases this may involve the inhibiting of natural tendencies at odds with Rousseau's declared wishes. Thus, Martin holds, whether one agrees or not with the education or with the social roles Rousseau assigns to males and females, either for his own time or any other, this education and these roles are not rooted in their different natures as Rousseau alleges. They are founded on culturally rooted gender biases.[19]

If Plato's proposals for the same education for men and women falls short of the ideal form of education for girls—in part because it is the same as that for men—and Rousseau's proposals for different education for boys and for girls also fall short—notwithstanding the fact that it is not the same as that for boys—the question arises, what conception of education for girls will fit the bill. Already, Martin has intimated that it is possible to conceive of a suitable education for girls, but that it might not be the same as education for boys. Thus, she writes, in an important departure from Adler, "the educational treatment given males and females may have to be different if equivalent results are to be achieved"; that is to say, "an education in Sophie's virtues for females may have to proceed differently from one designed for males."[20] Martin's elaboration on this point in *Reclaiming a Conversation* follows from her careful analysis of the educational thought of the three women writers whose works she examines alongside that of Plato and Rousseau, namely Wollstonecraft, *A Vindication of the Rights of Women*; Beecher, *A Treatise on Domestic Economy*; and Gilman, *Herland*.[21]

Wollstonecraft's Daughters

As with Plato and Rousseau, according to Martin, Wollstonecraft adopts a production model of education. Unlike Plato's guardians or

Rousseau's Sophie, however, Wollstonecraft's educated woman is to occupy two roles in society: those of citizen and wife-mother. Accepting that the nurturing capacities do not arise naturally even in women, Martin argues that education for both roles is necessary. The problem, according to Martin, is that Wollstonecraft's proposed form of education, being based on those of the philosopher-king and of Emile in regard to its intellectual content, and being the same as for men, will fit her only for the role of citizen. This is the central point of Martin's criticism of Wollstonecraft's ideal of the educated woman, the consequences of which she considers perilous, especially in the rearing of children. Granted Wollstonecraft's beliefs on this matter, and given in particular her view that women have primary responsibility for childrearing, Martin believes that Wollstonecraft's "theory of female education must include education for mothering."[22]

Her reservations notwithstanding, Martin sees a number of positive and highly beneficial aspects in Wollstonecraft's rationalism. That rationalism enables Wollstonecraft to claim the rights of men for women and brings women into the domain of citizenship. It also demonstrates the compatibility of the roles of citizen and wife-mother in a way that neither Plato nor Rousseau did. Despite its shortcomings when it comes to fashioning a vision of women's education, Wollstonecraft's rationalism serves to illuminate intelligence and a certain stability of character as aspects of mothering often overlooked. It also shows the place of reason and self-control in the educative aspects of mothering. Finally, for Martin, Wollstonecraft's rationalism "inspires her to claim for women the academic education historically reserved for men and, like Plato, to recommend a system of coeducation."[23] This is so even though this very rationalism does not allow Wollstonecraft to envision a kind of education that is fully suitable for women, lacking as it does the virtues of Sophie that are necessary for carrying out the reproductive processes.

Wollstonecraft's ideal of the educated woman is that of a liberal education: a traditional, intellectual education. Accordingly, for Martin, Wollstonecraft "presents us with an ideal of female education that gives pride of place to traits traditionally associated with males at the expense of others traditionally associated with females."[24] As a function of its gendered origins, it is one-sided and lacks the emotional content necessary for the reproductive processes that the role of mother requires. Presumably because Plato's female guardians, unlike Wollstonecraft's educated woman, will not marry or engage in childrearing, in the final analysis, Martin concludes, a society "that does not abolish the institutions of private marriage, home, family, and childrearing cannot afford to take as its model the education Plato devised for his guardian class."[25]

Beecher's Homemakers

For Beecher, education is the vital moving force in society. Her ideal is that of a woman who is both well educated and a professional by virtue of her study of domestic economy. Crucial to her role is the education that she gives her sons and daughters to ensure that they become moral citizens for the well-being of the state. This is the educational role of the mother, born not of mere skill, but of reason, understanding, and character. This conscious joining together of reason and domesticity in Beecher is for Martin a breakthrough. It shows that theoretical learning, associated with men, and domestic activity, associated with women, do not stand worlds apart. Women's roles also call for educated reason. For Beecher, civil society is constituted of both the domestic and the public spheres; there should be education for the roles required by each. Beecher also suggests that a liberal education of the kind envisioned by Wollstonecraft needs to be supplemented by a form of practical education aimed at preparation for the reproductive processes, one akin to that body of knowledge once defined by Beecher as domestic economy.[26]

Her important practical and theoretical contributions to the education of girls and women notwithstanding, Beecher ultimately fails in one crucial respect in Martin's eyes. Despite her strong emphasis on moral, liberal, and professional education, in the final analysis Beecher fails to provide for education in the three Cs of care, concern, and connection.[27] For this reason, the liberal and professional education of the wife-mother figure envisioned by Beecher and the moral education she receives in the home fall short. They do not, in Martin's view, make adequate provision for the development of the "kindly feelings" and "sympathetic emotions" that Beecher herself says are necessary to be a good wife and mother. Because of this lack of attention to the "gentler feelings," Martin finds Beecher as guilty as Wollstonecraft of the "fallacy of false dilemma" and a too-heavy reliance on reason, even though both emphasized the educative role of the mother.[28]

Given the difficulty that the attention to reason over the gentler feelings appears to present for both Wollstonecraft and Beecher in their efforts to fashion a suitable concept of the educated woman, Martin asks if we should change our attitude to reason itself. If such a change appears fanciful given the claims for the education of women's reason that have already been presented, no less imagination is required as one contemplates Gilman's invitation to depart from the reality of a gendered world.[29]

Gilman's Mothers

Gilman agrees with Beecher that those entrusted with the rearing and education of children should have the kind of specialist knowledge that

Beecher came to associate with domestic economy, although Gilman does not accept Beecher's assumption that all women should be entrusted with the education of the young. For Gilman, the rearing and education of the young is the most valuable role of all and is reserved for specialists. Education forms a seamless web of experience in which there is to be no separation of school from the world. Education embraces a wide range of knowledge and physical activity. Mother-love is Herland's overarching cultural and educational ideal, and the Herland Dream is "neither the accumulation of private wealth nor an increase in the gross national product; rather, it is the growth and development of children."[30] Reason is "at all times harnessed to the practical goal of making the best kind of people,"[31] hence the emphasis in education "on the development of 'a clear, far-reaching judgment and a strong, well-used will.'"[32] By contrast with Wollstonecraft, in Gilman the nurturing capacities traditionally associated with women come first, they being the "fundamental elements of an improved social order."[33] Not surprisingly, to be a good mother in Herland is to be a good citizen and vice versa.[34]

According to Martin, the identification of the interests of women with those of the state found in Gilman, to which Gilman brings a particular image of family relationships, makes her utopian vision special. It resonates with Martin's own appeal in *The Schoolhome* for a rewritten domestic tranquility clause of the U.S. Constitution, in which the values of domesticity—namely, care, concern, and connection—will be prominent.[35] Not only does Gilman see the state as family but, for Martin, she also includes in it the very family members that Plato, Dewey, and other social philosophers who invoke the family ignore: "mothers and daughters, particularly mothers."[36] Rousseau would criticize Gilman's extinction of private family, since he sees the traditional family as a necessary breeding ground in love and respect for the state. As Martin argues, however, while this criticism may be correct if applied to Plato, it does not hold up against Gilman, because she builds in a mother love and "large family" love missing in Plato. That is to say, for Gilman, expressing a viewpoint toward which Martin herself leans, the world is family in a way that for Rousseau only the immediate family was.

A crucial question for Martin, especially given the failure of Wollstonecraft and Beecher in this context, is whether Gilman makes adequate and appropriate provision for the three Cs in her educational ideal. Undeniably she does. Yet, their significant contributions notwithstanding, Martin does not believe that any of the educational theorists she examines in *Reclaiming a Conversation* have said all that needs to be said about the ideal of the educated woman. It is evident from their work, Martin concludes, that we still must consider "both what would constitute a proper preparation for performing those [reproductive] processes and to whom such preparation should be extended."[37] This consideration leads Martin to an exploration that takes her beyond the question of the ideal of the educated woman pursued in *Reclaiming a Conversation* and beyond the ideal of a liberal education as conceived in Newman and Adler. The outcome, as we shall see, is a reenvisioning of the education of both women and men and a redefinition of the idea of a liberal education itself.

TRADITIONAL LIBERAL EDUCATION

In the years preceding the publication of *Reclaiming a Conversation*, Martin devoted close attention to the ideas of Hirst and Peters. Central to the work of both were the questions of what constituted the ideal of the educated person, what form that education should take, and what the implications were for liberal education.

Peters's Educated Man

In Martin's view, Peters's concept of the educated man[38] raises troubling questions that demand a response from a feminist perspective. This response she provides in the form of her Presidential Address to the Philosophy of Education Society in 1981. As Martin sees it, Peters's concept of the educated man represents widely held thinking in the field on a number of fundamental gender-related issues in education that were in need of rebuttal.[39] The first objective of her response to Peters is to challenge the adequacy of the traditional ideal of the educated man as propounded by Peters and others. This she does by examining its suitability for the education of both boys and girls. Martin is less concerned with the gender-biased language employed by Peters than with the gender-biased content of his ideal. The second objective is to fashion a new educational ideal and to indicate some of its qualities. The male-based ideal represented by Peters, which is essentially the ideal of liberal education co-championed by Hirst and Peters, Martin argues, does harm to boys and men as well as girls and women, the harm it does to men being intimately tied up with the injustice it does to women. The female-based ideal that was the focus of attention in *Reclaiming a Conversation*, it appears, is also considered inadequate. Taking up and even anticipating a theme that emerges toward the end of *Reclaiming a Conversation*, the new ideal would be a gender-sensitive view of education.

According to Martin, Peters and others conceive an educated person as viewing things in a certain way, resulting from their study of the academic disciplines. From the standpoint of the ideal of an educated person, however, the disciplines are in several respects seriously flawed, because they contain a thoroughly male cognitive perspective.[40] They have a male image of women and they focus on the public world and its productive societal processes, as opposed to the private world and the reproductive processes. In sum, Martin writes, the disciplines into which one must be initiated in order to become an educated person exclude women. They further "*construct* the female to the male image of her and *deny* the truly feminine qualities she does possess."[41] One may add that school subjects are likely to share this characteristic.

According to Martin, the masculinity of Peters's model of the educated man does not derive only from the content of the academic disciplines: the traits attributed to this educational ideal are male as opposed to female. Even though the ideal of the educated man may be attained by women, as was the case with Plato's guardians, it is genderized in favor of males, and a woman possesses the traits of an educated man at her peril. For Martin, therefore, the ideal held up by Peters puts women in a double bind. If they are to be educated, they must forfeit their own way of experiencing the world, thereby alienating themselves from themselves. Failing that, they must remain uneducated.[42] Such a view Martin sees as just another example of our willingness to impose male models on females. Not only are women devalued as a consequence, but males are likewise deprived of an education in the reproductive processes of society. Males are damaged because the masculine ideal creates people lacking in emotions and feelings.[43]

For Martin, Peters's concept of the educated man is yet another example of education viewed in terms of production. Peters's educated man, Martin argues, no less than Plato's guardians or Rousseau's Emile, "is designed to fill a role in society which has traditionally been considered to be male."[44] The educated man, accordingly, is not equipped to carry out roles associated with the reproductive processes in society traditionally considered to be women's. For Martin, people need to be educated in the reproductive roles, such as parenting, roles not intuitively known. Excluding such education implies an unwarranted negative value judgment about the tasks, activities, traits, and dispositions associated with reproductive roles.[45] The inhabitants of the educational realm, by which Martin appears to mean those in the public world who control schooling, are actually insensitive to its biases, she maintains. They will tell you that in the less civilized domain of the home, the main commodity is socialization not education, and child-rearing activities are so instinctual, effortless, and lacking in purpose that they do not constitute teaching.[46] This is why Peters could deny that rearing was part of education. But for Martin, an adequate ideal of the educated person must do more than give the reproductive processes their due. We must avoid the trap of assigning males and females to different processes and at the same time not ignore one of the processes.[47]

Hirst's Ivory Tower People

Up to this point, Martin's critique of selected philosophers of education and of liberal education has been largely shaped by her attention to a variety of exclusions of women and women's experience from the discourse on education and by the desire to rectify this exclusion. Her critique of Hirst's influential theory of a liberal education has a wider focus and is as much an epistemological as a gender critique. More wide ranging in scope than the gender critique presented already, it is still inspired by Martin's feminist leanings and elaborates important new dimensions in her critical analysis of liberal education. Finally, in the context of her critique of Hirst's theory, Martin reveals the nature of her own commitment to liberal education and provides the broad outlines of an alternative view of liberal education, an outline on which she builds in her later works, as we shall see.

Martin takes Hirst's forms of knowledge theory of liberal education to be broadly representative of that body of philosophical thinking that enjoyed a renewed prominence throughout the 1960s and 1970s, in which the school curriculum is viewed chiefly in terms of academic or discipline knowledge.[48] Her critique of the Hirst position bears much of the burden of showing the weaknesses of this way of thinking. So one may ask, what so concerns Martin about Hirst's curriculum theory and the mainstream curriculum theorizing of the second half of the twentieth century that she takes it to represent? After all, the values highlighted in Hirst's thinking, values such as rationality, logic, breadth of knowledge, and depth of understanding, are widely respected. They are largely upheld by Hirst's contemporaries and by others who engage the topic, including Adler; Harry S. Broudy, B. Othanel Smith, and Joe R. Burnett; Philip H. Phenix; John White; Allan Bloom; E. D. Hirsch; and Ernest Boyer.

This being so, it is not surprising that the thrust of Martin's critique is not against Hirst's advocacy of such values. Her concern lies in the exclusion of other important values, such as those represented by practicality, feelings and emotions, and the three Cs, values decidedly lacking in historical models of liberal education. Such values, she argues, have been omitted from mainstream curriculum theory, and specifically from Hirst's forms of knowledge theory, because the focus has not been upon the goals of education as the foundation for the curriculum but upon the nature, structure, and uses of knowledge. Accordingly, for Martin, Hirst's curriculum theory is rooted in a fallacy, what she terms the epistemological fallacy. Those of Hirst's critics who have been preoccupied with his account of the forms of knowledge have failed to recognize the fallacy and are likewise guilty of perpetuating the faulty theory of curriculum that it supports.

According to Martin, Hirst's critics have concentrated largely on analysis of the forms of knowledge, whereas for her, falling afoul of the epistemological fallacy is the basic issue. "Behind Hirst's theory," she writes, "lies a conception of liberal education as the development of mind and the identification of the achievement of knowledge with that development."[49] It is around this conception that Hirst constructs his thesis that a liberal education consists in an initiation into the forms of knowledge. Hirst, she adds, has made the "mistaken assumption that the nature and structure of knowledge determines the nature and structure of a liberal education."[50] Hence the fallacy of arguing from a theory of knowledge to what Hirst concludes regarding the content of an education.[51]

According to Martin, it is epistemological rather than moral considerations that, in Hirst's view, are fundamental in determining the content and objectives of the curriculum, meaning that what is put into the curriculum depends upon one's theory of knowledge. In Hirst's case, as Martin sees it, epistemological considerations are decisive, or so it would appear, and value judgments are dispensed with.[52] The philosopher as epistemologist is merely telling it as it is. While this may simplify life for the curriculum maker, Hirst is not actually telling it as it is, as Martin sets out to demonstrate in her analysis of his argument.

Hirst's theory of a liberal education, Martin argues, only gives the appearance of dispensing with value judgments. As she sees it, if we choose Hirst's account of knowledge as a basis for curriculum over other accounts, we do so on based on our aims and purposes. We cannot choose an account of knowledge to justify those aims because any such justification entails value judgments regarding the lives people should live and the kinds of societies in which they should live. Those falling afoul of the epistemological fallacy decide what constitutes a liberal education in terms of the kind of lives people should live and the kinds of societies in which they should live. They then tailor their accounts of knowledge in accordance with this. In effect, Martin continues, "being worthy of inclusion in a liberal education is sufficient for something to be knowledge for them."[53] This is why they argue at such length that art, religion, and moral judgment are forms of knowledge.

The consequences of Hirst's fallacious reasoning for the curriculum are devastating, according to Martin. The kind of knowledge that Hirst's theory of liberal education accepts is so limited that it leads to the formation of lopsided human beings. Because of its emphasis on propositional knowledge and its narrow view of mind, other values such as feelings, emotions, and other so-called noncognitive states of mind often associated with education, such as caring for others, are omitted. Knowledge-how and education for action are also overlooked, as well as physical education, vocational education, artistic performance, languages, and civic education.[54] In "The Disciplines and the Curriculum," in which she offers a studied critique of the academic disciplines as curriculum content,[55] Martin decries the omission of such subject matter from the curriculum, for its content addresses some of the legitimate needs and interests of school-goers. These include topics such as friendship and relationships, matters not addressed at all by the theoretical academic disciplines. Hirst seems unconcerned, as his theory of liberal education produces what are but caricatures of humankind, what Martin terms "ivory tower people." Such people may possess knowledge, but they do nothing: they have no commitment to action and lack know-how.[56]

Recognizing a difference between education and schooling, as she increasingly and forcefully does in her more recent work,[57] Martin also acknowledges that Hirst does not claim that liberal education is a theory of all education deemed valuable. Neither does he deny that there could be different forms of worthwhile education or schooling; they simply would not be liberal education. Yet she adds that not everyone has been so exact on this point and that Hirst's theory has become "the received theory not just of intellectual but of that education deemed valuable." This, she adds, is due at least in part to Hirst's own use of the honorific label, liberal education.[58] The educational values overlooked by Hirst are similarly overlooked and even castigated, Martin further points out, by bureaucrats in the world of the public schools, even though Martin's focus of attention is not school practice but the dominant theory of liberal education. Nor does she deny that good practice around these values also survives. When it does, however, Martin argues that it cannot be attributed to this theory. She is even willing to grant that some who are educated according to the theory will become competent makers and doers, and some may even become moral agents and agents of social change. But, from the standpoint of the theory of a liberal education "in its role as paradigm of education deemed valuable," this will be accidental. All that matters for this theory of liberal education is that the forms of knowledge be acquired.[59]

The dualism between mind and body identified by Martin in Hirst's theory and the theory of liberal education as a whole separates reason from emotion, thought from action, and education from life, she maintains. It does so by excluding knowledge-how and noncognitive states and processes from its idea of mind and thereby from liberal education.[60] Yet it goes farther still. By relying on a theory of education that divorces mind from body, this inherent dualism declares education of the body to be nonliberal, and thereby denies its value. Since action usually involves bodily movement, it follows that education of and for action is denied value, too.[61] If this explains why ivory tower people are apathetic, it also has serious social ramifications, for it means that the theory commits one to political models that require, or at least desire, that people be passive participants in the political process.[62] This, in combination with an education that separates reason and emotion as well as mind and body, leaves us with people who are uncaring and inactive. Far from being willing to engage in the political process, such people are politically docile and even incapable of action, a far cry from the ideal of civic engagement often proclaimed even by advocates of liberal education itself.[63]

Evaluating Martin's Critique of Liberal Education

Drawing on a distinction between liberal and professional education, in *Knowledge, Gender, and Schooling* I discussed Martin's argument that liberal education produces only the ivory tower person and suggested that while liberal education viewed on its own may produce only ivory tower people, those incapable of action for any cause, liberal education has rarely been seen as existing within a vacuum.[64] To view it in this way, which Martin does when she maintains that her critique of liberal education is directed toward liberal education understood strictly as a theory,[65] is almost to construct a straw man, I suggested. In Plato's plan of education as generally understood, for example, liberal education is seen as the third stage in a four-stage process designed for the formation of the philosopher-king. It is located within the context of the other three parts of education, all of which were considered necessary in the education of the philosopher-king. Whatever one may wish to say of the ivory tower person, Plato's philosopher-king was no such person, prepared as he or she was for citizenship and for conducting the practical affairs of governance in the other three stages of education. Neither was Newman's celebrated idealization, the gentleman, whose liberal education was situated in the context of a well-recognized moral and religious formation.

Martin's ivory tower criticism is irrefutable if one accepts Martin's critique of liberal education as a concept standing alone. But liberal education is not always a concept standing alone, Plato's theory being a conspicuous case in point. A key element of basic education in Plato, namely, the stage required of all citizens approximately from age five through sixteen, was an education in patriotism and in a life of morally acceptable behavior. That is why Plato sanctioned censorship while promoting the knowledge, attitudes, values, feelings, emotions, and modes of behavior dedicated to the well-being of the state. In the second stage, which was reserved for the future philosopher-king and the auxiliary, there was a military education in preparation for service in defense of the state. And in the fourth stage there was the preparation of the philosopher to become king, to become a just ruler in the just state.

Martin sometimes overlooks and at other times strips from Plato's theory elements of education in attitudes and feelings, in action and behavior, and in caring and commitment to a cause, those elements that she criticizes the theory for not possessing. She also minimizes the possibility of the person of a liberal education applying reflection and critical thought to matters of home and family life. To education in the feelings and emotion overlooked by Martin, moreover, Plato added an education for action that Martin found lacking in Hirst's ivory tower person and which she also overlooks in the education of the philosopher-king. This is not to suggest that Plato attended to the full range of dispositions involved in care, concern, and connection and preparation for family living as Martin delineates them. He did not. Martin is also correct in saying that the emphasis in Plato was on preparation for service in the public world rather than in the private world of home and family.

The interpretation I have just presented challenges Martin's criticisms of omissions or oversights in Plato. At the same time, it accepts a number of her more specific charges. This being so, what are we now to make of Martin's critique of the theory of liberal education in general and of Hirst's theory of liberal education in particular? Hirst has provided a highly articulate reformulation of the historical ideal of liberal education and Martin a thoroughgoing critique of this ideal when compared to broader conceptions of education. Both positions are classic statements. They are also erroneous, for they claim too much. Martin overstates her case in claiming to discover limiting features of liberal education that we have known all along; Hirst errs in asserting that his definition of liberal education is a stipulative definition,[66] one in which a new meaning is assigned to the term. Hirst's claim is the crux of the matter. Yet it entices Martin to repeat his mistake of forgetting for the moment what they both surely know of the history of liberal education.

When Hirst draws upon the idea of liberal education in developing his own position on the curriculum, he elaborates the new in the context of an old and highly regarded way of thinking about education, one in a continuous process of evolution. In spelling out the details of his own position, like others before and since, Hirst alters the old and introduces new elements, reflecting the times and the changed philosophical understandings of his own day. In particular, he attempts to make the idea of liberal education independent of an Aristotelian metaphysics of the kind accepted by, for example, Newman and Adler. This he accomplishes in a postmodernist departure from the philosophical realism of Aristotle, which holds that knowledge is a true account of reality. He argues that over time we have created a number of different modes of interpreting and elaborating our view of the world we seek to know and understand. In all, we have thus far created seven such modes of knowledge.

But no claim is made by Hirst that these modes of knowledge contain knowledge that is true. This is not to say that our understanding them has no value. On the contrary, even if the accounts they provide are not true, they are accounts to which we can refer and thereby support an objectively grounded public discourse and openly verifiable methods of investigation and proof for the knowledge claims that we do make. In addition to this objective and verifiable basis for public discourse about our world to which every suitably educated person can relate, the forms of knowledge that have been created throughout history and identified by Hirst capture ways that the human mind thinks and comes to know. They also provide a necessary foundation upon which to initiate the young into ways of thinking and creating knowledge. Such initiation constitutes their education.

Hirst's rejection of the Aristotelian underpinnings of liberal education that had long been relied upon by many and openly embraced by Newman does not therefore cause him to reject the value of acquiring knowledge and the intellectual development that accompanies it. He simply values knowledge and understanding for different reasons. In a manner that is important to any theory of liberal education, he holds on to commitment to the pursuit of knowledge for its own sake rather than for any ulterior purpose. For this reason, his search for the seven forms of knowledge and understanding is a search for a kind of knowledge that is considered worthwhile in itself. It is, in Hirst's own words, knowledge that is logically basic.[67]

Hirst knows well that he is not the first to seek and characterize such knowledge. Plato's identification of that knowledge located in the upper half of the divided line, namely, science, mathematics, logic, and dialectical reasoning, was but one attempt to formulate such a theory of the nature and structure of higher knowledge in relation to an educational plan. The institutionalization of the liberal arts and sciences in the university at its birth in Europe in the twelfth century or thereabouts was another. Newman's nineteenth-century view of the circle of the sciences consisting of literature, science, and theology as forming the necessary substance of liberal education, was yet another. It is precisely because such knowledge was considered logically basic, as Hirst puts it, that it has been considered a necessary foundation for later studies. Similarly, because it is thought to be logically basic and at the same time pure, or theoretical as distinct from applied, knowledge, it often was and still is considered by many to be useless. Yet, this very uselessness notwithstanding, it is the logically basic character of such knowledge that makes it also the most valuable in the educational sense. Once mastered, through the knowledge it supplies and the intellectual development that attaining it demands, it enables students to grow in what Newman refers to as philosophical knowledge or illumination. In this way, students come to see the connections among the various branches of knowledge, to evaluate the importance of each in relation to the other, to grow, as Hirst and Peters put it, in knowledge and understanding. Such knowledge and understanding is, once again in Hirst's and Peters's words, a liberal education. It is free and freeing, liberal and liberating. It is free from the constraints of being shaped by practical ends. It is freeing because it empowers the mind.[68]

When Hirst claims to establish a stipulative definition of education, therefore, he is doing nothing of the kind, at least as it relates to liberal education. Neither is he, as Martin asserts, merely trading on the term liberal education. Rather, he is drawing on and expressing anew that long and winding tradition reaching all the way back to Plato and Aristotle. For these are the very claims he makes in defense of his theory of liberal education: it is free and freeing. It is essentially in his novel account of the nature and structure of knowledge, that is to say his account of the logically basic forms of knowledge and the altered nature of the truth claims he attributes to them, that he differs from the preceding tradition of liberal education. It is not that he provides a definition of liberal education as something other than an education that is free and freeing, one characterized by knowledge and understanding in depth and breadth. If one accepts Israel Scheffler's characterization of stipulative definitions as ones that "do not purport to reflect the predefinitional usage of the terms they define,"[69] then Hirst has not introduced anything remotely resembling a stipulative definition of liberal education.

Hirst's theory of liberal education expresses aspects of both its educational and philosophical character in a way not necessary in earlier times, and it is in this regard that Martin's critique is valuable, too. For Martin's critique of Hirst is as much a critique of a twentieth-century view of liberal education as it is of Hirst's version of it, a point Martin herself makes.[70] The validity of this critique, strictly speaking, rests largely on the grounds of Martin's comparison of Hirst's theory not with other theories of liberal education but with other educational ideals or accounts of what she terms "the whole of education."[71] It also suggests that the title of Martin's original article, "Needed: A New Paradigm for Liberal Education," could have been considered something of a misnomer and the position it enunciates a departure from the historical idea of liberal education. For that reason it could also be considered much closer to a stipulative definition than that put forth by Hirst.

Theories of liberal education—as distinct from the practice of liberal education in a particular context—have long been grounded in theories of the nature and structure of knowledge and to that extent have been guilty of Martin's epistemological fallacy. They have typically erected a dualism between mind and body and between reason and emotion and have been primarily focused on education for reflection rather than action. As such, they came to be labeled theories of liberal education as distinct from theories of vocational or some other form of education. To argue that it is a failing in liberal education to possess the qualities it does, therefore, is somewhat beside the point. To say it possesses these qualities is simply an articulation of what liberal education has meant. To identify the distinctive qualities of liberal education, moreover, with a view to locating it within the context of the whole of education, for example, is not to deny the possibility or even the desirability of other forms of education. This said, it must also be acknowledged that the idea of liberal education has normally been articulated as a statement of the preferred or the best form of education, Adler's claim being a case with which we are readily familiar.

Plato's proposal for the third stage in the education of the philosopher-king—what might be termed the stage of liberal education—is a notable case of locating liberal education within the context of a broader education. By the time Plato's philosopher-kings or future guardians get to this point in the educational process, they have been initiated, as have all other citizens, into the values, customs, and mores of society and have already completed a basic education. To view the proposal for the liberal education that follows as not taking place within such a context is therefore to ignore an important feature of their education. As applied to Martin's critique of Hirst, it is to deny his explicit recognition, which Martin herself acknowledges, that a liberal education does not claim to be the whole of education. Nonetheless, Martin proceeds to do exactly that. She picks out that part of the whole of education that liberal education claims to be and then criticizes it for not possessing the qualities of the other parts. As was seen already in the discussion of Adler's curriculum stance, Hirst knew very well that his theory of liberal education excluded certain elements of a broader education.[72]

So, one may reasonably ask, why is Martin's contribution so valuable? It is important because while Hirst is not merely trading on the term liberal education, as I have already suggested, accompanied by Peters, he sees liberal education both as education and as general education, understood as a total education. This is so despite their protests to the contrary in *The Logic of Education*.[73] This point makes Martin's contribution valuable for two reasons: Firstly, because Hirst wants it both ways, as I have just suggested, and she is unwilling to let him get away with it. That is to say, Hirst wants to hold both that his theory of liberal education does not claim to be a total or general education and that it is one. Secondly, because she articulates forcefully the deficiencies of a theory of liberal education understood as a theory of the whole of education. This she achieves by detailing her objections to Hirst's position in terms of the epistemological fallacy, the ivory tower person, and the dualism between mind and body. Hirst alludes to deficiencies in his own theory; Martin elaborates on them skillfully and insightfully. Having openly asserted that his theory of liberal education is not to be considered a theory of total or general education, Hirst proceeds to ignore this admonition, notably but not exclusively in *The Logic of Education*.[74]

In various references to the concept of education, Hirst specifically identifies it with both liberal education and general education. He also makes clear that, whatever limitations he acknowledges in his theory of liberal education by comparison with a broad or total education, he persists in characterizing education and general education as he understands it in terms of his own theory of liberal education.[75] In doing so, he insinuates or at least leads others to conclude that it is the only kind of education that really matters, an insinuation rejected by Martin. In invoking the epistemological fallacy, moreover, Martin makes clear that Hirst's insistence on grounding his theory of liberal education "fairly and squarely on the nature of knowledge,"[76] rather than in the goals and purposes of education, denies his position a source of ultimate moral and educational justification.

Martin's critique of Hirst bears out her observation that philosophical investigation of curriculum in the mid to late twentieth century endorses a theory of curriculum that she considers deficient. While Hirst's theory of liberal education highlights important aspects of the intellectual growth long considered a mark of the person of a liberal education, true to that tradition, it overlooks the development of the emotions and other noncognitive aspects of human development. As Martin points out, however, Hirst's theory is but one of many, such as those set forth in the United States by Broudy, Smith, and Burnett; Phenix; and Adler, that are open to her critique. All of these are based largely in one or another theory of the nature and structure of knowledge. All similarly fail to take fully into account aspects of human development that are recognized by Martin in a wider concept of personal development that emphasizes emotional formation and the importance of action and interpersonal relations in human affairs.

I have argued that Martin's critique of Hirst's theory of liberal education at once recognizes and downplays Hirst's own early acceptance of the limits of his theory and that she is unduly selective in her critique of Plato, because she fails to recognize the importance Plato attaches to education for action and for service to the common good. While this is so, Martin is much more committed to a detailing of the kinds of education for caring, for action, and for serving others than is Plato or even Hirst following his retraction of his own theory of liberal education. Plato and Hirst may recognize elements of education for action and service to others and even for moral formation, but Martin's elaboration of these dimensions of education is much more explicit, well developed, and clearly articulated than is either Plato's or Hirst's theory. This is especially so when it comes to spelling out what is actually entailed in education in the three Cs and education for action, for family life, and for domesticity. Similarly, she is intent on portraying an idea of education that is more fully developed than that presented by Rousseau or Beecher with regard to education for family and more comprehensive than that presented by Hirst with regard to liberal education.

THE IDEA OF A GENDER-SENSITIVE EDUCATION

If there are serious shortcomings of the kind implied by Newman and made explicit in Martin with regard to the idea of a liberal education, the question arises as to the continuing usefulness of liberal education as a construct. If there is a neglect of education in the three Cs and all that entails, for example, how might we replace or better conceptualize liberal education to overcome these oversights and other shortcomings? How, for example, might one educate future generations for carrying out the reproductive processes in society and combine the rational and emotional elements that Martin clearly considers essential to the ideal of the educated person? In her examination of the ideal of the educated woman as it has been variously treated by the writers she considers, Martin does not directly attempt to answer the question of how these shortcomings might be overcome in a theory of women's education. This, of course, does not blind her to the fact that similar omissions are common to idealizations of the education of men. So important are they that these failings lead Martin to conclude in *Reclaiming a Conversation* that the educational ideal to which primary attention ought now to be given is not the idea of the educated woman but the idea of a gender-sensitive education.

The Search for a New Ideal

Although she had not yet fully formulated the question as one of gender-sensitive education, in her early attempt to map out the general features of such an idea, "Needed: A New Paradigm for Liberal Education," Martin portrays the task as one of rethinking and redefining liberal education.[77] We know Martin is dissatisfied with the idea of the educated man as portrayed by Peters. If the task for Martin has now become that of redefining liberal education rather than pursuing the idea of the educated woman, one may ask if this is because she is also unhappy with the ideal of women's education as expressed by those writers considered in *Reclaiming a Conversation*.

As portrayed by Martin, there appear to be three crucial elements in the ideal of the educated woman: intellectual formation, emotional formation, and education for domesticity in the specific sense of good housekeeping, childrearing, and caring for the needy. It would appear from Martin's account that she does not find all three elements to be present in any one of the portrayals examined in *Reclaiming a Conservation*. Taken together, however, it would seem that all three elements are present in those portrayals as a group and it remains for someone else to present an appropriate formulation by combining them all in the one idealization of the educated woman. For her part, Martin backs away from such an undertaking. In its place, she turns her attention to her new but related quest: the consideration of an entirely new ideal of the educated person.[78] This is an ideal that holds out the prospect of answering a question that none of the other thinkers has considered. For her it now becomes the overriding question: how can we educate both men and women for carrying out the productive and reproductive processes in society, for living well in both the public and private worlds? Martin, like Carl Bereiter, may have seen this as a question of what it should mean to be an educated person in the twenty-first century. But her focus and orientation is markedly different from Bereiter's. Where Bereiter draws heavily on notions such as capital and production deeply rooted in the public sphere, Martin draws on notions associated with the private sphere, such as care, concern, and connection.

It is not because Martin is dismayed by the ideal of women's education presented by the writers examined in *Reclaiming a Conversation* that she turns her attention beyond the question of the education of women. It is that she has come to the realization that the more wide-ranging and universally encompassing question is also more pressing. Enter the ideal of a gender-sensitive education. Enter, too, Martin's account of how the traditional concept of liberal education needs to be expanded to serve the purpose of articulating and justifying a more comprehensive educational ideal.

A Gender-Sensitive Ideal

So, what is this new ideal and how adequate is it as a concept of liberal education? For Martin the idea of a gender-sensitive education becomes a "governing educational ideal." It is an idea that recognizes both the individual and collective educational needs of boys and girls and those educational needs that derive from their interdependency.[79] It is, moreover, a response to her recognition of the need for a new ideal or paradigm for liberal education. It is an ideal all the more pressing given the altered conditions of life in the twenty-first century, conditions in which a key question is who will look after the children as women follow men into the world of work outside the home. In approaching this question, Martin relies heavily on the distinctions she draws between the productive and the reproductive processes in society and between the public world, the world of work dominated by men, and the world of the home, the private world dominated by women. With women increasingly occupying a place in the world of work outside the home, the work of the home is under threat, not least the educational work of the home. In approaching this question, Martin alters her earlier stance on the role of the school as an agent of caring. That is to say, notwithstanding the school's pronounced disinclination to concern itself with the affairs of the home,[80] suitably constructed as in the Schoolhome, it may be embraced as a moral equivalent of home, that is to say an ideal home, "a home that is warm and loving, and neither physically nor psychologically abusive; and a family that believes in and strives for the equality of the sexes."[81]

In delineating the central characteristics of her new idealization, Martin is specific in treating of those learnings that fall outside of the subjects normally associated with liberal education. By contrast, her treatment of the traditional learning associated with the academic disciplines and liberal education is lukewarm and less settled. Accordingly, when it comes to the specifics of her alternative ideal, unlike Adler and to a lesser degree Newman, Martin does not give sustained attention to the academic studies, liberal education as traditionally understood, or cognitive growth. Instead, the focus is largely on how the ideal is shaped by domesticity and its associated values of care, concern, and connection; inclusion, as applied to gender, race, ethnicity, religion, sexual orientation, class, and socioeconomic status; the integration of the productive and reproductive processes in the formation of boys as well as girls; education for action and participation and not mere observation; the enormous extent and variety of our cultural wealth; and the role of a diverse range of competing educational agents in transmitting cultural assets and liabilities. By and large, these concerns fall well outside the boundary of liberal education as usually understood.

Martin found Hirst's theory of a liberal education to be unduly narrow as an account of the whole of education. For this reason, she called on philosophers of curriculum to broaden their horizons and consider forms of education that might be deemed valuable. Martin herself attempts to do this when calling for a new paradigm of that education deemed valuable. She presents her conclusions in embryonic form in the essay on Hirst's theory of a liberal education and in a more developed form in *The Schoolhome* and elsewhere.

For Martin, the concept of liberal education set forth by Hirst, a concept of education based squarely on the nature of knowledge itself, is not adequate for all possible forms of education. The inadequacy arises in large part from Hirst's focus on the nature of knowledge rather than the purposes of education. The failure to devote adequate attention to the question of the aims of education was not confined to Hirst and like-minded philosophers of education, however. It was also a feature of educational policy making that by the 1990s Martin had come to argue was quite unacceptable. The failure to attend to the question of goals or purpose may be addressed, she suggests in "The Radical Future of Gender Enrichment," by making an addition to those goals normally accepted by the public schools.[82] One goal in particular needs to be incorporated along with the usually accepted goals: preparing children for family life, which she enumerates as goal e. Stated more fully, this goal emphasizes education for the three Cs, on which Martin elaborates on a number of occasions, and it includes education for the reproductive processes in society. Accordingly, Martin attempts to expand the historical idea of liberal education based largely on a reconsideration of the purposes or goals of education. What is added is largely what is needed to provide for goal e, the education of students for family life and care, concern, and connection.[83]

Martin is insistent on the essential features of her new, alternative theory. She spells them out in a manner that shows how they reach well beyond the limits of liberal education as it is traditionally understood. Accordingly, this new concept, while not ignoring the forms of knowledge, sees them as but one part of a person's education. Such an education, she continues, identifying the ways in which it extends beyond the traditional conception, is one that "integrates thought and action, reason and emotion, education and life"; it does not divorce people from their social and natural contexts and it embraces individual autonomy as just one of many values.[84] The young and not-so-young alike must be educated in ways of living in the world as well as knowing about it, in action as well as thought. It was on this point that Martin took issue with Martha Nussbaum's plan for the reform of liberal education.[85] It is likely that Martin would level this criticism even at Broudy's advocacy of the study of molar problems, but unlikely that she would extend it to Theodore Brameld's curriculum designs for a transformative culture, which may be more accommodating toward some kinds of education for action.[86] What is clear, however, is that, for Martin, to base education exclusively on academic studies is to teach our young about life: it is to fall into the trap of turning out observers, not participants. And if we do not teach the young to apply intelligence to living, they will fall victim to life.[87] This is so serious and of late so recurring a challenge to the academic tradition that one may speculate even now that any successful new conceptualization of liberal education needs to deal with it.

Reinventing Domestic Tranquility

Before turning to consider how Martin provides for educating the young to apply intelligence to living and how she proposes to implement her program of gender-sensitive education, there are two further aspects of her thought whose implications for the theory of liberal education require attention. Both of these aspects speak to the question of how she is to realize her hopes for education and schooling in a world already gone wrong. The first has to do with domestic tranquility and the second with Martin's idea of cultural wealth and the related idea of multiple educational agency.

There is goodness, kindness, and friendship in our world, but there is also greed, ambition, and violence. So, how can we foster in the private world of the home the care for every human being that Martin seeks if that care is out of step with the values, priorities, and *modus operandi* of the public world? And how can we justify it in school programs? If we are to achieve a caring society, a fundamental restructuring of the social and political order is as important as the new ways of viewing education and schooling that Martin envisages. In such a society, the values of the private world of home become the bedrock values of a new political order, of the public world. In a crucial and imaginative move in *The Schoolhome*, Martin invokes the nation's past and turns to the U.S. Constitution for answers, believing that in the Constitution we already possess the necessary basis on which to establish this new order. We can establish it by embracing the notion of the school as a moral equivalent of the home. To do so necessitates "a remapping of the logical geography of education as well as a revisioning of the public world." The Schoolhome can play its part in bringing the values of the home, the school, and the world into alignment "by deriving its overarching aim from a rewritten domestic tranquillity clause."[88] How can this be so? For Martin, what she terms "the *civic* form" of domestic intranquility about which the founding fathers were concerned may not be extinct, but domestic intranquility of another kind poses the greater threat today. This is an antisocial form of domestic intranquility that seemed of little concern to the founding fathers. It tears the social fabric just as rebellion unties civic bonds. Domestic violence of all kinds, Martin maintains, "violates the very rights of life, liberty, and the pursuit of happiness" that the Constitution sought to protect.[89] For the homeless, the poor, the abused, there is no domestic tranquility. For the framers of the Constitution, however, the public or civic realm was the domestic realm. Domesticating the concept of domestic tranquility produces a society in which social and personal values of caring replace those of cold politics and economics[90] and a constitutional basis for promoting the values of domesticity through schooling.

As Martin introduces the idea of a reinterpretation of domestic tranquility, she is clear that the role of the school ought not be to prepare students for the public world as it now stands. Neither does she wish to leave this world unchanged. The point of rewriting the domestic tranquility clause is to indicate that it allows for a social and political ideal supportive of the educational ideal represented by the Schoolhome, an educational ideal grounded in care, concern, and connection. If the work of social reform is to be undertaken, we must therefore "remap the public world." Instead of rejecting the Schoolhome because of a conflict between the values, attitudes, and behaviors it promotes and those of the public world, we should instead reshape the values, attitudes, and behaviors of the public world in accordance with those of the Schoolhome.[91]

In making the notion of domesticity fundamental to both the gender-sensitive educational ideal and the remapping and regeneration of home, school, and society, the influence of Maria Montessori on Martin's thinking is powerful.[92] When we realize that Montessori saw school as being modeled on the home, the various parts of her system may be viewed differently,

Martin tells us.⁹³ Of course, Montessori did not model her school on just
any home. She modeled it on a version of home that many of its inhabitants would not have known, that is, a caring, nurturing, warm, welcoming,
joyful place. She also thought of the home—and now, by extension, the
school—as a second womb, where children were transformed into peaceful
persons, not the vandals they were likely to become if left to the streets.⁹⁴
For Montessori, the children belonged to the school and the school belonged to the children. They formed one school family. Following Montessori, as is made clear in *The Schoolhome* and in "Women, Schools, and Cultural Wealth," Martin has no doubt that to attain the goal of developing
each person as a member of a home and family, some values ought to be
chosen over others. Referring to the kind of home—and school—she has in
mind, she writes, "when I propose that our schools be home-like, I have in
mind ideal, not dysfunctional, homes."⁹⁵ Without going into the challenging issues of justification that arise, she assumes homes that are warm and
loving. The ideal of domesticated nation as home and family, we are led to
expect, would be similarly characterized.

Cultural Wealth, Multiple Educational Agency, and Curriculum

In Martin's search for a gender-sensitive ideal of education, the concept
of domesticity and the three Cs of care, concern, and connection are central. For this reason, special care is needed in expressing exactly what is
meant by domesticity, for the term domesticity is open to conflicting interpretations. It is clear from everything she writes that Martin sees domesticity as an enriching and empowering concept, at a far remove from Paulo
Freire's notion of education for domestication. From a societal perspective,
domesticity is even viewed by Martin as a source of transformation, unrelated in any way to the notion of subjugation, which is sometimes associated with the term and with the domestic sphere itself. In fact, Martin considers that Dewey himself repressed what she views as the domestic aspects
of the early American home: "Focusing on its disciplinary features—the industry, responsibility, habits of observation it taught," she writes, he overlooked other qualities that domesticity possessed. Highlighting the qualities she wishes to emphasize, Martin, by contrast, uses the term to refer to
"the intimacy and affection of family relationships and to the shared day-
to-day living that constitutes domesticity."⁹⁶

With domesticity understood in this way, it becomes clear that gender
sensitivity alone is not sufficient. There must also be sensitivity to race, ethnicity, religion, class, physical abilities, sexual orientation, and other salient
dimensions of people's lives.⁹⁷ Because of neglect in this area even now, the
school curriculum is, for many, unrelated to their lives. They feel excluded
and they underperform, though some master its content.⁹⁸ Showing an

affinity with critical pedagogy and criticizing the exclusionary and self-focused character of Hirsch's plan for "cultural literacy," Martin wishes to include the voices and stories of all, not just those of the dominant, cultural elite.[99] She also wishes to push further ahead by examining more closely the notion of culture itself.

Since presenting the notions of domesticity and of a gender-sensitive education in *The Schoolhome*, Martin has added substantially to the fundamentals of her educational thought by developing her cultural wealth thesis and by committing to the notion of educational metamorphosis. The cultural wealth thesis and the related notions of multiple educational agency, the educational problem of generations, and what she terms "the new problem of curriculum,"[100] are set forth at greatest length in *Cultural Miseducation*. They provide important clarifications of her theorizing about the content and structure of the school curriculum. Of particular relevance are the implications of her cultural wealth thesis for the idea of the well-rounded community—as distinct from the well-rounded individual—of which she now speaks. The idea of educational metamorphosis is exemplified in *Educational Metamorphoses* and raises new questions regarding the place of purpose in education.

While not directly connected by Martin to a society deficient in domestic tranquility, the idea of multiple educational agency is intended, in part, to heighten awareness of the manner in which our society unwittingly transmits to the young cultural liabilities rather than cultural wealth. According to this view, the transmission of cultural liabilities is accomplished most conspicuously through various media agencies and technologies that are not held to the same standards of accountability or responsibility as educational agents, such as schools and universities, which are expected to transmit cultural assets.[101] In the course of determining how we can most effectively maximize the transmission of cultural wealth, rather than connecting to domestic tranquility or gender sensitivity, Martin embarks on yet other imaginative explorations in quest of fresh avenues of curriculum theorizing. Central to a position in which she extends her earlier thinking is the proposal that the one curriculum for all is not the best path to follow in seeking improved directions for liberal education or the betterment of society.[102]

A differentiated or elective curriculum of the kind intimated in *Cultural Miseducation* departs from the notion of democracy in which each individual is seen as supremely self-reliant. According to Martin, such a view of individual self-reliance flies in the face of both community experience and the model of science, where the community or team draws upon the varying kinds of expertise of its participants. This expertise in turn reflects the interests and talents of community and team members. Given the cultural superabundance we possess, the existence of multiple intelligences, the precedent of teamwork and its dependency upon varying areas of expertise among the participants, and rejecting the notion of supreme self sufficiency, Martin argues against the idea of the one curriculum for all. Rather than attempting to transmit the same selected fraction of cultural wealth to every individual, leaving to chance that which is not passed on to all, she suggests we transmit all or a much greater proportion of the cultural wealth to the community as whole. This may be justified in the knowledge that not all will possess the same cultural stock or knowledge but all will have a contribution to make to the goals and purposes of the community as a whole. Martin acknowledges that this does bring with it the serious challenge of transmitting different portions to each rather than the one portion of our cultural wealth to all "without sacrificing the ideals of political democracy and social equality."[103] That is to say, those who possess the most valuable cultural stock may be at an advantage over others, and there is the risk that they will not share its benefits freely with all others, thereby threatening political democracy and social equality. If that challenge can be overcome, however, society will be the better served by this approach.

The Curriculum of a Gender-Sensitive Education

In moving forward to consider the implications of the foregoing discussions of gender sensitivity, domestic tranquility, and cultural wealth as well as the kind of curriculum they suggest, one must face the ongoing evolution of Martin's own thought. This evolution is not inconsiderable. Realizing that attempting a summary of Martin's position today, especially as it relates to the curriculum, is skating on thin ice, one could envisage at least two parts that are somewhat inconsistent with each other. The first, dealing with the broad scope of her position, would of necessity be general and, especially since the appearance of *Cultural Miseducation*, somewhat tentative on aspects of the curriculum. The second, dealing with the details of her stance on gender-sensitive education, could be more specific and internally consistent if also somewhat speculative.

Referring first to the broad scope of Martin's position, the aims of education are several, if not endless.[104] They include preparation for family living and promoting the three Cs of care, concern, and connection alongside the more traditional goals of an academic and civic nature. The implications drawn by Martin for curriculum are less clear-cut.[105] Whatever its eventual curricular form or its pattern of distribution among students, nonetheless, content could be expected to extend beyond disciplinary knowledge to include a wide range of cultural content characterized by Martin as being akin to that uncovered by the anthropologist. It could represent cultural wealth, including high culture. At the same time it could accommodate student participation in activities while also providing for their emotional formation.

Schools would not be viewed as the sole agents of education, however, and particular attention would need to be given to the educational agency of television and the Internet and their potency as countercultural forces.[106] Given all of this, how might one decide what to incorporate into the curriculum? Since Martin has long argued that we should shape school programs not on the basis of what knowledge exists but on the basis of our goals, such goals should be the basis on which curriculum content is chosen.[107] Knowledge can be viewed as a human or social construction, and all knowledge or any particular subject does not have an *a priori* claim on the curriculum. Accordingly, Martin once sought a curriculum that emphasized a commonality of attitudes, skills, and values rather than bodies of knowledge.[108] It was to blend science with humanity and affection, recognize individuality and tolerance, and have a respect for nature and joy.[109] Such a curriculum would also be one that speaks to all students, addresses common themes and great questions, and—more important than itself being unified—unifies all.[110]

Attempting to be more concrete and yet provide an overall view, one may reasonably ask, what specifically are to be the subjects of the curriculum, of say, the Schoolhome? There is no ready answer to this question, in part because Martin's recommendations in this regard, unlike Adler and others, are not set out in tabular form, but also because of her unsettled position on the question of a common core curriculum for all.

Unexpected as it may have been even before *Cultural Miseducation*, it once appeared that, for all its failings, liberal education and the disciplines it draws upon should be, in one way or another, a necessary part of the curriculum. Whether education would be organized in the form of a selection of academic disciplines or "the discipline" that Martin once spoke of,[111] it should be supplemented by education for domesticity and the three Cs. The curriculum of the Schoolhome, we are told, would feature reading, writing, friendship, conversation, music and singing, camaraderie, spontaneity, and gym. The Schoolhome itself would be a happy place where all would belong and where all could achieve and form positive memories of the experience. Having recognized that we need to teach children human activities, since they are not born with them, Martin mentioned theater and journalism as suitable for this purpose. She also saw these, in turn, as leading into language, literature, social studies, and even science, mathematics, building, designing, and every human emotion, joining head and hand to heart. They have the potential to lead to political science and civics, too.

Turning more specifically to gender-sensitive education viewed within the broader context just set forth, how might Martin's gender-sensitive ideal be translated into practice and be reflected in the school curriculum? Will gender sensitivity or domesticity be a school subject and, if so, in what form? Martin has argued for the inclusion of a subject entity embracing, for example, gender, women, and the three Cs. It is difficult, she admits, to find a suitable name for such a subject entity—perhaps home economics or family studies.[112] Care would be needed, moreover, since such a study could fall prey, as other practical subjects do, to becoming a study of theory, with students mere observers. It would be important, therefore, that "boys and girls alike learn to exercise the virtues which our culture thinks of as housed in our private homes."[113] What would be the subject matter of such family studies? Given the abusive attitudes toward girls and women that boys are universally exposed to from their earliest years, there could first be a focus on gender intended to promote respect for others of both sexes. Second, there could be a study of child care, housework, and the reproductive processes of society in general. Third, there could be attention to the three Cs.[114] Martin provides no extensive analysis regarding the epistemological and moral character of these areas. Aside from insisting that there may need to be different approaches to teaching for boys and girls, she gives only slight attention to the pedagogical characteristics and methodological aspects of those approaches.[115]

The inclusion of home economics in the school curriculum, or at least some of the elements of it such as cooking, might not rise to the order of a challenge to all schools today. For theorists such as Phenix, Hirst, and Adler, whose theories marginalize if not debar it, it does. Yet Martin wants to go much farther than home economics in its conventional sense as well as how it is understood by scholars in the field.[116] She wants to introduce the culture of the ideal home into the curriculum, along with its values of care, concern, and connection, as well as respect for gender differences. Through the school, she wants to bring domesticity into the nation and the world. Then, "when the civic 'sphere' is seen as a domestic domain, as I am recommending it should be," Martin writes, "domestic education in the limited sense of home economics becomes one among many elements of domestic education writ large."[117] To view the matter in this way is clearly a challenge to the theorists. It may be an even greater challenge to the schools, to those who make school policy, and to the politicians.[118]

MARTIN'S REDEFINITION OF LIBERAL EDUCATION

With the continuing evolution of Martin's educational thought, her overall position has become increasingly complex. This is especially so in regard to the school curriculum, where there clearly is some indecision on her part. But one need not be deflected by any of this, for her position still represents both a thorough and broadly based critique of the traditional idea of a liberal education and a range of imaginative possibilities regarding how to think about it anew. Nor is Martin alone in attempting a redefinition of liberal education. The ongoing search for alternative approaches to the education of the young shows widespread concern regarding the continuing usefulness of liberal education as traditionally understood. Earlier we saw the rich menu of suggestions for redefinition offered up by educational theorists of varying persuasions. Educational bodies too have contributed. In a recent publication of the Association of American Colleges and Universities, to pick one such presentation, there is a clear commitment to liberal education. But when liberal education is defined as it is there by Debra Humphreys, vice president for communications and public affairs of the Association, it is not the liberal education of Adler or Newman or of Hirst and Peters that is presented. It is liberal education redefined to include, among other accomplishments, creative thinking, teamwork and problem solving, civic knowledge and engagement, ethical reasoning and action, synthesis and advanced accomplishment across general and specialized studies.[119]

The search for new conceptualizations and definitions has been associated with liberal education throughout its long history[120] and for this reason all of this comes as no surprise. Yet, one can almost hear it whispered by the wary: "Has Martin gone too far?" Whether schools and colleges should or can provide education for the three Cs or family living or domesticity is open to question; it is a separate matter whether the comprehensive education of the young should include such a goal. Martin has made an impressive case that it should. She has also made the point that this view is not reflected in the goals commonly adopted for schooling in our society. Nor is it remotely aligned with traditional conceptions of liberal education in either schools or colleges. This is not to say that other educational theorists do not accept it, for some do. Aside from pedagogical matters, the line between those who do and those who do not usually has two prominent characteristics when it comes to the purpose and content of the curriculum. These are the inclusion or exclusion of practical education and the inclusion or exclusion of what Martin has labeled the concerns, interests, and ethos of the private world of the home.

As I have pointed out already, Martin does not sing the praises of traditional liberal education or dwell upon its desirable qualities. She does, however, draw attention to the emotional, behavioral, and attitudinal rather than cognitive nature of the more practical forms of education that she has argued ought to be added on to a redefined notion of liberal education if we are to provide a good education. She singles out for special attention the benefits of such education for both the public and the private worlds. In doing so, she also broadens considerably the range of legitimate discourse on liberal education, adding serious weight to what may be termed the minorstream tradition in educational theory whose voice has been muted over the years.

Martin broadens the range of legitimate discourse in a second and related area as well. Whether or not one agrees with the particular values and the strong commitment to education for domesticity, for care, concern, and connection, that Martin seeks to advance, serious questions of practicality and justification arise regarding the educational stances she adopts and the models of curriculum she envisions. But neither should this be surprising. If schools and colleges are to be places of education, they have to stand for something. "It comes with the territory,"[121] as David Purpel and Kevin Ryan put it in writing of moral education. This being so, the question is not whether schools and colleges should embrace or reject any particular values, be they values of the Schoolhome or the ivory tower; rather, the question is what values and how. Education is a value-laden enterprise by its nature. For this reason, the kinds of questions of practice and principle posed for Martin will still need to be addressed, whatever the stand of the school or college and whatever its stance on liberal or general education. What Martin has done is to push these questions out into the open and to challenge those who think about these matters to consider an extended range of educational values and principles.

In his retreat from liberal education, Newman raised several questions about the value or reliability of notional or theoretical knowledge in the conduct of human affairs. He also pointed to the possibilities raised by possessing real as distinct from notional knowledge. Martin goes beyond Newman—and considerably beyond the highly rationalist conceptions of liberal education once presented by Hirst and Peters and Adler—in identifying specific elements of a nonacademic kind that she argues are necessary in the education of the young. She does so in her analysis of the deficiencies of liberal education and does so again in identifying essential elements to be included in a gender-sensitive education, her reformed concept of liberal education.

Of the concepts introduced by Martin, none is more original or far reaching in its suggestive potential for rethinking liberal education than the ideal of a gender-sensitive education. The outgrowth of her insight that once women are brought into the debate, what constitutes an educated person is clear: gender-sensitive education, in its strictest construction, means simply taking gender differences into account in the design of educational programs. These differences will sometimes necessitate different approaches to ensure equality for all. But while the ideal of how to educate women may differ somewhat from the ideal of how to educate men, in Martin's view its aim is to ensure equality, for being treated equally sometimes means being treated differently. In Martin's hands, the ideal of the educated woman—and one might add, the ideal of the educated man, too—merges rather than conflicts with her ideal of a gender-sensitive education. It culminates in an educational ideal ranging far beyond what has traditionally been associated with the idea of a liberal education, and it resonates with many others in search of new interpretations.

NOTES

1. D. G. Mulcahy, *Knowledge, Gender, and Schooling: The Feminist Educational Thought of Jane Roland Martin* (Westport, CT: Bergin and Garvey, 2002).
2. Jane Roland Martin, *Changing the Educational Landscape: Philosophy, Women, and Curriculum* (New York: Routledge, 1994); Jane Roland Martin, *The Schoolhome: Rethinking Schools for Changing Families* (Cambridge, MA: Harvard University Press, 1992); Jane Roland Martin, *Coming of Age in Academe: Rekindling Women's Hopes and Reforming the Academy* (New York: Routledge, 2000); Jane Roland Martin, *Cultural Miseducation: In Search of a Democratic Solution* (New York: Teachers College Press, 2002); Jane Roland Martin, *Educational Metamorphoses: Philosophical Reflections on Identity and Culture* (Lanham, MD: Rowman and Littlefield, 2007).
3. Jane Roland Martin, *Reclaiming a Conversation: The Ideal of the Educated Woman* (New Haven, CT: Yale University Press, 1985).
4. See Martin, *Changing the Educational Landscape*, 70–87, 88–99, 170–186.
5. Martin, *Reclaiming a Conversation*, 171–199.
6. In her later work, Martin prefers to use the phrase "public world of work, politics, and the professions" in place of "productive processes of society." See Jane Roland Martin, "Women, Schools, and Cultural Wealth," in *Women's Philosophies of Education*, ed. Connie Titone and Karen E. Moloney (Upper Saddle River, NJ: Merrill/Prentice Hall, Inc., 1999), 155.
7. Martin, *Changing the Educational Landscape*, 13, 79, 116.
8. On this point see Mulcahy, *Knowledge, Gender, and Schooling*, 101–108.
9. See Robin Barrow, *Plato and Education* (London: Routledge and Kegan Paul, 1976), and any of a number of treatments of Plato's educational thought such as Gerald L. Gutek, *Historical and Philosophical Foundations of Education* (Upper Saddle River, NJ: Prentice Hall, Inc., 2001), 9–26; Edward J. Power, *A Legacy of Learning* (Albany: State University of New York Press, 1991), 29–37; and Henry J. Perkinson, *Since Socrates* (New York: Longman, 1980), 14–30. See also, of course, Plato, *The Republic*, trans. Benjamin Jowett (New York: Airmont Publishing Company, Inc., 1968).
10. Martin, *Reclaiming a Conversation*, 12–17.
11. Martin, *Reclaiming a Conversation*, 17–23.
12. Martin, *Reclaiming a Conversation*, 26. Mary Warnock adopts a broadly similar stance in *Education: A Way Ahead* (Oxford: Basil Blackwell, 1979), 47–54.
13. Martin, *Reclaiming a Conversation*, 26–34. Martin's reference to the experience of Rosalind Franklin, 31–34, highlights this.
14. Martin, *Reclaiming a Conversation*, especially 19–20, and Jane Roland Martin, "Bringing Women into Educational Thought," *Educational Theory* 34, no. 4 (Fall 1984): 341–343.
15. Martin appears ambivalent on this point, calling at times for a somewhat differentiated curriculum and at other times for essentially the same curriculum for both boys and girls. See, for example, Martin, *Cultural Miseducation*, 130–142;

Martin, *Changing the Educational Landscape*, 133–153; and Martin, *The Schoolhome*, 49–84.

16. See Martin, *Changing the Educational Landscape*, 53–69, and Martin, *Reclaiming a Conversation*, 38–69.

17. Martin, *Changing the Educational Landscape*, 66.

18. Martin, *Changing the Educational Landscape*, 61–66, and Martin, *Reclaiming a Conversation*, 38–43, 47.

19. Martin, *Reclaiming a Conversation*, 38–53. It is important for Martin's position that she establishes that the education and roles set for Emile and Sophie are not rooted in their different natures but in culturally based gender biases.

20. Martin, *Reclaiming a Conversation*, 195.

21. See Martin, *Reclaiming a Conversation*.

22. Martin, *Reclaiming a Conversation*, 97 and 91–99.

23. Martin, *Reclaiming a Conversation*, 99.

24. Martin, *Reclaiming a Conversation*, 100.

25. Martin, *Reclaiming a Conversation*, 101.

26. Martin, *Reclaiming a Conversation*, 127–128, 134–138.

27. Martin, *Reclaiming a Conversation*, 103–138.

28. Martin, *Reclaiming a Conversation*, 128–132.

29. Martin, *Reclaiming a Conversation*, 132.

30. Martin, *Reclaiming a Conversation*, 140–141. See also 139–148.

31. Martin, *Reclaiming a Conversation*, 149.

32. Martin, *Reclaiming a Conversation*, 151.

33. Martin, *Reclaiming a Conversation*, 141.

34. Martin, *Reclaiming a Conversation*, 151. See also Charlotte Perkins Gilman, *Herland* (New York: Pantheon Books, 1979).

35. Martin, *The Schoolhome*, 161–204.

36. Martin, *Reclaiming a Conversation*, 155–156.

37. Martin, *Reclaiming a Conversation*, 170.

38. See especially R. S. Peters, "Education and the Educated Man," in *Education and the Development of Reason*, ed. R. F. Dearden, P. H. Hirst, and R. S. Peters (London: Routledge and Kegan Paul, 1972), 3–18. See also Jane Roland Martin, "Transforming Moral Education," *Journal of Moral Education* 16 (October 1987): 204–213.

39. Martin is not alone in characterizing Peters' concept of the educated man as representing a dominant viewpoint. See also Eleanor Kallman Roemer, "Harm and the Ideal of the Educated Person: Response to Jane Roland Martin," *Educational Theory* 31, no. 2 (Spring 1981): 117.

40. For a discussion of the debate that grew up around Martin's use of the term male cognitive perspective, see Mulcahy, *Knowledge, Gender, and Schooling*, 40–44. Of particular importance in this debate is Harvey Siegel, "Genderized Cognitive Perspectives and the Redefinition of Philosophy of Education," *Teachers College Record* 85, no. 1 (Fall 1983): 100–119.

41. Martin, *Changing the Educational Landscape*, 74.

42. Martin, *Changing the Educational Landscape*, 77.

43. Martin, *Changing the Educational Landscape*, 170–186.

44. Martin, *Changing the Educational Landscape*, 79.

45. Martin, *Changing the Educational Landscape*, 80.

46. Martin, *The Schoolhome*, 140.

47. See Martin, *Changing the Educational Landscape*, 80–81.

48. Contributions of particular note dating from the 1960s and 1970s, when Martin first became interested in the subject, include Harry S. Broudy, B. Othanel Smith, and Joe R. Burnett, *Democracy and Excellence in American Secondary Education: A Study in Curriculum Theory* (Chicago: Rand McNally & Company, 1964), and Philip H. Phenix, *Realms of Meaning* (New York: McGraw Hill, 1964). Important works in the same time frame by English scholars include R. S. Peters, *Ethics and Education* (London: George Allen and Unwin, Ltd, 1966); R. F. Dearden, *The Philosophy of Primary Education* (London: Routledge and Kegan Paul, 1968); P. H. Hirst and R. S. Peters, *The Logic of Education* (London: Routledge and Kegan Paul, 1970); J. White, *Towards a Compulsory Curriculum* (London: Routledge and Kegan Paul, 1973); and P. H. Hirst, *Knowledge and the Curriculum* (London: Routledge and Kegan Paul, 1974).

49. Martin, *Changing the Educational Landscape*, 171.

50. Martin, *Changing the Educational Landscape*, 172.

51. Martin, *Changing the Educational Landscape*, 176.

52. Martin, *Changing the Educational Landscape*, 176–177. On this point, see also Andrew Davis and Kevin Williams, "Epistemology and Curriculum," in *The Blackwell Guide to the Philosophy of Education*, ed. Nigel Blake, Paul Smeyers, Richard Smith, and Paul Standish (Oxford: Blackwell Publishers, 2003), 253.

53. Martin, *Changing the Educational Landscape*, 177. For a fuller treatment of this and related points regarding Martin's critique of Hirst's theory, see Mulcahy, *Knowledge, Gender, and Schooling*, 2–13.

54. Martin, *Changing the Educational Landscape*, 173.

55. Martin, *Changing the Educational Landscape*, 133–153. See also Mulcahy, *Knowledge, Gender, and Schooling*, 13–20.

56. Martin, *Changing the Educational Landscape*, 173–176.

57. Martin's reluctance to recognize the distinction in many of her writings is considered in Mulcahy, *Knowledge, Gender, and Schooling*, 101–108. It should be said, however, that in Martin, *Cultural Miseducation*, and Martin, *Educational Metamorphoses*, which have appeared since then, there is no such reluctance. In fact, the distinction is emphasized.

58. Martin, *Changing the Educational Landscape*, 173–174.

59. Martin, *Changing the Educational Landscape*, 175. It should be noted that in Hirst and Peters, *The Logic of Education*, it is made clear that, in addition to a knowledge of the seven forms that are central to the theory of liberal education, students are also expected to grow in their respect of persons. For a further consideration of this and related points, see Mulcahy, *Knowledge, Gender, and Schooling*, 10–13.

60. Martin, *Changing the Educational Landscape*, 179.

61. Martin, *Changing the Educational Landscape*, 179. Martin's accounts of action and participation call for a much higher level of "bodily" engagement, or activism, than that found in other writers. See, for example, Yusef Waghid, "Action as an Educational Virtue: Toward a Different Understanding of Democratic Citizenship Education," *Educational Theory* 55, no. 3 (August 2005): 323–342, and Yusef Waghid, "University Education and Deliberation: In Defence of Practical Reasoning," *Higher Education* 51, no. 3 (April 2006): 315–328. See also Mulcahy, *Knowledge, Gender, and Schooling*, 9.

62. Martin, *Changing the Educational Landscape*, 180.

63. Martin, *Changing the Educational Landscape*, 179–180. For a view of liberal education other than Adler's that highlights education for citizenship, see Martha C. Nussbaum, *Cultivating Humanity: A Classical Defense of Reform in Liberal Education* (Cambridge, MA: Harvard University Press, 1997).

64. Mulcahy, *Knowledge, Gender, and Schooling*, 44–49.

65. Martin, *Changing the Educational Landscape*, 175. In this connection, see Lionel Elvin, *The Place of Commonsense in Educational Thought* (London: Allen and Unwin, 1977), 52–53.

66. Hirst, *Knowledge and the Curriculum*, 96.

67. In this connection see, R. S. Peters, "Ambiguities in Liberal Education and the Problem of Its Content," in *Ethics and Educational Policy*, ed. Kenneth A. Strike and Kieran Egan (London: Routledge and Kegan Paul, 1978), 3–21. Unfortunately, Peters does not dwell here upon how knowledge that is considered logically basic might throw light upon the phrase "knowledge for its own sake."

68. On the nuances of the term 'liberal' in association with liberal education, see, for example, Jacques Maritain, "Thomist Views on Education," in *Modern Philosophies and Education*, 54th Yearbook of the National Society for the Study of Education, Part I, ed. Nelson B. Henry (Chicago: The University of Chicago Press, 1955), 77–83; Mortimer J. Adler, *Reforming Education: The Opening of the American Mind*, ed. Geraldine Van Doren. (New York: Macmillan Publishing Co., Inc., 1988), 283; Nussbaum, *Cultivating Humanity*, 293–301; Peters, "Ambiguities in Liberal Education," 3–21; Martin, *Changing the Educational Landscape*, 181–182; and Lars Lovelie and Paul Standish, "Introduction: Bildung and the Idea of a Liberal Education," *Journal of the Philosophy of Education* 36, no. 3 (August 2002): 317–340, which traces many of the various influences upon and elements within the idea of liberal education over the past century or so. For a comprehensive historical treatment, see Bruce A. Kimball, *Orators and Philosophers: A History of the Idea of a Liberal Education* (New York: College Entrance Examinations Board, 1995). This is the expanded second edition. The original edition was published in 1986 by Teachers College Press.

69. Israel Scheffler, *The Language of Education* (Springfield, IL: Charles C. Thomas, 1960), 15.

70. Martin, *Changing the Educational Landscape*, 171.

71. Martin, *Changing the Educational Landscape*, 173. In fact, Martin uses a number of phrases to capture this notion, including "all education deemed valuable," "that education which is valuable," "education deemed valuable," and "the whole of valuable education." See Martin, *Changing the Educational Landscape*, 174–175, 180.

72. Hirst, *Knowledge and the Curriculum*, 96.

73. Hirst and Peters, *The Logic of Education*, 66–67.

74. See D. G. Mulcahy, "Jane Roland Martin and Paul Hirst on Liberal Education: A Reassessment," *Journal of Thought* 38, no. 1 (Spring 2003), 25–28.

75. There are several passages in *The Logic of Education* where the concept of education is identified with liberal education as understood by Hirst. See, for example, Hirst and Peters, *The Logic of Education* 19, 25, 66–67. In the original piece on liberal education upon which Martin's analysis is largely based, "Liberal Education and the Nature of Knowledge," Hirst says that the outcome of his idea of liberal educa-

tion is best summed up by Oakeshott when Oakeshott spoke of education as an initiation into the skill and partnership of the intellectual adventure of conversation. In the very paragraph quoted by Hirst, however, Oakeshott uses the word education not the phrase liberal education. See Hirst, *Knowledge and the Curriculum*, 52.

76. Hirst, *Knowledge and the Curriculum*, 30.

77. Martin, *Changing the Educational Landscape*, 170–186.

78. Martin, *Reclaiming a Conversation*, 193–199, and Martin, *Changing the Educational Landscape*, 70–87.

79. This latter point is especially well brought out in Martin, "Women, Schools, and Cultural Wealth," 150–155

80. Martin, *Changing the Educational Landscape*, 228–241.

81. Martin, "Women, Schools, and Cultural Wealth," 162.

82. Martin, *Changing the Educational Landscape*, 231–233.

83. Martin, *Changing the Educational Landscape*, 231–233.

84. Martin, *Changing the Educational Landscape*, 183, and Martin, "Women, Schools, and Cultural Wealth," 163.

85. Martin, *Coming of Age in Academe*, 138, and Martin, *The Schoolhome*, 85–87.

86. Broudy, *The Uses of Schooling*, 103–106; Broudy, Smith, and Burnett, *Democracy and Excellence*, 233–243, 272–274; and Theodore Brameld, *Patterns of Educational Philosophy* (New York: Holt, Rinehart and Winston, Inc., 1971), 475–511.

87. Martin, *The Schoolhome*, 87–91, and Philip O'Hear, "Coherence in Curriculum Planning," in *Assessing the National Curriculum*, ed. Philip O'Hear and J. White (London: Paul Chapman Publishing, Ltd., 1993), 15–24, where O'Hear concurs on this point in his critique of the national curriculum in England

88. Martin, *The Schoolhome*, 203.

89. Martin, *The Schoolhome*, 165–166.

90. Martin, *The Schoolhome*, 161–204.

91. Martin, *The Schoolhome*, 161–204.

92. Martin, *Changing the Educational Landscape*, 88–99.

93. Martin, *Changing the Educational Landscape*, 89.

94. In *The Schoolhome*, for example, Martin accepts that re-creating the school as a moral equivalent of home will have to address the issues of whether this can be done in a place of such diversity and violence as the school itself, that postindustrial homes have often lost the ethic of caring, and that the school may have to compensate for this lost ethic and provide the respite and recreation from the cruel world once found in the home, at least the idealized, model home. At the same time, she believes, it is possible, with hard work by faculty, to develop a curriculum suitably designed for this purpose. This would be a curriculum that speaks to all students, addresses common themes and great questions, and unifies all.

95. Martin, "Women, Schools, and Cultural Wealth," 162. See also Martin, *The Schoolhome*, 46, and Martin, "Women, Schools, and Cultural Wealth," 159–164.

96. Martin, *The Schoolhome*, 126.

97. Martin, *The Schoolhome*, 118.

98. See, for example, Martin, *The Schoolhome*, 52–57.

99. Martin, *The Schoolhome*, 65–70, and Martin, "Women, Schools, and Cultural Wealth," 149–175.

100. See, for example, Jane Roland Martin, "The New Problem of Curriculum," *Synthese* 94, no. 1 (1993): 85–104.

101. Martin, *Cultural Miseducation*, and Martin, "Women, Schools, and Cultural Wealth," 167–177.

102. Martin, "The New Problem of Curriculum," and Martin, *Cultural Miseducation*, 130–142.

103. Martin, "The New Problem of Curriculum," 102.

104. Martin, *Educational Metamorphoses*, 151.

105. These seem to range from a common core for all to an ambivalence to the idea. See, for example, Martin, *The Schoolhome*, 77–84, 104–119, and Martin, *Cultural Miseducation*, 130–142. See also Mulcahy, *Knowledge, Gender, and Schooling*, 65–66, 75 n. 124, 150–151, 156.

106. See Martin, "Women, Schools, and Cultural Wealth," 167–175, and *Cultural Miseducation*, 32–61.

107. In *Cultural Miseducation*, Martin's position on aims seems to shift away from the primacy of aims or purpose, a stance that is basic to her important critique of Hirst; that shift becomes even more pronounced in her latest book. In *Educational Metamorphoses*, she writes that "although some of the education a person receives over the course of a lifetime is a conscious, deliberate undertaking, some of it happens accidentally and occurs unbeknown to the educator or the learner." Later she continues that for anyone who thinks she has made discussion of the aims of education pointless, "the moral to be drawn from our case studies of educational metamorphoses is not that goals cannot be set, but that there are many more aims to choose from than are listed in most philosophies." Martin, *Educational Metamorphoses*, 21, 151. See also, for example, Martin, *Changing the Educational Landscape*, 133–153, 170–199, 212–227.

108. Martin, *The Schoolhome*, 84.

109. Martin, *The Schoolhome*, 18–19, 31–40.

110. See Martin, *Changing the Educational Landscape*, 212–227, and Martin, *The Schoolhome*, 49–84.

111. Martin, *Changing the Educational Landscape*, 146–150.

112. Martin, *The Schoolhome*, 91–98, 150–160, and Martin, *Changing the Educational Landscape*, 228–241.

113. Martin, *Changing the Educational Landscape*, 233.

114. Martin, *The Schoolhome*, 91–98, 150–160, and Martin, *Changing the Educational Landscape*, 228–241.

115. Martin, *The Schoolhome*, 91–98, 111–119, and Martin, "Women, Schools, and Cultural Wealth," 164–165.

116. See Linda Peterat, "Family Studies: Transforming Curriculum, Transforming Families," in *Gender In/forms Curriculum*, eds. Jane Gaskell and John Willinsky (New York: Teachers College Press, 1995), 174–190.

117. Martin, "Women, Schools, and Cultural Wealth," 166.

118. Alongside the theoretical positions Martin adopts there is also the question of implementation. On this point, see Benjamin Levin, "*Changing the Educational Landscape*," *Journal of Educational Thought* 30, no. 1 (April 1996): 79–81.

119. Debra Humphreys, *Making the Case for Liberal Education: Responding to Challenges*. (Washington, DC: Association of American Colleges and Universities, 2006), 3. For a view of liberal education that envisions a connectedness of service-learning, civic education, and liberal education, see Joseph L. DeVitis, Robert W. Johns, and

Douglas J. Simpson, eds., *To Serve and Learn: The Spirit of Community in Liberal Education* (New York: Peter Lang Publishing, Inc., 1998).

120. See Kimball, *Orators and Philosophers.*

121. David Purpel and Kevin Ryan, "It Comes with the Territory: The Inevitability of *Moral Education in the Schools,*" in *Moral Education. . . It Comes with the Territory,* ed. David Purpel and Kevin Ryan (Berkeley, CA: McCutchan Publishing Corporation, 1976), 44–54.

5

Liberal Education as
a Preparation for Life

However well and with whatever degree of inclusiveness they do so, suc-
ceeding generations have the opportunity to decide for themselves what are
their educational aspirations as they contemplate their own values and
broad social goals and responsibilites. It is appropriate, therefore, to consider the implications of the foregoing discussion of liberal education for
how we conceptualize the education of the young as we make our way
through the twenty-first century. It is a measure of the extent of the task that
our future brings with it not only unknown possibilities and challenges, but
also serious questions about the inherited traditions of a liberal education
that have long been looked to as a guide to the way forward with this vital
undertaking.

Purpose and Pedagogy

In *Democracy and Education*, John Dewey objects to the separation of subject matter and method,[1] and in *Experience and Education*, he writes "there is
no subject that is in and of itself, or without regard to the stage of growth
attained by the learner, such that inherent educational value can be attributed to it."[2] This is because the content of the curriculum cannot be adequately discussed in isolation from pedagogy or teaching, a point raised by
Madeleine Grumet in responding to *The Paideia Proposal* and one to which
Padraig Hogan has drawn attention more recently.[3] Much depends on how
the content can be integrated into the knowledge and experience of the student. Picking up on this point, Ira Shor quotes Dewey to the effect that finding material for learning within experience is but the first step. The next one
is the progressive development of what has been previously experienced

into a richer and more organized form. Shor continues, "the goal is structured, critical knowledge, but that cannot be the starting point. Student experience and understanding are the foundations into which academic material and structured knowledge are situated."[4] Though Dewey has been criticized as being weak on academics,[5] both Shor and he have the highest regard for academic or organized knowledge; they also realize that higher or more formalized knowledge is the goal, not the starting point. Grasping this core pedagogical feature of the educational process is a persistent challenge for the public, for legislators, and for educators, and yet it is essential to success in any educational endeavor.

I accept that this is so, but this study is based on the understanding that the curriculum and its content may also be considered in the broader context of aims and purpose. In fact, it often is. Unfortunately, because the constraints imposed by the crucial pedagogical dimension just alluded to are often overlooked, such considerations are less useful than they might be.[6] This said, the discussion of liberal education in the preceding chapters points to a number of ways in which the reconceptualization of liberal education may be advanced by focusing directly on questions of the purpose and general content of the curriculum. This discussion suggests, moreover, that in the terms of Thomas Kuhn's theory of scientific revolutions,[7] we may be at the threshold of a wholly new paradigm in liberal education. For that matter, Jane Roland Martin has already linked the two ideas.

Continuity and Change in Liberal Education

So what have we learned about liberal education from our study of the educational thought of John Henry Newman, Mortimer Adler, and Martin, and what does it suggest for the future? We have learned that there remains a strong commitment to intellectual development or cultivation of the intellect. Newman and Adler stress the requirement of broad knowledge of a generally academic kind, a requirement modified in Martin. Appealing to the notion of culture in the anthropological sense, she seeks recognition of an even broader knowledge base while restricting the dominance of the academic disciplines.[8] Adler emphasizes the connection between education and preparation for citizenship in a democratic society and a commitment to the same course of study for all aimed at developing the essentially human in all of us. This same course of study for all is justified on these grounds and on the necessity in a democracy to treat everyone equally, and it is built around the study of academic subjects and the great works of Western civilization.

Notwithstanding his commitment to a broadly based knowledge, to the cultivation of the intellect traditionally associated with liberal education, and to the idealization of liberal education to which he contributed so substantially, Newman recognizes several limitations of liberal education. These include its failure to deal directly with moral and religious formation, aspects of education for which he turned to the college within the university as a sort of home away from home that, along with its tutorial side, possessed a moral and spiritual dimension. But even beyond these limitations that Newman expressly recognizes, wittingly or unwittingly, and accompanied by little or no fanfare, he also raises serious doubts about the capacity of theoretical knowledge of the kind associated with liberal education to enable the individual to deal with the real world. This is because, for Newman writing in this vein, notional or theoretical knowledge of the kind sought in liberal education deals with abstractions and does not reach as far as concrete reality. Newman's favorable evaluation of knowledge of the real as distinct from the notional left no doubt in his mind that there is considerable value in forms of education that build directly upon concrete experience.[9] Newman never addressed the tension in his educational thought to which this point gave rise, a tension that is broadly attributed by Jay Newman to John Henry Newman's tendency to ambiguity on these issues and, surprisingly perhaps, his anti-intellectualism.[10]

Martin does not directly address this tension in Newman's thought, yet her view of the educational landscape does accommodate it. It does so by accepting with reservations the merits of the traditional ideal of liberal education as propounded by Newman and others. Martin then adds forms of education that address the emotional and practical sides of human nature, for some of which Newman himself had certain sympathies. These additional elements attempt to address Martin's reservations regarding the limitations of liberal education in its traditional form, notably its separation of thought from emotion and body from mind, its neglect of the practical, and its gender biases. In her idea of a liberal education, Martin argues for the development of human beings as caring individuals, educated for participation in a world that calls for action as well as thought. This she envisages in an education that draws on the historical experiences of men and women, educates boys and girls alike for both the public and the private worlds, and is committed to equal respect for all human beings: men and women, tall and small: people of all races, religions, ethnicities, and social and economic backgrounds.

In the past quarter of a century or so, many new and overlapping elements have been added onto—or at least proposed for consideration with—these components. These include the introduction in many institutions of interdisciplinary areas such as women's studies and African-American studies along with the intellectual orientations and skills associated with them. Those associated with critical pedagogy have highlighted the study of power relations in society and how these may be viewed from the perspective of their impact on the self, the disenfranchised, and both the oppressed

and the oppressor in society. To this, Carl Bereiter has added the broadly related idea of "enlarging liberal education so as to encompass both the
grasping of what others have already understood and *the sustained, collective
effort to extend the boundaries of what is known*" (italics added).[11]

To the examples given above, Thomas Green[12] has added an emphasis on
developing capacities of craft, judgment, and taste, the need for a social
memory, and an engaging pedagogy. Ernest Boyer[13] and Joseph L. DeVitis,
Robert W. Johns, and Douglas J. Simpson[14] and others added on the idea of
service-learning, contending that service may contribute to heightened understanding in a way that socratic teaching, reading the classics, and participating in artistic activities was intended to do by Adler. In addition, it is
claimed, service-learning may enable students to contribute to the community while also becoming caring and developing interpersonal skills not
normally associated with liberal education. To the element of service,
DeVitis, Johns, and Simpson add activism or participation, as do Shor and
Martin. And John White and others have highlighted the place of the practical in general education. Regarding all of this and other developments
combined, Bruce Kimball has observed, "it might even be said that pragmatism is now infusing liberal education."[15]

This wide array of elements recently introduced, often in the face of some
controversy and alongside the ideals of liberal or general education expounded by Newman, Adler, and Martin, are now exerting their particular
influences on liberal education. It is the coalescence and even the contradictions among these elements that bring us to the threshold of a new paradigm of liberal or general education. In what follows, I am attempting to
push over the line. In doing so, I shall be drawing on the analysis presented
in the foregoing chapters and adding to it, bearing in mind the pedagogical
dimension to which I have alluded.

THE CHALLENGE

At the beginning of this book, I raised several questions regarding the continuing relevance and usefulness of the idea of a liberal education. I asked
how the idea still speaks helpfully to educational challenges enumerated at
the outset. I also asked how it assists us in addressing the question raised by
Bereiter, namely, "what should it mean to be an educated person in the
twenty-first century?"[16] This remains the central question. It is very much a
question of the aims and content of the curriculum with which, modified
for the times, the tradition of liberal education has been exclusively concerned throughout its long history.

As regards the aims of education, liberal education has been resolutely
committed to the overriding goal of cultivation of mind understood as the

development of intellectual skills and the enlargement of understanding and, as Lars Lovelie and Paul Standish have put it, has been "unlike any education geared solely to extrinsic ends."[17] The development of intellectual skills and understanding has drawn in varying ways upon a curriculum comprised of a broad theoretical knowledge base. Addressing the question of the knowledge base, Hirst once expressed better than anyone a contemporary view of the nature and structure of the kind of knowledge entailed in the prevailing idea of a liberal education. Hirst's account was presented in his celebrated if contested analysis of the forms of knowledge developed in support of the theory of liberal education that he has now retracted.[18] According to Hirst, there are seven different forms of knowledge, namely, logic and mathematics, physical sciences, history or interpersonal knowledge, moral knowledge, aesthetic knowledge, religious knowledge, and philosophical knowledge.[19] While the characterization of the nature and structure of knowledge as presented by Adler is considerably more general than that of Hirst, Adler's model does describe very well both the knowledge base and the intellectual skills as traditionally conceived in the idea of liberal education. These are knowledge as organized into language, literature, and the arts; mathematics and science; and the social studies. The related skills are language skills, mathematical and scientific skills, and skills of analysis and critical judgment.

However one may evaluate these broad expressions of the traditional aims and content of liberal education, they have garnered considerable agreement over the centuries. For some, they have stood the test of time. For others they are acceptable as far as they go. For still others they do not go far enough to provide clarity or address the need to articulate policy and guide practice. Judging by our earlier review of emergent conceptions of liberal education and the requirements placed upon it, neither do they go far enough to embrace a range of new viewpoints and address pressing challenges to contemporary educational thought. Thus, while the attention given to aims and content in the tradition of a liberal education is helpful to us today in focusing on these two essential elements, care is needed to delve below the surface of varying articulations of the aims of liberal education.

If standing the test of time were a helpful criterion, one would be slow to jettison those attempts at formulating the goals of education traditionally associated with a liberal education. Yet the times are changing. One of the new requirements accompanying the changing times is more explicitness in formulating even broad aims of education, where such formulation may require a consideration of the implications for the curriculum. An example that addresses both this issue and the issue of whether traditional articulations of the purpose of liberal education go far enough may be helpful at this point.

Following Dewey and Richard Pring, Shor strenuously rejects as inappropriate and ineffectual any approach to education that does not grow out of the experience of the student. Accordingly, Shor is dismissive of the traditional curricular canon with its affinity for "academic themes" and disinclination toward "generative themes." He also disagrees with the kind of comprehensive range of curriculum content mandated both by Hirst in his early work and by Adler on the basis of their various characterizations of the nature and structure of knowledge. Moreover, in addition to studies leading to higher forms of knowledge, Shor, in a manner somewhat akin to Bereiter, envisions students engaged in solving problems encountered in their own experience and thereby adding to the body of knowledge. He also insists that students be educated for activism. All of this Shor advocates in the name of empowerment or personal liberation, education for critical thinking, and education for democratic citizenship in much the same manner as Dewey or Paulo Freire might have done.

One could be forgiven for thinking it was Adler rather than Shor who suggested that the objectives of liberal or general education were personal liberation, critical thinking, and democratic citizenship. By contrast, there could be no forgiveness for thinking Adler advocated the same curriculum path as Shor does. The course of studies envisaged by Adler, it will be recalled, highlighted a study of a comprehensive range of the core academic disciplines and the great works of Western civilization with little evidence of an opportunity for student input to the selection of such content. Accordingly, what we have in the case of the differences between Adler and Shor is largely a disagreement about curriculum and pedagogy, not a disagreement about aims or objectives. In fact, it is likely that one could line up on the one side of a similar divide such figures as Jean Jacques Rousseau, Dewey, Freire, Pring, and Shor and on the other side Adler, Robert Hutchins, Jacques Maritain, Harry S. Broudy, Philip H. Phenix, Hirst, E. D. Hirsch, and Allan Bloom. These two groupings may view the content of the curriculum and its associated pedagogies very differently from each other. It is much less clear that they would be similarly at odds on the matter of aims or objectives, as long as these were stated at the more general level. This is why it may not be sufficient to rest an exploration of varying ideals of liberal or general education at the level of aims without pursuing how those who adopt them translate them in terms of curriculum and general pedagogy.

This example also throws light on the observation that broad statements of the aims and content of liberal education are acceptable as far as they go. It may even bring into question W. B. Carnochan's contention that we ought to focus on purpose rather than content. One can imagine that both Adler and Shor (or Hutchins and Dewey or Hirst and Freire) could subscribe to the aim of "the development of mind" or "the cultivation of intellect" and consider it to be an acceptable formulation, as far as it goes. The problem is that it does not go far enough, that is to say, far enough to expose the considerable differences in the positions of Adler and Shor when it comes to translating these aims into content or curricular terms. In setting out in this chapter to contemplate the theme of education as a preparation for life[20] as a way of conceptualizing liberal education today, it will be necessary, therefore, to explore more fully than is done in *The Paideia Proposal*, for example, the questions left unanswered by Adler's treatment of the aims or objectives of basic schooling and their justification. Similarly, it may be necessary to examine how those objectives may be linked to the content of the curriculum and more broadly to its pedagogy.

This will call for a balancing act of sorts. On the one hand, in the interests of clarity, there is the need to be sufficiently specific, as I have just indicated. But the objective here is not to present a curriculum proposal for liberal or general education.[21] It is to attempt a new conceptualization of the idea, making reference to the implications for curriculum as required. The moment this attempt at a new conceptualization becomes a set of recommendations for particular content, the project is jeopardized, as it may be seen as no more than taking sides in an ongoing curriculum debate.

More importantly, perhaps, a set of recommendations for particular content cannot be presented here without disregarding a commitment made earlier. That was to abide by the notion of Dewey, Pring, and Shor that the content to be introduced into the curriculum for any particular student needs to be individualized to reflect his or her experience. Faced with this same predicament, Pring observes, "I cannot lay down what precisely should be the content of the curriculum." This is so because a main feature of his argument has been the need to shape the curriculum to reflect the already active mental life of particular individuals. "Without knowing these individuals and the particular context in which they are to be educated," he continues, "I cannot say what should be the content of *their* education."[22] Not only does this contrast markedly with the approach of Adler but, as Pring himself points out, it also deviates greatly from curriculum theorizing in the mainstream tradition of liberal education. Accordingly, what is aimed at here is the articulation of an idea of liberal or general education that accommodates a curriculum stance allowing for variety within certain broad parameters without becoming unduly prescriptive regarding the content of that curriculum. As a stance that is shaped by theory rather than actual practice in schools and colleges, it will, in turn, need to accommodate the considerable requirements of translating or implementing educational ideas into practice.

A STARTING POINT

In his celebrated paper "Liberal Education and the Nature of Knowledge," Hirst sets forth a concept of education he claims to be "based fairly and squarely on the nature of knowledge itself."[23] This concept he labels liberal education. In her critique of Hirst's concept, Martin argues that there are serious shortcomings in the theory of a liberal education, and she calls for new thinking in the field.[24] Taking what Martin calls Hirst's forms of knowledge theory as the dominant one among contemporary theories of liberal education, and yet broadly representative of them, Martin argues that this theory is unduly narrow, fails to provide an adequate justification, and erects an untenable dualism between mind and body in its exclusive concern for education of the mind.

The force of Martin's critique derives not from any shortcomings in Hirst's original theory of liberal education, as I argue in *Knowledge, Gender, and Schooling*, but from the shortcomings of that theory judged as a more comprehensive or all-embracing theory of education.[25] As Martin acknowledges, Hirst himself never claims in his original presentation of his theory that it is a theory of the whole of education, and on a number of occasions he explicitly says so.[26] As I have also suggested elsewhere, Hirst, writing with R. S. Peters in *The Logic of Education*, did convey the impression that liberal education is the most valuable and true form of education and, moreover, that there is little or no distinction between it and general education as he understood it.[27] It is this that gives force to Martin's critique.

If the force of Martin's critique of liberal education derives from the shortcomings of Hirst's theory judged on broader grounds, the important question arises as to how one might set about developing and justifying a more broadly based theory or concept of education. Hirst himself did not deny the need for such a theory, and Martin agrees when she suggests that there is a need for a new paradigm for liberal education. She makes clear how inadequate she considers the traditional idea of liberal education—and specifically Hirst's version of it—as a theory of the whole of education. In her critique, she does not go so far as Nel Noddings, who asserts that liberal education is a false ideal for universal education.[28] In fact, building on the idea of liberal education, Martin indicates some directions that a new conception of liberal education might take. In summary, she states, the idea of liberal education should begin with a view of liberal education as the development of a person. Then she continues:

> add to it an analysis of the concept of a person in which mind and body are inseparable, mix in the value judgement that the purpose of a liberal education ought to be to develop us as persons and not simply as minds. Guidelines for a liberal education that drives no wedge between thought and action, between reason and emotion begin to emerge.[29]

If the concept of liberal education based on the nature of knowledge set forth by Hirst is unsuitable, the question arises if there is not some basis other than the nature of knowledge itself upon which an adequate concept might be developed? Even if there is such a basis, a prior question still arises: adequate for what purpose? The purpose with which Hirst is originally concerned, Martin suggests, is the development of mind as he portrays it. For Martin, the primary concern is the development of a person of intellect who is also caring, emotionally mature, and action oriented. But these are not the only purposes for which an education may be conceived and fashioned. To these may be added purposes reflecting the increasingly varied expectations for education and schooling that are held out today by governments, industry, and society at large. This is to say nothing of the many and sometimes more specific purposes—such as producer of knowledge—contained in the additional dimensions more recently associated with the notion of liberal education, all of which only add to the questions.

Of the additional questions raised, two are of particular interest here: What basis for curriculum other than the nature of knowledge can be formulated or created to accommodate the varying expectations now held out for liberal or general education? And what are the prospects for conceiving and articulating a similarly accommodating new paradigm for liberal education? Given all of this, a pressing challenge facing those wishing to revitalize liberal education is to fashion a conception of the aims of education (and the general implications for curriculum) that meets the exigencies of our times as reflected in the emergent aims now associated with the idea of liberal education.

RECONCEPTUALIZING LIBERAL EDUCATION

Noddings has remarked that "criticizing liberal education within academe is like criticizing motherhood in a maternity ward," but she proceeds to argue that liberal education is not an ideal for everyone, drawing as it does on only a narrow set of human capacities.[30] But there is also the possibility of envisioning a new or revitalized concept of liberal education, one that accommodates the emergent diverse aims now associated with liberal education and even the reservations of Noddings. Here I shall pursue just one such possibility by starting out with an idea raised but not pursued by Adler. This is Adler's idea of education as embracing personal as well as social goals and taking its direction from the widely espoused though rather ill-defined notion of education as a preparation for life. Adler referred to this as a preparation for the vocations or callings of life common to all. Ill defined though it may be, education as a preparation for life does not necessarily mean preparation for some distant and even uncertain future, a charge that is sometimes brought against this notion.[31]

While it may seem reasonable to expect that schools and colleges should provide an education that prepares students for life and personal fulfillment, it is not at all clear nor widely agreed upon how one might conceptualize education for this purpose. What form might such an education take and how might it be justified? At least since Newman's time, these are questions about whose answers there was for many years no serious doubt among theorists of liberal education. Not so in regard to efforts aimed at conceptualizing education as a preparation for life. Even as central, state, and local governments; concerned citizens; corporations and professional bodies; and educators themselves are predisposed to the idea of preparing students for the economy, and maybe even for citizenship, they flounder in search of common understandings.

Adler intended his ideal to incorporate preparation for work alongside personal development and preparation for democratic citizenship. At the same time, his analysis erects a dichotomy between the idea of liberal education as general academic formation and that of an education more focused on specialization and practical forms of education such as vocational education, an analysis taken to task by Christopher Winch in his argument regarding the economic aims of education.[32] Fortunately, although Adler himself overlooks the possibility, there is room in his formulation to arrive at a position between the extremes he posits. The basis for such a centrist position lies in the notion already referred to and set out in *The Paideia Proposal*, namely, that the objectives of schooling are determined by the vocations or callings common to all. A broadly similar stance is hinted at in the notion of human tasks spoken of by Noddings. The vocations or callings Adler identifies as citizenship, work, and personal development. But while Adler speaks of these as callings common to all, he does little by way of analysis of these callings to determine the kind of education that a preparation for them might necessitate. As a result, possibilities raised by him for conceptualizing education as a preparation for life and developing a position on the matter by responding to the educational demands of a preparation for life for each and all students are not pursued. It would be incorrect, moreover, to conclude from what Adler does say that he is entirely guided in the positions he adopts by the notion of grounding the objectives of schooling in the vocations or callings common to all.

The three objectives of schooling identified by Adler are elaborated in his proposed course of studies in terms of the three goals of the acquisition of organized knowledge, the development of intellectual skills, and the enlarged understanding of ideas and values. This course of studies is intended to provide a preparation for the callings of life. If the actual objectives of schooling from which the course of studies is purportedly derived had, in fact, been determined by the vocations or callings common to all, the theory of education set forth by Adler could have taken a very different form.

What that form might be will now be pursued, for it raises the prospect of setting forth a concept of education that is based upon an explicit view of the nature and purposes of living, the demands it makes upon the individual, and what a preparation for living broadly entails. It also raises the prospect of accommodating the varied expectations placed upon liberal education today.

Even before Adler entered the debate, there were those such as David Snedden, Franklin Bobbitt, and W. W. Charters who saw the activities of everyday living, or the callings that are common to all people, as the proper determinants of the objectives and content of schooling.[33] In the face of rapid social change, immigration, and industrial growth and their implications for education, citizenship, and work, many in the United States in the mid-nineteenth century questioned the benefits of classical education for all. In such circumstances, the radical educational ideas of the nineteenth-century English social philosopher, Herbert Spencer, attracted attention.[34] Their implicit challenge to the dominant classical tradition in secondary education was to prove persuasive, at least in the shorter term. This was nowhere more evident than in the *Cardinal Principles of Secondary Education*.

According to Spencer, there are five leading kinds of activity that constitute human life. These are i) activities that minister directly to self-preservation, ii) activities that minister indirectly to self-preservation by securing the necessities of life, iii) activities that have as their end the rearing of children, iv) activities that maintain proper social and political relations, and v) miscellaneous activities that make up the leisure part of life.[35] Insofar as education is to prepare us for complete living, it should prepare us in each of these areas. Writing in the 1920s in the United States and clearly influenced by this way of thinking, Franklin Bobbitt suggested the following ten general activities as a basis for a curriculum: i) language activities, ii) health activities, iii) citizenship activities, iv) general social activities, v) spare-time activities, vi) activities for maintaining mental fitness, vii) religious activities, viii) parental activities, ix) unspecialized practical activities, and x) the labors of one's calling.[36]

This same general approach characterizes the *Cardinal Principles of Secondary Education*. Here, also in a modification of Spencer's formulation, preparation for the activities of everyday living is adopted as a guiding principle for the curriculum. As set out in the *Cardinal Principles of Secondary Education*, these activities are health, command of fundamental processes, worthy home-membership, vocation, citizenship, the worthy use of leisure, and ethical character.[37]

The principles enunciated in the *Cardinal Principles of Secondary Education* had a lasting effect on the organization and practice of secondary education in the United States. Yet, by the mid-twentieth century, under the leadership of a number of outspoken conservative critics, attention had shifted away from a concern for education in accordance with the perceived activities of everyday living. Once again, boosted by the reaction to Sputnik, the call went out for greater attention to academic education and a return to intellectual discipline.[38] For whatever reason, life-adjustment education, as it was called, fell into disfavor, and the movement was faced by a range of difficult questions with which it never fully came to grips.[39] These same questions still face those who frame their justification and proposals for education in terms of preparing students for life. That is to say, if the purpose of education is to prepare students for life, if the objectives of schooling are to be determined by the callings common to all people, a number of important questions arise. Among them are these three: What are the activities or callings of living for which preparation is deemed necessary or desirable? What demands do they make upon people and how do the goals of personal development and preparation for the demands of living relate to one another? And how might these demands be satisfied through education? Adler addresses to a greater or lesser extent the first and third of these, but not the second. The adverse effects of this omission seriously undermine his answer to the third.

It will be evident from a moment's reflection that the circumstances and activities of living and the demands that they make upon us are legion, varied in character, and of different orders of importance. To attempt a detailed listing would appear to be a hopeless undertaking. Moreover, wonderful as may be the *Cardinal Principles of Secondary Education,* as Noddings has observed,[40] a listing of activities or tasks alone is insufficient. Such are the activities and the demands of living and such are the changing and different circumstances in which people live that new activities and callings emerge and others die out. Many specific activities that once were part of everyday living no longer exist. How can one be sure, then, which activities should be perpetuated? What guarantee have we that preparation to deal with existing activities prepares one for new activities and demands in the future? Besides, it is unlikely that everyone will be required to engage in all of the same activities or be faced with all of the demands in the same manner. Furthermore, it would be impractical to develop a curriculum or approach to schooling that attempted to respond to every possible activity or demand. So what is one to do?

One way of dealing with these important and pertinent questions is found in the approach taken by Florence Stratemeyer and her colleagues some years ago. That is to say, whatever the demands or activities of living for which it is deemed desirable to provide a preparation, it would be wise that these should be largely common to all people, possess what Stratemeyer termed a persistent quality,[41] and be central or essential to living well.

While this may be helpful, even this approach leaves out a vital question surrounding what is meant by life or living well, or work, or citizenship. It is easy to be lured into the expectation that the life for which students are to be prepared is self-evident and uncontested. This sentiment is found in the *Cardinal Principles of Secondary Education*, for example, in its reference to such values of everyday living as "worthy home-membership," "worthy use of leisure," and "ethical character," as if what constitutes worthiness or ethical character is unproblematic.[42] In reality, of course, there are many different kinds of life that one may lead and be prepared for, all of which have a bearing on one's personal growth and fulfillment. Indeed, it has long been a matter of serious philosophical inquiry and dispute as to what constitutes the "good life" and how it might be distinguished from what Charles Taylor has eloquently characterized as "ordinary life."[43] Accordingly, those who advocate education as a preparation for life—or for work or citizenship—may be asked what they mean by life, by work, by citizenship. By what values is life and personal development, for example, to be characterized, and by what arguments are such values to be justified? Once one has begun to deal with these questions, one then needs to inquire by what kind of education can one's view of the good life be promoted and even ask if liberal education is the answer at all?

It is a weakness of the *Cardinal Principles of Secondary Education* that it does not take these considerations into account. It is a further weakness of the seven objectives identified there and the corresponding areas of activity that they do not always correspond to actual activities of living. Ethical character, one of the seven objectives set forth, for example, does not point to activities or behaviors at all in the way that could conceivably be true of objectives intended in the health, vocational, or civic domains.[44] Ethical character is primarily concerned with a value orientation rather than with particular activities or behaviors. Besides, it seems from the document itself that ethical character is a prerequisite for learning to behave ethically. Objections may also be raised against the objectives of worthy use of leisure and worthy home membership. As was just pointed out, there is the assumption in these notions that what constitutes worthy use of leisure or worthy home membership is self-evident rather than problematic and dependent upon a particular philosophical or moral viewpoint. As we also know very well from the political squabbling surrounding the use of such terms as "family values," whether any particular set of family values is considered worthy or contemptible has become very much a matter of debate.

For these reasons, the kind of objectives or activities of living envisaged in *Cardinal Principles of Secondary Education* is not a suitable basis for characterizing the demands, activities, or callings of everyday living by which a conceptualization of education as a preparation for life and personal fulfillment might be informed. Neither are the identification of the vocations or callings of life, or their corresponding objectives for schooling, as set forth by Adler fully acceptable, although they do point a way. These are insufficiently elaborated in the case of the objectives of preparation for work and for citizenship and too narrowly based in the objective of personal development, where forms of personal development other than the cognitive are slighted.

Given these deficiencies, yet cognizant of the generally critical view taken toward a life-adjustment approach, I shall propose a modified view of the activities or demands of living as a basis for a new conceptualization of liberal education. While recognizing the centrality of the question, it is a view that leaves open what constitutes the good life and builds on Nodding's notion of common human tasks. It attempts to avoid the pitfalls of earlier efforts of this kind and is intended merely to exemplify how such an approach might be employed. It also aims to accommodate emergent demands made on liberal education as identified already.

Of course, it may not be possible to accommodate all of the sometimes conflicting ideals represented in the varying emergent conceptions of liberal education that have presented themselves. The kinds of demands or activities of living that will be identified in the view presented here, however, are commonplace and persistent across all lives. As such, they provide a basis to pursue the idea of education as a preparation for life in which there is an affirmation of ordinary life and in which personal fulfillment has a special importance. Accordingly, the following identification and general classification of the activities or demands of living is presented: the work demands of living, the recreational demands of living, the miscellaneous social and practical demands of living, and the philosophical demands of living.

In order to pursue the idea of liberal or general education as a preparation for life, it is necessary to consider the nature of these demands or callings and the implications they have for the idea of education as a preparation for life. In doing so, it will be necessary to avoid the failing I pointed out in Adler, namely, providing an insufficiently explicit characterization of the various callings or vocations common to all. Accordingly, in examining the demands of living it will be necessary to analyze and characterize them in sufficient detail that they provide a reasonably clear idea of what it means to be a worker, for example. It will then be evident that the manner in which these demands are understood holds important implications for both the nature and purpose of education and for the curriculum.[45]

THE DEMANDS OF LIVING[46]

By the demands of everyday living, what Adler terms the callings or vocations of life through which we become embroiled in the activities of ordinary life, I understand those circumstances in life encountered by everyone that necessitate a response from us. These demands may be personal or social in origin. Our need for knowledge, for example, constitutes a demand that is rooted in the individual person; as if intuitively, we seek knowledge. It is the same with our need for food and shelter. These are not requirements or obligations imposed upon us by membership in a family or social group but by intellectual and biological forces, respectively, that govern our nature. Some of the demands made upon us—such as the demand made on all of us to abide by the laws, customs, and mores of society—do have social or group origins, of course. To fail to comply with these demands may not always have grave consequences. Taken together, the demands of living that we encounter—the callings or activities of living in which we either are required or desire to engage—make it imperative that we respond successfully in one way or another. The point of education conceived in terms of preparing students to deal successfully with the various callings or activities of everyday living is, then, to enable them to develop ways of dealing with these demands and, through the forces of initiative and will, even surpassing them.

It may be considered a failing of the conceptualization of education in terms of the demands or callings of living that it is open to a view of human beings as passive responders to their social and physical environments who may even appear unwilling or incapable of initiating action themselves and are devoid of spontaneity or a creative urge of any kind. No such view is necessary or intended. The demands of living may sometimes be set in motion by forces beyond our control, and they often are. They may even be conceptualized in such terms alone. Alternatively, these demands may also be seen as brought on by or originating within oneself. The urge to explore, to create, to invent is sometimes occasioned by necessity, but it may also be the result of curiosity or the desire to seek a different explanation, a new perspective, a better way. The call to invent may originate from within, the demand for perfection in what we do uncalled for by external circumstances. To say that the demands of living may be personal or social in origin, therefore, is not to subscribe to a fatalistic or passive conception of human nature and social interaction. These demands can sometimes be occasioned by external circumstances and at others the result of human volition and initiative, of the search for personal fulfillment and the good life. But even when originating in personal initiative—as in the urge to explore and create—certain demands are still placed upon the initiator in achieving his or her goals.

The Vocational and Work Demands of Living

With the demands or callings of living understood in this general sense, one of the most visible of all the demands or callings made upon the great majority of people is the call to work.[47] There are, of course, different kinds of work and it is helpful to distinguish between the idea of work in general and the idea of work for a living or employment. Work for a living or employment, namely paid work, is what is meant by work as the word is commonly used. Work in this sense is largely equated with employment or having a job, and everywhere schools are being called upon by employers, government leaders, and others to prepare students better for work in this sense. In a second and less widely used sense of the word, work refers to a wide range of undertakings in which we engage to provide for the necessities of life, fulfilling responsibilities as a member of a family or of the community, out of a commitment to attaining some particular goals, or following a personal interest. Work in this sense may embrace one's job, that is, one's work for a living. This is often true, for example, of those artists, businessmen, scholars, or craftsmen, whose work for a living or job coincides with the work or undertaking in life from which they derive much of their enjoyment in living. Work in this sense, akin to what John White calls autonomous work,[48] of course, may not coincide at all with one's everyday employment and it may not have any direct pecuniary advantage. Yet it may still be a vehicle that affords satisfaction and a sense of fulfillment, as in the case of the work of a mother in the home or that of a voluntary community worker. Even if not considered a human need, work may take the form of a freely chosen creative activity.[49]

In whatever sense work is understood, it assumes significance in the life of the individual, and it makes a variety of demands on the worker. It may become a major factor in creating one's sense of identity and in developing a sense of esteem for oneself, and, as has been nicely pointed out by Paul Standish, for example, vocation may well contribute to the meaning a person finds in his or her life.[50] It may be a source of happiness or of dismay and upset.[51] It may have important implications, too, for the non-working and non-job facets of one's life and for how free time or leisure is spent.[52]

Whether work is enjoyable or not, obligatory or voluntary, paid or not, it makes a variety of demands on the worker. Some of these are largely common to all forms and places of work, others peculiar to particular forms. Some aspects of the workplace and the demands it makes are largely persistent from one age to another; others are more fleeting and subject to change over time. Already it has been suggested that a particular feature of liberal education, as opposed to specialized, vocational, or professional education of one kind or another, is its capacity to prepare students for dealing successfully with the persistent and common demands of living. Even at a time of increasingly differentiated, specialized, and advanced forms of work, many aspects of work have a lasting quality, are common to various forms of work, and may be encountered by most people in the course of a working life. It is these aspects of work that become the main focus of attention when considering the implications for education for the demands of working life, not the particular requirements of specialized forms of work, such as may be found in a particular job.

Among the demands or requirements of the workplace are communications with others, working and cooperating as a member of a team, taking on responsibility, and perhaps the exercise of initiative, leadership, diplomacy, and tact. They also include dealing successfully with practical problems involving conceptual, manual, or social skills, adaptability, and a willingness to go on learning. It is a requirement of all work that it be done with at least a minimum level of competence. This may require the worker to see a task through to completion, to stick to the task at hand even if it holds little interest or the worker has temporarily lost such interest. Likewise, work may entail persisting with a task in the face of difficulties, unpleasantness, and even adversity.[53]

A fuller appreciation of the nature and demands of work and the potential contribution of work to society and to the individual in highly sophisticated working arrangements of advanced societies necessitates additional understandings and commitments by the worker. These include an understanding of the diversity of work in contemporary society, the place of science and technology in work, the nature of decision making within the workplace, the nature and processes of labor relations, and the implications of these for work and for the worker. An understanding of the place of work in the life of the individual—as a potential source of personal enrichment and achievement and not merely as a possible source of income—may also be seen as a more advanced and sophisticated demand made by work on the individual. Much the same may be said of understanding the place of work as a source of communal prosperity and well-being in the life of the community. It may be particularly important for high school and college students to have a general understanding of the nature, range, and suitability of various forms of work for themselves and for their future careers.

Knowledge, attitudes, and skills of the kinds indicated above are required of or at least desirable in the worker. There are, as has been amply pointed out by critics of objectionable workplaces and work practices, many aspects of workplaces that are sometimes unethical, undesirable, and even degrading, and these also have implications for the worker and for the education of workers. Even the once-hallowed Protestant work ethic, for example, has not escaped criticism for its antipathy toward the interests of women and minority workers.[54] And, as investigations of misconduct among elected officials, the Enron case, and the exposing of cheap labor camp practices have highlighted, unethical or degrading practices may be as true of the boardroom and agencies of government as of the sweatshop. This being so, there is clearly a moral dimension to what constitutes an education for work and understandings of the workplace considered desirable for workers. It centers

on the issue of what is legitimate work and what is considered dehumanizing. In an age of increasing technology and unemployment, and even the
possibility of an end to work in the sense of having a job as Jeremy Rifkin
envisions,[55] questions of the relationship between work and labor and between technology and unemployment, and their far-reaching personal and
societal implications, arise in even more compelling form.

The Recreational Demands of Living

If we live in a world of work, in varying degrees many also live in a world
of increased free time, whether because of favorable working conditions or
unemployment.[56] As a result, and given the ease of access to recreational activities, the need to prepare the young for the proper and beneficial use of
spare time is probably greater than ever. Given the potential for personal
growth and social benefit or, conversely, for stagnation and even destruction, depending upon how free time is spent, education must play a crucial
role in preparing students to make the most constructive use of leisure.[57]
The increased availability of free time is not the only reason why schools
and colleges should concern themselves with preparing students to make
the best possible use of leisure. Leisure and its beneficial uses are imperative for people as a corollary of work.[58] For as people need to work, so also
they need to rest from work for recreation or refreshment.

People have always had a need for rest and recreation for the mind and
the body after the toils and labors of the day and in preparation for those
of tomorrow. For many sleep was often the only refuge. But if free time is
now available on a large scale, and if it has brought with it possibilities for
freedom previously unimagined, it has also brought with it perplexing challenges and its own unique demands. These are challenges and demands
whose seriousness is sometimes heightened by unemployment. Not least
among them is striking a balance between recreational activities and other
activities of living.

In the case of work, whether in the home, in government, in business, or
elsewhere, individual or societal needs may be sufficient to indicate a clear
purpose for engaging in it. Unlike the question of work, that which constitutes recreation is largely determined by one's view of the nature and purpose of life itself. More specifically, it is determined by our view of how
spare time can best be channeled toward enabling us to achieve what we see
as the purpose of living. What is recreational is not fixed, but depends at
least in part upon one's purposes and values. Seeking a direction or a purpose for one's recreational use of free time is essentially an ethical or philosophical quest, then, in much the same way as is determining what is and
what is not acceptable work. It entails an understanding of the nature and
place of leisure and recreation in the life of the individual and of society.

This is not to say that one has to become a philosopher before going for a swim or a round of golf. Yet, as with many activities recreational choices do reflect values, and they contribute to quality of life.

Responding to the recreational demands of living, as distinct from the work demands of living, has a special relationship to the goals and purposes of education. As understood here, the overarching goal of education as a preparation for life is the attainment of our fullest potential as human beings within the challenges and constraints imposed by personal, biological, social, environmental, and other factors. Similarly, responding to the recreational demands of living involves availing of free time and opportunity in such a way that it, too, promotes the attainment of our fullest potential by meeting needs and aspirations through the recreation of our minds and bodies. Activities that may appear to be recreational but which detract from the attainment of our potential would be considered abusive or destructive rather than recreational. Responding well to the recreational demands of living, therefore, entails having a reasonably clear idea of the purpose of living with a view to selecting those forms of leisure activity that are genuinely recreational, and ideally it calls for a knowledge of the comprehensive range of such recreational activities and pursuits. It also calls for an understanding of and skills in a range of these activities and pursuits.

Enormous possibilities for the recreational use of leisure exist. These include time-honored, so-called cultural activities such as music, art, theater, literature, and film. While such pursuits are often honored for their esthetic appeal and recreational potential, as has been highlighted by Hirst and Broudy among others, they also have the capacity to heighten understanding and enlighten feeling.[59] Wide ranges of other potential recreational activities, pastimes, and avocations also have considerable recreational value. These include a variety of pursuits, such as sports, hobbies, travel, and outdoor pursuits. Even some forms of work may be recreational.

The Practical Demands of Living

What I term the miscellaneous practical demands of everyday living is an area that, with a few exceptions, has received little explicit attention in the considerable literature dealing with the idea of a liberal education. It is also an area that traditionally has not merited inclusion in liberal education even if it has more recently begun to attract attention.[60] Yet the nature and significance of the practical in life and in reasoning has been an object of philosophical inquiry ever since the Greeks contemplated its place in the hierarchy of human activity. In view of the pervasiveness of the practical in life, moreover, it is difficult to justify the neglect of attention to such an element in programs of liberal or general education. If liberal education purports to provide general knowledge and understanding, it is inconceivable that practical knowledge and understanding, and its contribution to the attainment of our fullest human potential and broad preparation for life, should be disregarded.

Living is both a reflective and a practical affair. It calls for forethought, decision making, and action on a wide range of issues. It has powerful emotional and spiritual dimensions as well as cognitive and behavioral aspects that deeply influence and shape our thoughts and actions. The conduct of our daily lives, be it in conventional places of work or in work at home with the family, in our social relations with others or in the pursuit of personal goals and interests, is as much if not more a practical as a theoretical matter. In an endless range of everyday activities from rearing a family or preparing a meal to running a business, serving the public, defending the nation, paying one's bills, negotiating the traffic, creating art or making music, elements of planning or forethought, decision making, feeling, and action are involved. To live as a human being is to be seeking goals and to be active, often in mind and heart and body, in their pursuit. It is to be engaged with the world at various levels from the activities of ordinary living to the sublime, with fellow human beings and with family and friends.

In the educational context, education for practical affairs is frequently associated with so-called practical subjects, such as those included in the auxiliary studies identified by Adler.[61] Most people would not object to speaking of such everyday activities as driving a car, using the telephone, making a sandwich, or maintaining a garden as practical activities. There can be, accordingly, a physical dimension to the practical, but practical in the sense used here has a wider meaning than physical. To take a simple example, the maintenance of one's personal or family finances in a healthy condition may be considered to be a practical activity of no little consequence. It may be no more an intellectual activity than gardening is, but it is surely a less physical one. While it calls for no identifiable physical activity, it does call for a certain amount of forethought and planning as well as the monitoring and periodic review of plans and practices and possibly their readjustment from time to time. In certain circumstances, it might necessitate the application of elementary principles of accounting, taking note of one's past experiences, discipline or restraint in handling one's affairs, and almost invariably the use of elementary mathematics. While practical undertakings as envisaged here, then, may have a physical element, they are not confined to the physical. They will also typically include a cognitive dimension and frequently a social or emotional one. In addition, they may be of a moral character, depending on the kind of practical activity in question, a point that will be taken up presently.

Practical activity in the sense understood here does not therefore necessarily possess a major moral or even a physical dimension, although it often does. Portrayed more positively, practical activity does involve two necessary aspects: first, making decisions regarding the selection of means to be taken to achieve certain ends in view; and, second, actually taking the means considered suitable to attain the ends in view. This latter aspect may or may not necessitate the taking of specific physical measures. The first of the two steps may be said to constitute *practical judgment*, the second *practical action*.[62] Accordingly, to say that life is a practical affair is to say that life, or at least the rationally inspired life of a human being, demands of us that we engage in purposeful action. Specifically, it requires of us that we select means appropriate to the ends that we have in view and that we take steps suitable for achieving our ends in view. There are, of course, other activities of living that are not practical in this way. Activities of a recreational or relational kind engaged in for the sheer enjoyment they afford are a case in point. Nor is this to say that nothing of benefit ever accrues from such activities. It is simply to say that they are activities engaged in for no purpose beyond themselves. Neither is it suggested that practical activities in which we engage cannot also be enjoyed. Work in any form may be a case in point.

To master the various practical demands made upon us in all walks of life requires a range of knowledge, understandings, attitudes, and skills that is varied in character and that is appropriate to dealing with the matters on hand. It also requires us to call upon a range of personal resources of mind and body. In any view of liberal education as a preparation for life and personal fulfillment, then, it is unimaginable that education for this purpose could be omitted.

At a more concrete and immediate level, many are coming to this conclusion regarding basic or common schooling. In the past, school was not always recognized as having the primary responsibility for preparing young people to deal with many of these demands, especially those that were considered highly personal in character and for which other agencies in society, notably the family and the church, were considered better suited. It is also true that the school was not, and often still is not, well designed to deal adequately with education in this area. Changing circumstances of society, however, and the growing recognition of the importance of schooling in the practical aspects of everyday living suggest that schools and colleges should consider anew their role in this area, as many are. Witness the increased provisions in schools and colleges for pastoral care and counseling, increased recognition of the importance of transition arrangements from school to college, and growing support structures for the social and communal aspects of college life, all now well established. Witness, too, the calls for education in such areas as personal and social development, health education, and education for adult living and interpersonal relations. These are no less persistent than the recurring call of back to basics.

The practical demands of living are varied in character and not all necessitate the same degree of attention by the school. Yet practical demands of living that assume varying degrees of personal, social, or moral significance abound, and dealing with them requires a degree of emotional maturity and understanding, technical knowledge, and know-how in support of which formal education could be enlisted. Such practical demands of living include those that Adler recognized, in part, in his treatment of the auxiliary studies and that are also the focus of attention in critical pedagogy. They include demands relating to individual and community health, such as nutrition and diet, healthy living habits, and the welfare of the community. They also extend well beyond health demands to include demands in the areas of family life and interpersonal relations, politics, consumer and environmental affairs, the media, and personal finances, for example. Nowadays they also include a variety of increasingly sophisticated activities relating to communications technology and services.

In addition to practical demands of this kind that have a significance for us all individually, there are also practical demands of such gravity that they have a significance for us all collectively and have, in addition, important moral overtones. These demands take varying forms, but they center on a number of easily identifiable and increasingly pressing social concerns. These include, for example, abortion, war and peace, the efficacy of existing governmental institutions, terrorism, nuclear energy, the environment, violence and crime, poverty, race relations, and social justice, all of which everyone is called upon to deal with to a greater or lesser extent in his or her personal life.[63] Clearly there are moral as well as practical dimensions to questions raised by these matters, and they call for a knowledge and understanding of a kind that merge with the knowledge and understanding required for meeting what I have termed the philosophical demands of living. But in practical matters of the kind considered here, one may not be free to rest with knowledge and understanding; action may be required.

The moral dimension of social and practical affairs may be located both in the values or ends that are sought and in the means taken to achieve these values or ends. Not only is there a moral dimension to the goal of reducing high rates of violence and crime or the promotion of social justice for all, for example, but there are moral dimensions to the means chosen to pursue these goals. As in the case of work and recreation, moreover, in the moral dimension of practical affairs, the practical demands of living become inextricably linked with the philosophical.

Arguing that education has a role to play in preparing students for the practical demands of living is not to deny that programs drawn up to meet other demands of living, or even on the basis of the traditional justifications of knowledge in the curriculum, may contribute to education for this purpose.[64] In fact, Pring believes that there may be considerable overlap between liberal education and vocational education in regards to the knowledge content of a particular topic. In such cases, he suggests, it is in the attitudinal disposition toward the knowledge that the crucial difference between the two may lie, a point on which Adler and even Aristotle appear to agree.[65] It may also be that someone with a traditional form of education in the academic disciplines could deal successfully with practical problems and come to good practical judgments and be able to effect them. Parallels between liberal or academic education and practical or even vocational education, moreover, may be less than accidental. It is very likely, for example, that the making of good practical decisions has much to do with coming to grips with new concepts quickly, apprehending the relevant features of a problematic situation, having the ability to see significant relationships, and drawing valid conclusions.

Be this as it may, concern persists that traditional schooling, dominated as it is by the conceptual and the academic, is not conducive to practical education. For this reason, preparation for meeting the practical demands of living may warrant greater direct attention in its own right. There is also good reason to believe, as Alasdair MacIntyre suggests in his analysis of the pursuit of excellence in practical activities and the place of apprenticeship, rule making, and rule breaking therein, that acquaintance with and practice in the practical domain is necessary to increase understanding and to develop the facility to make good practical judgments and to give effect to them.[66]

The Philosophical Demands of Living

The work, recreational, and practical demands of living may pertain largely to meeting the demands of ordinary life if placed in the kind of hierarchy associated with the Greeks, for example. Yet dealing with them is fundamental to leading not only the ordinary but the good life, if one wishes to make that distinction, for as humans we are faced with the recurring challenge of making meaning in our lives, of deciding our system of values, and of determining what it is in fact that constitutes the good life for us. By the philosophical demands of living, I understand the need for each of us to come to grips with such questions, which permeate all facets of our lives and all of the demands of living. Dealing succssfully with these demands resembles Pierre Hadot's characterization of philosophy as a way of life.[67] Understood in this way, philosophical considerations dealing with meaning and values enter into the question of what constitutes humane or acceptable work and what is degrading and acting accordingly. Not only may philosophical considerations enter into the determination of what is humane or acceptable work; but as Eleanore Holveck has argued, philosophical considerations may just as readily be grounded in lived experiences.[68]

Philosophical considerations also arise in determining what constitutes the beneficial or constructive use of leisure, and they impinge directly upon the resolution of a broad range of issues of practical, everyday significance such as crime, economic policy, environmental protection, health, race relations, and war. As Hirst has argued in his characterization of the philosophy of education as the exercise of practical reason,[69] and as Oakeshott and MacIntyre—following Aristotle—have addressed the matter in broader settings, moreover, it may be that it is only within the contexts of lived experience, as in the practice of education or medicine, for example, that such philosophizing or practical reasoning can properly take place. It seems essential that students be educated accordingly.

Education aimed at enabling the young to deal with the philosophical demands of living highlights that aspect of education that has always been a primary goal of liberal education, namely, intellectual development and a general understanding of the world in which we live, including its moral components. It is a kind of education that Plato considered necessary for the philosopher-king if he or she were to become a just ruler in a just state. Newman paid particular attention to characterizing such understanding as the product of an education that was liberal in the sense that it was philosophical. Such philosophical knowledge or understanding assumed the quality of an architectonic science for Newman. It is this that A. Dwight Culler characterized as a sort of *tertium quid* of the intellectual world, a recombination of all the sciences in some sense embodying the materials of them all.[70] In Newman's hands, it became a form of knowledge or understanding that enables one to develop "a connected view of the old with the new; an insight into the bearing and influence of each part upon every other. . . . It is the knowledge, not only of things, but of their mutual relations."[71] It is, in Broudy's sense, the capacity to employ cognitive and evaluative maps so as to use knowledge or schooling interpretively in our daily lives.

Because of its association with the capacity to reflect and theorize regarding complex matters, liberal education, understood as a general knowledge and a cultivation of the intellect, gained over time the highest esteem among theorists of education and even among leaders of business and government. As general knowledge, it embraced the academic subjects considered most basic to developing understanding and intellectual skills. Such general knowledge was considered a direct asset in many places of work, not least in science and technology, in business and commerce, and in the professions. For this reason, such education achieved a place of prominence in the formation of those destined for positions of leadership.

In short, such education came to be seen as all that was required for a good education. It was a good education because it was a free and freeing education, not tied to particular outcomes yet imparting intellectual substance, versatility, and skill. Reflecting, perhaps, the emergent pragmatic tone of which Kimball speaks, one senses that things may have changed.

Studies once pursued for their inherent value and their capacity to promote intellectual skill and heightened understanding now appear more likely to be studied for what they can contribute to future professional prospects. Maybe this is not new. Yet the focus in school and college programs appears more short-term and more specific than before. To the extent that this is so, such education conforms less to the notion of preparing students for philosophy as a way of life and for the philosophical demands of living, as I have tried to portray it and as it has been presented by Newman.

THE FUTURE OF LIBERAL EDUCATION

Serious questions have been raised about the idea of liberal education by advocates and critics alike and grave doubts have emerged concerning the continuing viability of the traditional idea of liberal education to serve as a helpful guide to the way forward with the vital task of educating the young. A wide range of competing perspectives on how it might be viewed have also arisen. Taken together, these considerations highlight the need for a comprehensive review of the idea. The preceding examination of the idea of education as a preparation for life and of the demands of living suggests a new way of envisioning liberal or general education in the future. It also lays the basis for a new justification. Accordingly, it is necessary now to spell out more fully this new idea. In doing so, it will be necessary to pay particular attention to the questions of aims and content, pedagogy, and justification.

NOTES

1. John Dewey, *Democracy and Education* (New York: The Free Press, 1966), 164–170.
2. John Dewey, *Experience and Education* (New York: The Macmillan Company, 1963), 46.
3. Madeleine R. Grumet, *"The Paideia Proposal*: A Thankless Child Replies," in *Curriculum Inquiry* 16, no. 3 (Autumn 1986): 335–344, and Padraig Hogan, "Teaching and Learning as a Way of Life," in *Education and Practice: Upholding the Integrity of Teaching and Learning*, ed. Joseph Dunne and Padraig Hogan (Malden, MA: Blackwell Publishing, 2004), 30, where he draws attention to the inseparability of the why (purposes), the what (curriculum content), and the how (teaching) of education.
4. Ira Shor, *Empowering Education: Critical Teaching for Social Change* (Chicago: Chicago University Press, 1992), 84. For a helpful account of Dewey's pedagogy, see Donal E. Mulcahy, "John Dewey," in *The Praeger Handbook of Education and Psychology*, ed. Joe L. Kincheloe and Raymond A. Horn (Westport, CT: Praeger, 2007), 67–74.

5. For a perspective on this and other criticisms, see David T. Hansen, "John Dewey on Education and the Quality of Life," in *Ethical Visions and Education: Philosophies in Practice*, ed. David T. Hansen (New York: Teachers College Press, 2007), 32–34.

6. A case in point is the view of Robert Hutchins in *The Great Conversation: The Substance of a Liberal Education*, vol. 1 of Robert M. Hutchins, ed., *Great Books of the Western World* (Chicago: Encyclopedia Britannica, 1952), 49. There he writes that "the task of educators is to discover what an education is and then to invent the methods of interesting their students in it." The point here, as viewed by someone such as Dewey, Shor, or Pring, is that the determination of what an education is cannot be arrived at in isolation from a sustained consideration of the interests and experience of the student. Failure to recognize this and in its place to seek to have educators "invent the methods of interesting their students" in what the educators have decided their education will consist of is to overlook the pedagogical dimension of the educational situation.

7. Thomas S. Kuhn, *The Structure of Scientific Revolutions* (Chicago: University of Chicago Press, 1996).

8. In one of her earlier articles, Martin suggested gathering all of the academic disciplines into one school subject, to be called "the disiplines," in order to create space for other important material in the school curriculum. See Jane Roland Martin, *Changing the Educational Landscape: Philosophy, Women, and Curriculum* (New York: Routledge, 1994), 143–150. On the issue of culture as understood in the anthropological sense, see, for example, Jane Roland Martin, "Women, Schools, and Cultural Wealth," in *Women's Philosophies of Education*, ed. Connie Titone and Karen E. Moloney (Upper Saddle River, NJ: Prentice Hall, Inc., 1999), 167–175.

9. Surprisingly, this may place him alongside those such as Jean Jacques Rousseau, Dewey, Paulo Freire, Pring, and Shor in their constructivist leanings.

10. Jay Newman, *The Mental Philosophy of John Henry Newman* (Waterloo: Wilfrid Laurier University Press, 1986), 4–10.

11. Carl Bereiter, "Liberal Education in a Knowledge Society," in *Liberal Education in a Knowledge Society*, ed. Barry Smith (Chicago: Open Court, 2002), 25.

12. Thomas F. Green, "Needed: A Pedagogy Please!" in *The Condition of American Liberal Education*, ed. Robert Orrill (New York: The College Board, 1995), 238–243.

13. Ernest L. Boyer, *High School: A Report on Secondary Education in America* (New York: Harper and Row, 1983), and Ernest Boyer, *College: The Undergraduate Experience in America* (New York: Harper & Row, 1987).

14. Joseph L. DeVitis, Robert W. Johns, and Douglas J. Simpson, eds., *To Serve and Learn: The Spirit of Community in Liberal Education* (New York: Peter Lang, 1998).

15. Bruce A. Kimball, "Toward Pragmatic Liberal Education," in *The Condition of American Liberal Education*, ed. Robert Orrill (New York: College Entrance Examinations Board, 1995), 89.

16. Bereiter, "Liberal Education in a Knowledge Society," 11.

17. Lars Lovelie and Paul Standish, "Introduction: Bildung and the Idea of a Liberal Education," *Journal of Philosophy of Education* 36, no. 3 (August 2002): 326.

18. P. H. Hirst, "Education, Knowledge and Practices," in *Beyond Liberal Education: Essays in Honour of Paul H. Hirst*, ed. Robin Barrow and Patricia White (London: Routledge, 1993), 184–199.

19. P. H. Hirst and R. S. Peters, *The Logic of Education* (London: Routledge and Kegan Paul, 1970), 62–66.

20. For a view that questions the the notion of education as preparation, see, for example, the position of Oakeshott in Kevin Williams, *Education and the Voice of Michael Oakeshott* (Exeter: Imprint Academic, 2007), 27–44.

21. I presented such a proposal some years ago in D. G. Mulcahy, *Curriculum and Policy in Irish Post-Primary Education* (Dublin: Institue of Public Administration, 1981). That is also where I began to develop the notion of education as a preparation for life based on an analysis of the various demands of living.

22. Richard Pring, *Knowledge and Schooling* (London: Open Books, 1976), 115.

23. P. H. Hirst, *Knowledge and the Curriculum* (London: Routledge and Kegan Paul, 1974), 30.

24. Martin, *Changing the Educational Landscape*, 170–186.

25. D. G. Mulcahy, *Knowledge, Gender, and Schooling: The Feminist Educatinal Thought of Jane Roland Martin* (Westport, CT: Bergin and Garvey, 2002), 5–13.

26. See, for example, Martin, *Changing the Educational Landscape*, 174, 178, and Hirst, *Knowledge and the Curriculum*, 96.

27. In this connection, see D. G. Mulcahy, "Jane Roland Martin and Paul Hirst on Liberal Education: A Reassessment," *Journal of Thought* 38, no. 1 (Spring 2003): 25–29, and Hirst and Peters, *The Logic of Education*, 66–67.

28. Nel Noddings, *The Challenge to Care in Schools* (New York: Teachers College Press, 1992), 28.

29. Martin, *Changing the Educational Landscape*, 180–181.

30. Noddings, *The Challenge to Care in Schools*, 28.

31. This charge is associated with both Rousseau and Dewey. As understood here, equipping students to deal with their existing situations may be conceived as the way to prepare them for the future. This is consistent with Dewey's insistence that the best way to prepare the young for the future is to give them command of themselves in the present.

32. Christopher Winch, "The Economic Aims of Education," *Journal of Philosophy of Education* 36, no. 2 (February 2002): 101–117.

33. For an excellent account of the growth of the life-adjustment or social efficiency movement in education at the beginning of the twentieth century, see Herbert M. Kliebard, *The Struggle for the American Curriculum, 1983–1958* (New York: Routledge, 1992), especially 89–122. For a shorter discussion by Kliebard of the movement at the point of its demise, see *Changing Course: American Curriculum Reform in the 20th Century* (New York: Teachers College Press, 2002), 57–59. See also Donal E. Mulcahy, "Progressive Education: The Legacy and Current Challenges," in *2007 Yearbook of the South Atlantic Philosophy of Education Society*, ed. Kurt Stemhagen, 36–44.

34. Herbert Spencer, *Education: Intellectual, Moral and Physical* (Totowa, NJ: Littlefield, Adams and Co., 1955).

35. Spencer, *Education: Intellectual, Moral and Physical*, 32.

36. Franklin Bobbitt, *How to Make a Curriculum* (Boston: Houghton Mifflin Company, 1924), 8–9.

37. Commission on the Reorganization of Secondary Education, *Cardinal Principles of Secondary Education*, United States Bureau of Education Bulletin no. 35 (Washington, DC: United States Bureau of Education, 1918), 10–16.

38. Leading critics included Hyman G. Rickover, *Education and Freedom* (New York: E. P. Dutton and Co., Inc., 1959) and Arthur Bestor, *The Restoration of Learning* (New York: Alfred A. Knopf, 1955).

39. For a view of how this movement has sometimes been treated in historical scholarship, see William F. Pinar, *What Is Curriculum Theory?* (Mahwah, NJ: Laurence Erlbaum Associates, 2004), 165–168.

40. Nel Noddings, *Happiness and Education* (Cambridge: Cambridge University Press, 2003), 77.

41. Florence B. Stratemeyer, Hamden L. Forkner, Margaret G. McKim, and A. Harry Passow, *Developing a Curriculum for Modern Living* (New York: Bureau of Publications, Teachers College, Columbia University, 1957), 113–205. See also Harold Alberty, "Designing Programs to Meet the Common Needs of Youth," in *The American Curriculum: A Documentary History*, ed. G. H. Willis, W. H. Schubert, R. Bullough, C. Kridel, and J. Holton (Westport, CT: Greenwood Press, 1993), 335–353, where Alberty considers various forms of the core curriculum and their suitability for addressing the common needs of youth. The more progressive of some of these forms resonate with elements of critical pedagogy found in Ira Shor, for example.

42. Commission on the Reorganization of Secondary Education, *Cardinal Principles of Secondary Education*, 10–16.

43. Charles Taylor, *Sources of Self: The Making of the Modern Identity* (Cambridge: Harvard University Press, 1989), especially 11–19 and 209–302. In this connection, see also J. White, *Education and the Good Life* (New York: Teachers College Press, 1991); Harry S. Broudy, *Building a Philosophy of Education* (Englewood Cliffs, NJ: Prentice-Hall, Inc., 1961), 21–41; and Hirst, "Education, Knowledge and Practices," 184–187, where the concept is considered in the context of education.

44. For his part, Kliebard also considered "command of fundamental processes" to be an aim that might not have represented an area of life activity. See Kliebard, *The Struggle for the American Curriculum*, 114.

45. It will also be clear, whether or not one agrees with the idea of a national curriculum or national framework, that in addition to the implications for any given school, the conceptualization presented could also provide the basis for a national curriculum.

46. The general position adopted here is a development of that presented in Mulcahy, *Curriculum and Policy in Irish Post-Primary Education*, 73–97. It should also be acknowledged that the notion of the demands of living is influenced by the framework around which the book *Democracy and Excellence in American Secondary Education* was developed. See Harry S. Broudy, B. O. Smith, and Joe R. Burnett, *Democracy and Excellence in American Secondary Education* (Chicago: Rand McNally & Company, 1964).

47. Pertinent contributions to the literature on the relationship between work and education include Williams, *Education and the Voice of Michael Oakeshott*; Christopher Winch, "Work, the Aims of Life, and the Aims of Education: A Reply to Clarke and Mearman," *Journal of Philosophy of Education* 38, no. 4 (November 2004): 633–638; Peter Clarke and Andrew Mearman, "Comments on Christopher Winch's 'The Economic Aims of Education,'" *Journal of Philosophy of Education* 38, no. 2 (May 2004): 249–255; Winch, "The Economic Aims of Education"; Alison Wolf, *Does Education Matter? Myths about Education and Economic Growth* (London:

Penguin Books, 2002); Nadene Peterson and Roberto Cortez Gonzalez, *The Role of Work in People's Lives* (Belmont, CA: Wadsworth/Thomson Learning, 2000); J. White, *Education and the End of Work: A New Philosophy of Work and Learning* (London: Cassell, 1997); V. A. Howard and Israel Scheffler, *Work, Education and Leadership: Essays in the Philospophy of Education* (New York: Peter Lang, 1995).

48. White, *Education and the End of Work.*

49. In this connection, see J. White, "Education, Work, and Well-being," *Journal of Philosophy of Education* 31, no. 2 (July 1997): 233–247, and Geoffrey Hinchliffe, "Work and Human Flourishing," *Educational Philosophy and Theory* 36, no. 5 (November 2004): 535–547.

50. Paul Standish, "The Nature and Purposes of Education," in *A Companion to the Philosophy of Education*, ed. Randall Curren (Malden, MA: Blackwell Publishing, Ltd., 2003), 225.

51. On these points, see Williams, *Education and the Voice of Michael Oakeshott*, especially chapter 6, and White, "Education, Work, and Well-being."

52. Of interest here is the suggestion that for some, work may become a refuge from the home, a different sort of home away from home. See Peterson and Cortez Gonzalez, *The Role of Work in People's Lives*, 60.

53. In this connection, see, for example, Nancy Stewart Green, "Training for Work and Survival," in *Cultures of Curriculum* by Pamela Bolotin Joseph, Stephanie Luster Bravmann, Mark A. Windschitl, Edward R. Mikel, and Nancy Stewart Green (Mahwah, NJ: Lawrence Erlbaum Associates, Inc., 2000), 46–47.

54. Peterson and Cortez Gonzalez, *The Role of Work in People's Lives*, 47–54.

55. Jeremy Rifkin, *The End of Work: The Decline of the Global Labor Force and the Dawn of the Post-Market Era* (New York: Putnam, 1995).

56. A good deal of the work on recreation and leisure has its focus on the relationship with work and with later life. A classic in the field is Josef Pieper, *Leisure, the Basis of Culture*, trans. Alexander Dru (New York: Pantheon Books), 1963. Other helpful works include Michael J. Leitner, Sara F. Leitner, and associates, *Leisure Enhancement* (New York: Haworth Press, 2004); Douglas A. Kleiber, *Leisure Experience and Human Development: A Dialectical Interpretation* (New York: Basic Books, 1999); and Stanley R. Parker, *Leisure and Work* (London: Allen and Unwin, 1983).

57. Several of the essays in Rudy Koshar, ed., *Histories of Leisure* (Oxford: Berg, 2002) provide a refreshing overview of the landscape of leisure activities, including those that might be considered harmful.

58. The place of lesiure in relation to work is viewed very differently in different cultures, a point that is nicely made in Kumkum Bhattacharya, "Non-Western Traditions: Leisure in India," in *A Handbook of Leisure Studies*, eds. Chris Rojek, Susan M. Shaw, and A. J. Veal (Basingstoke, Hampshire: Palgrave Macmillan, 2006): 75–89.

59. The work of Harry S. Broudy is particulary noteworthy here. See Harry S. Broudy, *Enlightened Cherishing* (Urbana: University of Illinois Press, 1972), especially 53–66. For a view that draws attention to a certain incompatibility between liberal education viewed as promoting critical thinking and education for leisure, see Kevin Gary, "Leisure, Freedom, and Liberal Education," *Educational Theory* 56, no. 2 (May 2006): 121–136.

60. Of particular importance here is the work of Pring already cited, as is the position of Martin, who emphasizes the importance education for action and participation. See also Alasdair MacIntyre, "Practical Rationalities as Forms of Social Structure," *Irish Philosophical Journal* 4, no. 1 (1987): 3–19; J. White, *Towards a Compulsory Curriculum* (London: Routledge and Kegan Paul, 1973), 56–59; L. R. Perry, "Commonsense Thought, Knowledge, and Judgement and Their Importance for Education," *British Journal of Educational Studies* 13 (May 1965): 125–138; D. P. Gauthier, *Practical Reasoning: The Structure and Foundations of Prudential and Moral Arguments and their Exemplification in Discourse* (Oxford: Oxford University Press, 1963).

61. Mortimer J. Adler, *The Paideia Proposal: An Educational Manifesto* (New York: Macmillan Publishing Co., Inc., 1982), 33. In this connection, see also Joseph Dunne, "What's the Good of Education?" in *The RoutledgeFalmer Reader in the Philosophy of Education*, ed. Wilfred Carr (London: RoutledgeFalmer, 2005), 145–160.

62. The notions of action or intelligent action and practical reasoning elaborated by Waghid approximate more closely practical judgment than practical action as described here. See Yusef Waghid, "Action as an Educational Virtue: Toward a Different Understanding of Democratic Citizenship Education," *Educational Theory* 55, no. 3 (August 2005): 323–342, and Yusef Waghid, "University Education and Deliberation: In Defence of Practical Reasoning," *Higher Education* 51, no. 3 (April 2006): 315–328. In this connection, see also MacIntyre, "Practical Rationalities as Forms of Social Structure."

63. For a careful consideration of how such issues might be dealt with, see Broudy, Smith, and Burnett, *Democracy and Excellence in American Secondary Education*, 231–243.

64. On this point, see also White, *Towards a Compulsory Curriculum*, 56–57.

65. Pring, "Liberal Education and Vocational Education," 68; Mortimer J. Adler, *Reforming Education: The Opening of the American Mind*, ed. Geraldine Van Doren (New York: Macmillan Publishing Co., Inc., 1988), 283, and *Aristotle on Education: Extracts from the Ethics and Politics*, trans. and ed. John Burnet (Cambridge: Cambridge University Press, 1903), 108–109. See also Standish, "The Nature and Purposes of Education," 221–231, and Dewey, *Democracy and Education*, 306–320, where Dewey cautions against simplistic dualisms.

66. See, for example, Alasdair MacIntyre, *Whose Justice? Which Rationality?* (Notre Dame, IN: University of Notre Dame Press, 1988), 30–32. On this point, see also Pring, *Knowledge and Schooling*, especially 92–94, and Jonas F. Soltis, *Education and the Concept of Knowledge* (New York: Teachers College, Columbia University, 1979), 11–16.

67. Pierre Hadot, *Philosophy as a Way of Life: Spiritual Essays from Socrates to Foucault*, ed. Arnold I. Davidson and trans. Michael Chase (Oxford: Blackwell, 1995), especially 264–276.

68. Eleanore Holveck, *Simone de Beauvoir's Philosophy of Lived Experience: Literature and Metaphysics* (Lanham, MD: Rowman and Littlefield, 2002).

69. P. H. Hirst, "A Response to Wilfred Carr's 'Philosophy and Education'," *Journal of Philosophy of Education* 39, no. 4 (November 2005): 615–620.

70. A. Dwight Culler, *The Imperial Intellect: A Study of Newman's Educational Ideal* (New Haven: Yale University Press, 1955), 182.

71. John Henry Cardinal Newman, *Fifteen Sermons Preached before the University of Oxford* (London: Rivingtons, 1887), 287.

6

Toward a New Paradigm
for Liberal Education

If a preparation for life and the demands of living may be characterized broadly along the lines that have been suggested above, then the objectives of liberal education as envisioned here are primarily those of preparing students to deal successfully with the work, recreational, practical, and philosophical demands of living. Such an education, being determined by the demands of living—or the vocations of life common to all, to use Mortimer Adler's phrase—may then be characterized as a preparation for life and personal development. If education is to be determined by the demands or vocations common to all or by the requirements of a preparation for life, recognition of a new and broader idea of what it means to be well educated is called for. In response to Carl Bereiter's opening question, this suggests a new ideal of the educated person for the twenty-first century. Undeniably daunting in its scope, this new conception opens up the possibility of a transition to a new paradigm for liberal education. Most importantly, it calls for a new justification.

MANY-SIDEDNESS AND PRACTICALITY

In that version of the theory of liberal education once championed by Paul Hirst and considered by Jane Roland Martin to have dominated curriculum philosophizing,[1] the idea of the educated person was of one who possessed knowledge and understanding in depth and breadth in much the same way as had been envisaged by Adler and John Henry Newman before him. Not just any knowledge and understanding, but knowledge and understanding developed in relation to the forms of knowledge identified and elaborated by Hirst. It was through initiation into these forms of knowledge—disciplined, theoretical knowledge—that the mind was developed. The person who had attained such mental development was considered to be an educated person. This process of initiation had also been labeled variously 'education,' 'liberal education,' and 'general education.'[2]

If liberal or general education is to concern itself with preparing students to deal with the various demands or callings of living along the lines indicated here, it will be very different in character from what hitherto has held sway in the tradition of liberal education. It will be more akin to the idealizations set forth and justified by Martin and John White,[3] in terms of the range of values it espouses, the kinds of knowledge and other curriculum encounters it draws upon, and the justification it offers for itself. This is not to say that it will reject the values of a traditional liberal education. On the contrary, it will entail a broader and more encompassing view of education than that found in liberal education as championed by Newman, Adler, and Hirst. But it will also incorporate many of the values of liberal education as understood by them and the implications of these values for the curriculum. Given the differences between the historical idea of liberal education and its conception here, it is important to inquire more fully into the character of this new ideal of liberal education and its justification.

Among the values espoused by the idea of liberal education as a preparation for life, the most distinctive are the many-sided development of the individual, practicality, and respect for student experience. The range of knowledge, understanding, attitudes, and skills possessed by the person of many-sided development is determined by and developed in the context of learning to deal successfully with the varied demands of living. Accordingly, the ideal person of many-sided development will be one who has learned both to understand and to cope with these demands and to master the cognitive and emotional challenges they present. The person of many-sided development will be able to relate sensitively and successfully with others in a variety of contexts. He or she will be caring and able to manage the affairs of personal life in regard to health, family, financial matters, and the like. He or she will be able to deal with the full range of the practical demands of living in the public workplace and other settings.

This person will have an understanding of work and of its place in the life of the individual and of the community. He or she will possess a range of knowledge, attitudes, and skills that are of service in different kinds of working situations and will have developed a sense of initiative and responsibility required in a variety of undertakings. The person of many-sided development will possess the knowledge, attitudes, and skills of recreation across a range of interests and pursuits. He or she will possess knowledge and understanding of the world that enables him or her to form a system of values and a philosophy of life that provide a cognitive and evaluative interpretive guide to the conduct of everyday living and an appreciation for truth,[4] goodness, and beauty.

The person of many-sided development, then, will be more than what Martin has termed an "ivory tower person."[5] This person will be knowledgeable and thoughtful, to be sure; he or she will also be caring and sensitive and possess a strong moral compass. Not merely an ivory-tower person, he or she will be capable of purposeful action, with a controlled zest for life in its rich variety, skilled in dealing with the demands encountered in a life lived fully.

In the ideal of liberal education presented here, the person of many-sided development will yield nothing by way of understanding or cognitive development to the person who has had a traditional and more narrowly focused liberal education based on the academic disciplines. Time and energy spent on many-sided development that is not academic in character are not seen as time lost to the cause of cognitive growth. Even leaving aside questions of motivation and methodological considerations of the effectiveness of teaching, insights and understandings may often be gained more fully and more readily from active, practical, hands-on involvement in affairs than from the vicarious experience provided by books and lectures. Recall, for example, our earlier consideration of the impact on learning and understanding of service-learning. As service-learning bears out, education in practical affairs is not concerned merely with know-how. Rather, as Richard Pring has brought out, it can build upon know-how by enabling the student to "reflect upon, to look critically at, to make explicit the hidden assumptions beneath the know-how that the pupil undoubtedly possesses." This, he continues, "is the beginning of disciplined thinking, of systematic inquiry, indeed of theory."[6] Hirst appears, in his retraction of his original theory of liberal education, to concur with Pring.[7] Thus, Hirst writes "education may at many stages turn out to be best approached through practical concerns"; he considers "practical knowledge to be more fundamental than theoretical knowledge, the former being basic to any clear grasp of the proper significance of the latter."[8]

Contrary to the image, the historical tradition of liberal education was focused on a limited range of knowledge and understanding in promoting its central objective of the development of mind and understanding. The claim by its supporters always has been and still is that liberal education is the most valuable form of education, even as considerations of practicality play no part in the idea or in its implementation in curriculum form. The truth is that proponents of traditional liberal education, and the tradition itself, have been contemptuous not only of utility but of the practical as a defining characteristic of education.

Though education may contribute to enabling the student to achieve his or her full potential and to attain the good life, education in the sense of formal education or schooling is incapable on its own of achieving these goals. Engaging in activities such as work and service are just as necessary to attaining these goals, as they undoubtedly were also at the time of the emergence of the idea of liberal education. In the everyday world, we are all faced with an incessant array of demands, demands that do not always respect the interests or circumstances of the individual, demands that must be dealt with successfully if we are to achieve our fulfillment as persons. That is to say, there is more to life than the uninterrupted pursuit of personal development. By enabling the person to master the many and varied situations encountered in life, liberal education understood as a preparation for life makes its contribution to the attainment of personal fulfillment. By preparing the individual to deal successfully with the various demands of living, liberal education as conceived here both enables and frees him or her to develop a legitimate vision of the good life and, importantly, to pursue it. Those who call on education to provide an adequate preparation for life may not emphasize the full range of personal development entailed in a many-sided development of the person, focusing instead on job preparatory education. If this is a shortcoming, however, the importance of the more immediate areas such as work and recreation for which the young are thought to be in need of preparation—and the importance of being prepared to deal with them—ought not to be underestimated. These, too, contribute to aspects of personal growth and development without which the longer-term goals of attaining one's full potential or the good life may remain a distant ideal.

To say that liberal education as conceived here is a practical education, accordingly, is to say that it is concerned to promote the ability of the student both to understand and to engage successfully in the practical activities required of all of us. Without such engagement, attaining one's full potential becomes an illusion. In life, understanding alone is not enough. Insofar as the practical demands of living require action, an education aimed at preparing students for life cannot ignore the education necessary to promote the understandings, attitudes, emotional formation, knowledge, and skills needed for the successful conduct of practical affairs.

THE PEDAGOGICAL DIMENSION

In addition to its commitment to many-sidedness and practicality, liberal education as conceived here is committed to respect for the previous experience of the individual student. This means extending its distinguishing range of values beyond those represented by many-sidedness and practicality in that these imply content and outcomes more than process. Absorbing a process dimension into the conception of liberal education is a central aspect of what is attempted here and of the new paradigm of liberal education suggested by this work. That is to say, education must accommodate a pedagogical dimension[9] as well as an aims and curriculum dimension.

Students bring a great deal of experience and practical knowledge with them to the educational encounter, be it in school or college. This may be most evident or present in an enactive mode, as Pring suggests, and students may possess practical knowledge in a wide range of areas.[10] But this practical know-how or knowledge is not as informed as it may be, existing as it does at the commonsense level. The ideal is to bring it along the path from commonsense knowledge to organized, disciplined knowledge, or theory.

Theory as it exists in the academic disciplines is experiential knowledge become reflective, organized, scientific, and above all in this context, enriched and enriching. This is why students need to be brought to it and it to them, a point that has been made in a particularly helpful way by Joe Kincheloe, Shirley Steinberg, and Deborah Tippins with reference to the educational experiences and ideas of Albert Einstein.[11] But students can only be brought to theory from where they are. Hence the pedagogical reality and the pedagogical challenge overlooked so freely in theories of liberal education: to recognize that there is no preordained, universal curriculum of liberal education for schools and colleges. Any curriculum, to be fruitful, must depend on the student's level of experience and education and his or her capacity to interact beneficially with it. John Dewey put the point amusingly when he wrote, "it is no reflection upon the nutritive quality of beefsteak that it is not fed to infants." It is then that he went on to add that no subject, in and of itself, or without regard to the stage of growth of the learner, is such that inherent educational value can be attributed to it.[12]

But for Dewey, there are additional complexities associated with pedagogy that reach beyond the question of content, complexities that point to limitations of didactic instruction and academic themes. There is the crucial component of communication between educator and student.[13] For Dewey, this is a process that must be both cooperative and bidirectional: communication from teacher to student and from student to teacher. The curriculum must be fashioned anew by every teacher in accordance with the requirements of the instructional moment, not merely because each student brings a unique experience to the teaching and learning encounter, but because each communication between the teacher and his or her students is unique. It is in these senses that the curriculum poses its pedagogical challenge, and this must now be recognized in any new conceptualization of liberal education. It may be possible—as a practical matter, perhaps even necessary—to posit broad if tentative curriculum parameters within which to work, but these cannot be definitive.

One way or another, the implications for the curriculum and curriculum theorizing as we have known it are considerable. If only obliquely, they are captured by Thomas Green in his response to Bruce Kimball's essay on the rise of pragmatism in liberal education. What is needed for a resurgence of liberal education, Green argues, is not a fresh way of justifying a given body of content. We need, rather, an engaging pedagogy, a way of talking about what paths of learning are best suited to engaging the human capacities for the exercise of craft, judgment, and taste. Economy, polity, literature, religion, and the arts become the substance of such an education, not because they contain canonical statements of liberal education but because they engage these capacities. With a hint of exasperation he concludes: "Give me not a theory, but a pedagogy, please!"[14]

CURRICULUM CONTENT

So, as suggested by the criterion of preparation for life, what might these broad, tentative curriculum parameters referred to be? Closely determined by the values and objectives to which liberal education as a preparation for life is committed are the kinds of knowledge and encounters or environments for learning that will make up the curriculum. Depending upon how one views work and the demands it makes upon the individual, education for work would prepare students in the attitudes, knowledge, and skills required to meet the more fundamental, common, and persistent demands that work, be it paid or unpaid, makes upon the individual. These demands call for a general orientation of the student toward the idea of work, the significance of work in the life of the individual and of the community, and the personal attributes most suited to work of different kinds. General preparation for work could also endeavor to encourage students to develop a positive attitude to work as an inevitable and potentially rewarding feature of human existence. Likewise, such preparation would not overlook the sometimes undesirable aspects of the workplace. It would emphasize the dignity of the worker and describe what constitutes humanizing work, a persistent theme among those who are committed to the notion of education for social justice and those who see education as empowering students in all facets of their lives, including their employment.

What form might education for the recreational demands of living take? Given the potential range of recreational pursuits available, there is no shortage of possibilities. While such an education could include an initiation into a wide range of recreational and cultural activities, it could be cognizant, too, that in addition to being sources of enjoyment and pleasure these activities may also promote understanding. It could provide the opportunity for students to consider forms of recreational activity particularly suited to their interests and talents. This consideration could extend to examining the extent to which recreational activities should balance and complement the obligatory occupations of life, including family life, work, civic duty, and service to others, in which the individual is engaged. Such education could deal with the planning and organization of one's recreational activities. It might include taking various practical steps to ensure that such activities are a way of enriching personal and social life, avoiding boredom, and preventing the squandering of free time and opportunity in dehumanizing, abusive, and destructive behavior

The sorts of practical activities in which we are likely to be engaged in the course of our lives indicates the kind of education that would be shaped by the goal of preparing students to deal with the miscellaneous practical demands of living. They suggest, for example, that matters such as family life, personal and community health, media and communications, consumer affairs, and major social, economic, and political issues of the day ought to be dealt with. What they do not indicate so readily, perhaps, is the likelihood that these issues might be treated in such a way as to allow for students to engage in caring and other practical activities. It would appear that the absence of such practical involvement and responsibility has contributed, at least in part, to the inability of the school to deal satisfactorily with social and practical education.

This brings to mind the themes of activism and action for social justice associated with critical pedagogy. Since the appearance of *A Nation at Risk* in the United States and the passage of the Educational Reform Act of 1988 in England, there are strong indications in legislation and testing that there has been a slanting and narrowing of educational goals and curriculum content toward economic ends.[15] More or less simultaneously, there has been a neglect of those forms of education idealized by Thomas Jefferson and many others in the tradition of American public schooling aimed at education for citizenship and civic responsibility.[16] Some, such as Henry Giroux, suggest that there has been a disregard for principles of democratic citizenship, the equitable distribution of wealth, and the historic commitment to schooling as a public good. In a more universal context than that of the United States, Alasdair MacIntyre and Joseph Dunne and Padraig Hogan have expressed broadly similar concerns regarding the culture of Western modernity and the suppression of debate regarding substantive ends of education that do not meet the criterion of performativity.[17] If these concerns are well founded, the enrichment of social and civic education by reasserting the schools' former commitment to social and civic goals and the empowerment of teachers to be educational leaders offer an avenue of response. Adler was clearly committed in principle to such a response. So too were reconstructionist thinkers of the mid-twentieth century, such as George S. Counts and Theodore Brameld.[18] Today, those making the case for critical pedagogy and empowering education and advocates for social justice stand firmly on its side. On a closely related point, aside from feminist theorists such as Martin and Nel Noddings, less attention has been given to education for caring and home and family living. Education understood as a preparation for the demands of living makes no distinction between social and civic education and education for family living. It considers all such forms of education, even if contentious in schooling, as central to the very notion of liberal or general education.

Discussion of these matters also brings to mind a notable deficiency in the literature on liberal education considered here. Aside from the positions of Newman and Jacques Maritain, little or nothing has been said of religious formation, although it is listed by Franklin Bobbitt as one of the ten activities of living.[19] Yet reliance on religion is both a significant part of the lives of large numbers of people and a crucial element in understanding the cultural diversity of contemporary societies. Many, including Hirst, recognize religion as a distinct form of knowledge, of course, with religion being understood as a body of theoretical knowledge that resides in the academic discipline of theology. If mention of religion brings a deficiency to mind, it also brings a rather unique educational problem with it. It is this. Should religious education form part of the curriculum of liberal education as a preparation for life and, if so, what form should it take? This is a question to which I shall return.

A curriculum aimed at enabling students to deal with the philosophical demands of living will have much in common with the disciplined-based curriculum of liberal education, although here, too, individual interests, aptitudes, and background experience need to be recognized and accommodated. Unlike earlier versions, a curriculum so aimed at enabling students will recognize explicitly what it holds implicitly, that interdisciplinary studies, problem solving, and knowledge creation of the kind suggested by Bereiter are entirely compatible with growth in knowledge and understanding even if, at least in the case of knowledge creation, it may imply some specialization. Though the academic disciplines undoubtedly have a strong claim to be represented in the curriculum of liberal education, especially in relation to the philosophical demands of living as understood here, two related matters are of particular importance. The first is the pedagogical point raised by Dewey, Pring, and Ira Shor, emphasizing the necessity of grounding the curriculum in the experience of the student, a point not readily appreciated among advocates of the disciplines. The second is the fact that there are forms of experience, skills, attitudes, values, and knowledge, all of which have important philosophical import, that the academic disciplines do not encapsulate in their formal structures. There are insights, understandings, and capacities that can arise or grow only from relating with other people. They come from action—political or otherwise—from involvement, from undertaking responsibility, for example, a point brought out by Joseph L. DeVitis, Robert W. Johns, and Douglas J. Simpson and especially well represented in the article on service-learning by Oren W. Davis and Jennifer Dodge. It is to the credit of Adler that he, unlike others in the tradition of liberal education, recognized that participation in various artistic activities, such as acting, playing with an orchestra, and making art objects, are avenues to understanding.[20]

Clearly, the insights and understandings provided by such practical and artistic activities are largely overlooked in the tradition of liberal education. Yet forms of experience found in artistic and practical endeavors, which are indispensable to the growth of knowledge, wisdom, and maturity, are ones in which any education aimed at enabling students to deal with the philosophical demands of living could be expected to provide a rich environment for learning; they are experiences in which the philosophical formation of "plain persons" may take root.[21] That is to say, our understanding of the world, our views on the meaning and values of life, can also be fashioned through what James Marshall has referred to in the educational context as a philosophy of lived experience, our dealings with others, our work, and our various other commitments and everyday activities of living.[22] It was, ironically once again, none other than Newman who drew out in his more philosophical writings both the insights of practical knowledge and the shortcomings of the theoretical in achieving such understanding.[23]

Though not sufficient for gaining a full understanding of our world, theory and the academic disciplines adequately conceived constitute a necessary element in education for such understanding and for dealing with the philosophical as well as the practical demands of living. Pring, and more recently Hirst, join with Newman—and with Dewey and Shor it may be added—in recognizing the limitations of theory divorced from practical experience. But they assert, better than Newman perhaps in this context, the necessity for theory, for a knowledge of the academic disciplines.

It may be true that, as Pring writes, theory needs to be rooted in the practical form of life upon which it is very largely a reflection. But theory has an indisputable benefit, which "lies in the greater mastery over oneself and one's environment so that one can act more effectively within it and in the capacity for critical reflection that it provides."[24] More recently, Pring reasserted the same general point: "There is embryonic theory contained within intelligent practice. It becomes theoretical, and thus open to examination, reflection and criticism, once the understandings embedded within the practice are made explicit and systematically formulated."[25] Hirst essentially concurs. Recognizing now that personal development by initiation into a complex of specific, substantive social practices is fundamental to education, he continues:

> But worthwhile education conceived in these terms requires initiation into the
> practices of critical reflection on the fundamental substantive practices it

basically involves, not merely immersion in these basic practices. Such reflection, however, directed at the modification of basic practices both socially and personally, is itself a matter of practical reason, though this requires consideration of presuppositions within practice in the light of abstracted theoretical study.[26]

To draw attention to the limitations of theory and the academic disciplines, therefore, is not to object to relying on them in preparing students to deal with the philosophical and other demands of living. On the contrary, their limitations notwithstanding, academic disciplines are highly desirable as a means of developing the mind and as a means of enabling students to understand and deal practically with the world in which they live. The academic disciplines, imperfect as they are, are the storehouse of a cultural inheritance of inestimable value and a self-refining vehicle for the continued search for knowledge. They provide concepts and ways of understanding and dealing with the world that the human race has painstakingly built up throughout the course of history. As such, they are a part of reflective experience that has a unique contribution to make to dealing with the philosophical and, indeed, all other demands of living. One very concrete manifestation of the value of academic studies is the stunning capacity of disciplined inquiry to contribute to many forms of social, economic, and technological growth.

In general, then, the curriculum of a liberal education conceived as a broad preparation for life will be multifaceted and varied. It may include conventional curriculum content drawn from the established academic disciplines long supported by advocates of liberal education, but it will also necessarily range beyond this. The academic disciplines are desirable to promote the growth and development of the valued cognitive or so-called intellectual attributes of the liberally educated person as we have come to know that idealization. But as has been suggested already, they may not be adequate or suitable for developing the person of action and commitment, of emotional sensitivity, caring, and feeling. They may contain gender, racial, and cultural biases. These may be especially evident for those whose collective experience has not yet been adequately embraced by and reflected in the corpus of disciplinary knowledge. The authors of *Women's Ways of Knowing* put the point this way: "women, paddling in the bywaters of the culture, have had little to do with positing the questions or designing the agendas of the disciplines."[27]

A curriculum of the kind suggested by the idea of a preparation for life set forth here may be at a remove from the more conventional curriculum of a liberal education. It might not meet with favor by advocates of an exclusively or predominantly academic education. Yet the kind of curriculum mandated by a view of liberal education as a preparation for life, the values which it espouses, and the objectives it implies, is going to be different. It will be a curriculum, moreover, that will not only hope to escape the censure of Whitehead but that will respond positively to his assertion that "there is only one subject-matter for education, and that is Life in all its manifestations."[28]

Before turning finally to the crucial question of the justification of the form of education presented here, it will be helpful to reflect on how well this model responds to concerns regarding the historical idea and to the emergent adaptations of that idea. To begin, it must be stressed that preparation for meeting the various demands of living is open to a great variety of curriculum possibilities. It is an openness that would accommodate such concerns as those of Noddings, that liberal education has recognized only a narrow set of capacities, and of Shor, that general education is misguided in its insistence on detailed coverage of subjects in place of relevance and provocative debates.[29] As long as the knowledge and capacities an individual possesses are sufficiently developed to constitute a preparation for life or, in Dewey's words, to give the young command of themselves, the key criterion is met.

Liberal education understood in terms of a preparation for life may also accommodate the many emergent expectations laid upon it as these have already been characterized. The concept of liberal education set forth here is entirely consistent with the commitment to democracy and gender sensitivity. It accommodates the study of the academic disciplines and the development of intellectual attitudes and skills associated with them, as it does interdisciplinary areas such as women's studies, African-American studies, and Latino studies, along with the intellectual orientations and skills associated with them. It is similarly open to the three Cs of care, concern, and connection, and recognizes that they contain both a cognitive component and attitudinal, emotional, and interpersonal components. In its openness to building upon the experiences of students as the starting point for learning, liberal education as understood here accommodates the concern of advocates in the tradition of critical pedagogy. This includes those who see as important the study of power relations in society and how these may be viewed from the perspective of their impact on the self, the disenfranchised, and both the oppressed and the oppressor in society. Similarly, because it embraces both the experiences and interests of students and the idea of problem solving associated with critical pedagogy, the concept of liberal education presented here is also friendly to Bereiter's view that liberal education ought to provide for knowledge creation through problem solving by students themselves.

As will already be sufficiently clear, the approach to liberal education as a preparation for life also accommodates Green's emphasis on developing capacities. The same may be said of the idea of service-learning upheld by

DeVitis, Johns, and Simpson and others, and of a commitment to education for action or participation as proposed by Shor, Martin, and DeVitis, Johns, and Simpson. And, of course, it is committed to the education of practical reason.

JUSTIFICATION, EDUCATION, AND SCHOOLING

Justifying any view of education or schooling may be seen as a dynamic and ongoing activity because of changing values, advances in our understanding of human nature and society, and the changing circumstances of education and schooling, all of which are reflected in the position adopted here. The traditional justification of liberal education lies in the development of mind and the growth of understanding. The justification of liberal education as understood here is found, in part, in the development of mind and understanding, but it also has a more broadly based justification rooted in the aspiration to provide a well-rounded preparation for life; that is to say, a preparation for dealing with the major callings of life or demands of living as a necessary avenue to achieving the good life. Of course, if one defines liberal education in these terms, it follows that the justification of liberal education will be found in these terms. So the question arises, can one justify a view of liberal education that posits preparation for life, a preparation to deal with the major demands or activities of living, as its purpose?

As was pointed out in discussing Martin's position, education is a value-laden enterprise, committed to values by its very nature. In this sense, liberal education is distinguishable from liberal learning and ought not to be confused with it, for learning, unlike education, may be aimless, even accidental. To speak of liberal education as a means to some intended goal or outcome, therefore, is not to distort the meaning of liberal education, as may happen when it is wrongly equated with liberal learning. To speak in this way of education is to conceive of education as preparing us to learn about life and to learn to do what is necessary to achieve or participate in it. These are the values with which, as conceived here, this form of education is laden. Whatever our vision of the good life, we have to actively seek to achieve it; it is not simply presented to us. Typically, such a life will entail work, recreation, dealing with practical affairs, and dealing with moral and philosophical issues. If so, then one is justified in preparing students to engage in such activities. The justification lies in the fact that these elements are essential to attaining the good life, however defined, and even to envisioning it in the first place.[30]

In the final analysis, the ultimate purpose of liberal education as conceived here is to enable the student to define for himself or herself, and to pursue a vision of, the good life. In the nature of things, every student's vision of the good life and the primary values by which it is determined will be shaped to some extent by the school and more fundamentally by home and the broader culture. As viewed here, liberal education is obliged to take account of each student's voice or agency, which will be reflected in the shape of the student's own education while in school or college. Once a vision of the kind of life sought begins to inform the education of each student, the guiding moral stance by which education for each is shaped and directed will be refined.

This is not to say that students should have determined in detail what kind of life they wish to live before leaving school or even college. This is a lifelong search, as is the quest to attain it. Liberal education is expected to initiate the student into these processes as well as provide the wherewithal (including the wherewithal to deal with the demands of living the kind of life that is chosen) to advance both of these undertakings throughout life.[31] Determining the kind of life one wishes to live is the central philosophical task in any person's life, and education's role in initiating the student into this undertaking in the manner suggested here gives the lie to the charge that education as a preparation for life is focused merely on some distant future. By playing a supporting rather than a controlling role, moreover, educational institutions do not run afoul of the charge of moral imperialism raised by Bereiter, among others, some years ago or of a danger of invasion of the rights of the individual to shape his or her vision of the good life and to shape his or her own education accordingly.[32]

In these circumstances, a question arises of how the school can fulfill its responsibility for preparing the student to deal with this central philosophical task of living, granted that the student has not yet decided fully and finally the kind of life he or she wishes to live. The question of whether the school or college can in this respect carry out its responsibility to both the individual student and to society is beset by both theoretical and practical difficulties that revolve around the values and commitments of the society in which the school or college exists.

Unless the society is committed to the good of its citizens, it is unlikely that schools can be so. If it is so committed, the prospects that the school or the college may discharge its responsibility both to the individual student and to society are greatly improved. It can aim to do so by preparing the student to deal with the various demands of living, including the philosophical demands, by promoting that vision of the good life to which it subscribes and which is itself supportive of the good life of the student. That is to say, the school or college fulfills its responsibilities by shaping the education it offers in accordance with those value parameters within which the individual is allowed to shape his or her own destiny. These are values and ideals that, as found in the traditions of democratic self government, are broadly conducive to promoting self-actualization defined in terms of cognitive, moral, physical, spiritual, and emotional development. They are directed by a morality of respect for others, for self, and for justice, peace, and cooperation among all peoples for the well-being of each and all. Such an explicit moral stance of the school, and the emerging moral direction given by the student being educated, ensure that liberal education as a preparation for life will always assume the existence of a vision of the good life by which to become directed or informed.

This is tricky business at any time and in any society; it is especially difficult in highly multicultural contemporary societies, given the diversity of values and social practices that exist within them. Moreover, it calls for a special kind of democratic life in schools and society, as has been highlighted by Amy Gutmann. The kind of democracy that obtains in any community and the kind of democracy toward which children are educated, she has suggested, are intimately connected. Deliberative democracy, in which the citizens are partners and not mere subjects, "objects of legislation," underscores "the importance of publicly supported education that develops the capacity to deliberate among all children as future free and equal citizens."[33]

It is in this context, too, that provision for the religious formation of students may take place. The question of how the public school in the United States, for example, should respond to the requirements of the U.S. Constitution in regard to the teaching of religion has long been debated and is far from settled. Although the Clinton Administration attempted to clarify the situation,[34] in practice public schools by and large disavow any role in the religious formation of students. This is so even though many educators and thinkers believe that we are spiritual beings and to ignore the spiritual dimension of our world is to put us all at a disadvantage.[35] Yet even the study of religious questions has become a delicate matter. This in turn raises the question of whether the school can provide a complete education if it relinquishes a role in religious formation.[36] None other than Adler once suggested that we must ask whether education can be complete without religious education.[37] While the resolution of this matter in the public schools of the United States may ultimately be a legal matter, two observations are pertinent. First, the United States was in part founded on the aspiration to provide religious freedom to all, not to deny it. Second, in the view of Robert Cord,[38] it is not the teaching of any or every religion that is prohibited by the Constitution but the teaching of any *state* religion. If this is so, there seems no good reason based on the Constitution that the public school should not be in a position to provide for the general spiritual or religious education of the young. In fact, not to do so may well be a dereliction of duty—ironically, given where we find ourselves as a society on this issue. Accordingly as the student begins to contribute to the ideal of the good life and the form of education it suggests in his or her case, an appropriate approach to religious formation could be accommodated by the school or college. The school or college would serve in this role in much the same manner as it would with any other aspect of education, more in a supportive than a prescriptive role as the student matures.

Liberal education traditionally understood as merely the cultivation of the intellect has eschewed any role in the moral formation of the student, a stance on which both Newman and Adler are clear. It was because of this absence that Newman, in his more all-embracing idea of a university education, attempted to set the "morally neutral" liberal education that he idealized within the context of a form of moral education and pastoral care. This, for Newman, was rooted in religious belief.[39] Here the school or college is envisioned as having a moral stance of the kind suggested above, namely a commitment to freedom, respect for others, and the pursuit of the good life. From this stance the school or college is positioned to imbue the liberal education it offers with the kind of moral dimension lacking in traditional conceptions of liberal education.

CONCLUSION

Developing a view of liberal education that approaches the question from the point of view of preparing students to deal with the major demands of everyday living does not necessarily rule out an important role for liberal education in its traditional sense. The idea of liberal education adopted here departs from the traditional ideal of liberal education in the broader scope of its curriculum posture. But it is not narrowly utilitarian and it does not degrade the place of cognitive or so-called intellectual development in the life of the individual. It accepts as important the distinction between liberal education and vocational education, in which an essential difference between the two is located not in their content but rather in their attitude toward learning. It also goes farther, saying that it is not the practical nature of an area of study that is illiberal, for many practical activities can be engaged in for no reason beyond the knowledge and enjoyment they provide. It is, rather, the pre-assigned purpose and the attitude with which something is studied that makes a particular area of study liberal or illiberal. Studying so-called vocational subjects, just as engaging in service-learning, may be pursued so as to promote understanding of particular forms of work or social action (or in some cases, just for the fun of it). In that respect, these pursuits may be as liberal a subject of study as any.[40] Accordingly, the idea of general education presented here may be considered as liberal as any. Being open to practical forms of education, this model of liberal education may claim to be useful, too, with even greater confidence than the historical ideal of liberal education.

As set forth here, therefore, liberal education cannot be fairly said to ignore important goals of personal development for the sake of merely utilitarian, vocational education, or know-how. While the concept elaborated here embraces values that the liberal tradition incorporates, it also goes wider and explicitly provides for enabling students to deal with the demands of everyday living, in work, in recreation, in a variety of practical contexts, and in dealing with philosophical and moral questions. It is by enabling the student to deal with these immediate and tangible issues that it promotes the attainment of the good life. The concept of liberal education elaborated here provides a context within which education is defined and shaped. That context consists in its focus on educating the student for personal fulfillment, for achieving his or her vision of the good life, for dealing with the demands of living and with philosophical demands in particular. It issues in a moral stance that imbues liberal education with its sense of mission and direction, its ultimate justification, and its final end in view.

Rather than curtailing or impoverishing the traditional idea of liberal education, the position considered here enriches it. This it does by relating education to the actual concerns of everyday life, by providing a context of relevance and concrete experience for the cognitively oriented studies, and by introducing a necessary balance and interplay between academic or theoretical education and practical education. It also provides a coherence in the curriculum that, in turn, gives a rationale for the practical studies that often languish because of the absence of such support. It enriches the concept and emphasizes the centrality of practical education, and it raises it to a place of respectability in schools and colleges. Most importantly, it recognizes the contribution of students' experience to their own education.

In "Needed: A New Paradigm for Liberal Education," Martin laid out broad guidelines for the development of a new paradigm for liberal education. The concept of liberal education set forth here attempts to meet and, in its sensitivity to the pedagogical dimension, even exceed the requirements established by Martin, who wrote that such an education would include the acquisition of conceptual schemes and even some initiation into the forms of knowledge as envisaged by Hirst. But this would not be the whole thing, for she added:

> There would be initiation into various forms of skill, for example, artistic and athletic, linguistic and mechanical. In this liberal education there would also be room for feelings, emotions, and attitudes to flourish, for creativity and imagination to develop, for making and doing and moral commitment.[41]

Consistent with these considerations, the new paradigm I am suggesting views liberal education as retaining but going beyond the traditional emphasis on knowledge and understanding and the development of intellectual skills. It embraces a broader view of knowledge than that represented by the academic disciplines, one that includes practical knowledge and undestandings. To these it adds skills and understandings essential to active participation in the world, including the search for new knowledge, and caring broadly conceived along with the accompanying skills and sensitivites required in our dealings with others as individuals and in groups. It accepts that even liberal education is committed to values, elaborated here as the pursuit of the good life for self and others. And it is dedicated to accepting and responding to the pedagogical requirements of each and every educational encounter.

NOTES

1. Jane Roland Martin, *Changing the Educational Landscape: Philosophy, Women, and Curriculum* (New York: Routledge, 1994), 171.

2. P. H. Hirst and R. S. Peters, *The Logic of Education* (London: Routledge and Kegan Paul, 1970), 17–41, 60–73. See also D. G. Mulcahy, "Jane Roland Martin and Paul Hirst on Liberal Education: A Reassessment," *Journal of Thought* 38, no. 1 (Spring 2003): 25–29, and J. Mark Halstead, "Liberal Values and Liberal Education" in *The RoutledgeFalmer Reader in the Philosophy of Education*, ed. Wilfred Carr (London: RoutledgeFalmer, 2005), 115–116.

3. Martin, *Changing the Educational Landscape*, and J. White, *Education and the End of Work: A New Philosophy of Work and Learning* (London: Cassell, 1997), especially 69–96.

4. For an eloquent formulation of a concept of truth that is sensitive to both premodern and postmodern perspectives, see Padraig Hogan, "The Integrity of Learning and the Search for Truth," *Educational Theory* 55, no. 2 (May 2005): 184–200.

5. Martin, *Changing the Educational Landscape*, 78, 173–176. Martin uses both the terms "ivory tower people" and "ivory tower person."

6. Richard Pring, *Knowledge and Schooling* (London: Open Books, 1976), 122.

7. In Pring, *Knowledge and Schooling*, Hirst's original theory is subjected to sustained critique on these and other grounds.

8. P. H. Hirst, "Education, Knowledge and Practices," in *Beyond Liberal Education: Essays in Honour of Paul H. Hirst*, ed. Robin Barrow and Patricia White (London: Routledge, 1993), 197. See also Hirst, "A Response to Wilfred Carr's 'Philosophy and Education'," where Hirst elaborates on practical knowledge.

9. Pedagogy as understood here is quite different from what is understood in Geoffrey Hinchliffe, "Education or Pedagogy?" *Journal of Philosophy of Education* 35, no.1 (March 2001): 31–45, where it is seen as "instrumental learning" by contrast with education, which is seen as a "more disinterested endeavour in which teacher and pupil engage in a form of enquiry" (31).

10. Pring, *Knowledge and Schooling*, 84–128.

11. Joe L. Kincheloe, Shirley R. Steinberg, and Deborah J. Tippins, *The Stigma of Genius: Einstein, Consciousness, and Education* (New York: Peter Lang, 1999), especially 49–63.

12. John Dewey, *Experience and Education* (New York: The Macmillan Company, 1963), 46.

13. On this point, see Gert Biesta, "'Of all affairs, communication is the most wonderful': The Communicative Turn in Dewey's Democracy and Education," in *John Dewey and Our Eductional Prospect: A Critical Engagement with Dewey's Democracy and Education*, ed. David T. Hansen (Albany, NY: State University of New York Press, 2006), 23–26. See also John Dewey, *Democracy and Education* (New York: The Free Press, 1966), 1–40.

14. Thomas F. Green, "Needed: A Pedagogy Please!" in *The Condition of American Liberal Education*, ed. Robert Orrill, (New York: The College Board, 1995), 243.

15. The inconsistency between the rhetoric of the importance of civic education and the failure to provide adequately for it is brought out in John White, "What Place for Values in the National Curriculum?" in *Assessing the National Curriculum*, eds. Philip O'Hear and John White (London: Paul Chapman Publishing, Ltd., 1993), especially 12.

16. For a recent analysis of the impact of Jefferson's dream, see J. M. Beach, "The Ideology of the American Dream: Two Competing Philosophies in Education, 1776–2006," *Educational Studies* 41, no. 2 (April 2007): 148–164; for a consideration of issues raised in committing to civic education, see, for example, Richard Pratte, *The Civic Imperative: Examining the Need for Civic Education* (New York: Teachers College Press, 1988), and Grace Roosevelt, "The Triumph of the Market and the Decline of Liberal Education: Implications for Civic Life," *Teachers College Record* 108, no. 7 (July 2006): 1404–1423.

17. Joseph Dunne and Padraig Hogan, eds., *Education and Practice: Upholding the Integrity of Teaching and Learning* (Malden, MA: Blackwell Publishing, 2004).

18. In this connection see George S. Counts, *Dare the School Build a New Social Order?* (New York: John Day Co., 1932), and, for example, Theodore Brameld, *Patterns of Educational Philosophy* (New York: Holt, Rinehart and Winston, Inc., 1971).

19. Franklin Bobbitt, *How to Make a Curriculum* (Boston: Houghton Mifflin Company, 1924), 8–9.

20. Mortimer J. Adler, *The Paideia Proposal: An Educational Manifesto* (New York: Macmillan Publishing Co., Inc., 1982), 30–31.

21. Alasdair MacIntyre, "Plain Persons and Moral Philosophy: Rules, Virtues and Goods," *American Catholic Philosophical Quarterly* 66, no. 1 (Winter 1992): 3–19.

22. See James D. Marshall, "Simone de Beauvoir: The Philosophy of Lived Experience," *Educational Theory* 56, no. 2 (May 2006): 177–189. See also Eleanore Holveck, *Simone de Beauvoir's Philosophy of Lived Experience: Literature and Metaphysics* (Lanham, MD: Rowman and Littlefield, 2002); Pring, *Knowledge and Schooling*, especially 84–98; Richard Pring, "Liberal Education and Vocational Education," in *Beyond Liberal Education: Essays in Honour of Paul H. Hirst*, ed. Robin Barrow and Patricia White (London: Routledge, 1993), 49–58; Hirst, "Education, Knowledge and Practices"; and Jonas F. Soltis, *Education and the Concept of Knowledge* (New York: Teachers College, Columbia University, 1979), especially 11–16.

23. For a helpful treatment of the debate surrounding the relationship between theroretical and practical knowledge in the educational context, including the views of Joseph Dunne, Gilbert Ryle, and Michael Oakeshott, see the discussion of the theoretical foundations of practical knowledge in Theodore Lewis, "At the Interface of

School and Work," *Journal of Philosophy of Education* 39, no. 3 (August 2005): 433–438.

24. Pring, *Knowledge and Schooling*, 122.

25. Pring, "Liberal Education and Vocational Education," 71.

26. Hirst, "Education, Knowledge and Practices," 197.

27. Mary Field Belenky, Blythe McVicker Clinchy, Nancy Rule Goldberger, and Jill Mattuck Tarule, *Women's Ways of Knowing* (New York: Basic Books, 1986), 198.

28. A. N. Whitehead, *The Aims of Education* (New York: The Free Press, 1967), 6–7.

29. Ira Shor, *Empowering Education: Critical Teaching for Social Change* (Chicago: University of Chicago Press, 1992), 145.

30. Consider Christopher Winch, "The Economic Aims of Education," *Journal of Philosophy of Education* 36, no. 2 (February 2002): 101–117, in which there are some similarities to the argement presented here.

31. The treatment of Dewey's discussion of purpose in Douglas J. Simpson, Michael J. B. Jackson, and Judy C. Aycock, *John Dewey and the Art of Teaching: Toward Reflective and Imaginative Practice* (Thousand Oaks, CA: Sage Publications, 2005), 152–154, points to intricacies and to some of the ways in which educational institutions and teachers in particular can be of assistance to students in clarifying and reflecting on their goals and purposes. For an earlier discussion of the same point, see W. H. Schubert, *Curriculum: Perspective, Paradigm, and Possibility* (New York: Macmillan Publishing Company, 1986), 193–194. See also Dewey, *Experience and Education*, 67–72. For an extension of the point in relation to teaching as a practice that also bears on the role of the teacher as intellecual and moral guide, see Nel Noddings, "Is Teaching a Practice?" in *Education and Practice: Upholding the Integrity of Teaching and Learning*, ed. Joseph Dunne and Padraig Hogan (Malden, MA: Blackwell Publishing, 2004), 167–168.

32. The invasion of the moral rights of the individual was a central concern among many of the critics of schooling, including Carl Bereiter, during the 1960s and 1970s. The difficult philosophical and moral decisions entailed in the resolution of this issue are well illustrated in Harry S. Broudy, *General Education: The Search for a Rationale* (Bloomington, IN: Phi Delta Kappan, 1974). See also Carl Bereiter, *Must We Educate?* (Englewood Cliffs, NJ: Prentice Hall, Inc., 1973), and, more recently, Eamonn Callan, "The Great Sphere: Education against Servility," *Journal of Philosophy of Education* 31, no. 2 (July 1997): 221–232. For a reflection on the interplay of the formal curriculum and the philosophy of lived experience that touches on this point, see also the conclusion of Marshall, "Simone de Beauvoir: The Philosophy of Lived Experience," 188–189.

33. Amy Gutmann, *Democratic Education* (Princeton, NJ: Princeton University Press, 1999), xii.

34. *Religious Expression in Public Schools*. Issued by the U.S. Secretary of Education, May 1998, at http://www.ed.gov/Speeches/08-1995/religion.html (accessed July 25, 2007).

35. On this point, see Charles Taylor's interview on PBS Newshour, March 20, 2007, at http://www.pbs.org/newshour/bb/religion/jan-june07/templeton_03-20.html (accessed July 25, 2007).

36. For a fuller consideration of issues that arise here, see, for example, Suzanne Rosenblith and Scott Priestman, "Problematizing Religious Truth: Implications for Public Education," *Educational Theory* 54, no. 4 (Fall 2004): 365–380. For an English perspective, see Colin Wringe, "Is There Spirituality? Can It Be Part of Education?" *Journal of Philosophy of Education* 36, no. 2 (May 2002): 157–170. For an Irish perspective, see Kevin Williams, *Faith and the Nation: Religion, Culture and Schooling in Ireland* (Dublin: Dominican Publications, 2005), 118–120.

37. Mortimer J. Adler, "In Defense of the Philosophy of Education," in *Philosophies of Education*, 41st Yearbook of the National Society for the Study of Education, Part I, ed. Nelson B. Henry (Bloomington, IL: Public School Publishing Company, 1942), 220.

38. See Robert L. Cord, "Church-State Separation and the Public Schools: A Reevaluation," *Educational Leadership* 44, no. 8 (May 1987): 26–32.

39. On this point, see D. G. Mulcahy, "Personal Influences, Discipline and Liberal Education in Newman's Idea of a University," in *Newman Studien* 11, ed. Heinrich Fries, Werner Becker, and Gunter Biemer (Heroldsberg: Glock and Lutz, 1980), 150–158.

40. All of which brings us back yet again to *Aristotle on Education: Extracts from the Ethics and Politics*, trans. and ed. John Burnet (Cambridge: Cambridge University Press, 1903), 108–109.

41. Martin, *Changing the Educational Landscape*, 181.

Bibliography

Adler, Mortimer J. "In Defense of the Philosophy of Education." In *Philosophies of Education*, 41st Yearbook of the National Society for the Study of Education, Part I, ed. Nelson B. Henry, 197–249. Bloomington, IL: Public School Publishing Company, 1942.

———. *The Paideia Proposal: An Educational Manifesto*. New York: Macmillan, 1982.

———. "The Paideia Proposal: Rediscovering the Essence of Education." *The American School Board Journal* 169, no. 7 (July 1982): 17–20.

———. *Paideia Problems and Possibilities*. New York: Macmillan, 1983.

———. "The Paideia Response." *Harvard Educational Review* 53, no. 4 (November 1983): 407–411.

———. *The Paideia Program: An Educational Syllabus*. New York: Macmillan, 1984.

———. *Reforming Education: The Opening of the American Mind*. Ed. Geraldine Van Doren. New York: Macmillan Publishing Co., Inc., 1988.

Adler Mortimer J., and Robert Wolff. *A General Introduction to the Great Books and to a Liberal Education*. Chicago: Encyclopaedia Britannica, 1959.

Adler, Mortimer J., and Charles Van Doren. *How to Read a Book*. New York: Simon and Schuster, 1972.

Aristotle. *Aristotle on Education: Extracts from the Ethics and Politics*. Trans. and ed. John Burnet. Cambridge: Cambridge University Press, 1903.

Bantock, G. H. "Towards a Theory of Popular Education." In *The Curriculum: Context, Design and Development*, ed. Richard Hooper, 251–264. Edinburgh: Oliver and Boyd, 1971.

Barrow, Robin. *Common Sense and the Curriculum*. London: George Allen and Unwin, Ltd., 1976.

———. *Plato and Education*. London: Routledge and Kegan Paul, 1976.

Beach, J. M. "The Ideology of the American Dream: Two Competing Philosophies in Education, 1776–2006." *Educational Studies* 41, no. 2 (April 2007): 148–164.

Beecher, Catharine E. *A Treatise on Domestic Economy.* New York: Schocken Books, 1977.

Belenky, Mary Field, Blythe McVicker Clinchy, Nancy Rule Goldberger, and Jill Mattuck Tarule. *Women's Ways of Knowing.* New York: Basic Books, 1986.

Benard, Edmond Darvil. "Newman's Idea of a *Catholic* University." *American Ecclesiastical Review* 121 (December 1949): 447–468.

Bereiter, Carl. *Must We Educate?* Englewood Cliffs, NJ: Prentice Hall, Inc., 1973.

———. "Liberal Education in a Knowledge Society." In *Liberal Education in a Knowledge Society,* ed. Barry Smith, 11–33. Chicago: Open Court, 2002.

Bergson, Henri. *The Creative Mind,* trans. M. L. Andison. New York: Citadel Press, 1992.

Berliner, David C., and Bruce J. Biddle. *The Manufactured Crisis: Myths, Fraud, and the Attack on America's Public Schools.* New York: Basic Books, 1995.

Bestor, Arthur E. *Educational Wastelands: The Retreat from Learning in Our Public Schools.* Urbana: University of Illinois Press, 1953.

Bhattacharya, Kumkum. "Non-Western Traditions: Leisure in India." In *A Handbook of Leisure Studies,* ed. Chris Rojek, Susan M. Shaw, and A. J. Veal, 75–89. Basingstoke, Hampshire: Palgrave Macmillan, 2006.

Biesta, Gert. "'Of all affairs, communication is the most wonderful': The Communicative Turn in Dewey's Democracy and Education." In *John Dewey and Our Educational Prospect: A Critical Engagement with Dewey's Democracy and Education,* ed. David T. Hansen, 23–37. Albany: State University of New York Press, 2006.

Bloom, Allan. *The Closing of the American Mind.* New York: Simon and Schuster, 1987.

Bobbitt, Franklin. *How to Make a Curriculum.* Boston: Houghton Mifflin Company, 1924.

Bouyer, Louis. *Newman: His Life and Spirituality.* Cleveland, OH: The World Publishing Company, 1960.

Boyer, Ernest L. *High School: A Report on Secondary Education in America.* New York: Harper and Row, 1983.

———. *College: The Undergraduate Experience in America.* New York: Harper & Row, 1987.

Boyer, Ernest L., and Arthur Levine. *A Quest for Common Learning.* Washington, DC: Carnegie Foundation for the Advancement of Teaching, 1981.

Brameld, Theodore. *Patterns of Educational Philosophy.* New York: Holt, Rinehart and Winston, Inc., 1971.

Broudy, Harry S. *Building a Philosophy of Education.* Englewood Cliffs, NJ: PrenticeHall, Inc., 1961.

———. *Enlightened Cherishing.* Urbana: University of Illinois Press, 1972.

———. *General Education: The Search for a Rationale.* Bloomington, IN: Phi Delta Kappan, 1974.

———. *The Uses of Schooling.* New York: Routledge, 1988.

Broudy, Harry S., B. Othanel Smith, and Joe R. Burnett. *Democracy and Excellence in American Secondary Education: A Study in Curriculum Theory.* Chicago: Rand McNally & Company, 1964.

Bruner, Jerome S. *The Process of Education.* New York: Vintage Press, 1960.

———. *The Relevance of Education.* New York: Norton, 1971.

Cahn, Steven M. "Two Cheers for the Proposal." *Harvard Educational Review* 53, no. 4 (November 1983): 403–406.

Callan, Eamonn. "The Great Sphere: Education against Servility." *Journal of Philosophy of Education* 31, no. 2 (July 1997): 221–232.

Carnochan, W. B. *The Battleground of the Curriculum: Liberal Education and American Experience.* Stanford, CA: Stanford University Press, 1993.

———. "On the 'Purposes' of Liberal Education." In *The Condition of American Liberal Education*, ed. Robert Orrill, 182–188. New York: College Entrance Examinations Board, 1995.

Carter, Kathleen M. "Secondary-Postsecondary Partnerships: An Analysis of the Educational, Cultural, Economic and Political Characteristics of Blended Institutions." EdD diss., Central Connecticut State University, 2007.

Casella, Ronnie. *At Zero Tolerance: Punishment, Prevention, and School Violence.* New York: Peter Lang, 2001.

Clarke, Peter, and Andrew Mearman. "Comments on Christopher Winch's 'The Economic Aims of Education.'" *Journal of Philosophy of Education* 38, no. 2 (May 2004): 249–255

Clinton, Hillary Rodham. *It Takes a Village.* New York: Simon and Schuster, 1996.

Clinton, William J. *State of the Union Address, 1997.* <http://clinton2.nara.gov/WH/SOU97/> (25 July 2007).

Commission on the Reorganization of Secondary Education. *Cardinal Principles of Secondary Education.* United States Bureau of Education Bulletin no. 35. Washington, DC: United States Bureau of Education, 1918.

Committee of Ten on Secondary School Studies. *Report.* New York: Published for the National Education Association by the American Book Company, 1894

Coombs, Philip H. *The World Educational Crisis.* New York: Oxford University Press, 1968.

Corcoran, Timothy. "Liberal Studies and Moral Aims: A Critical Survey of Newman's Position." *Thought* 1, no. 1 (June 1926): 54–71.

Cord, Robert L. "Church-State Separation and the Public Schools: A Re-evaluation." *Educational Leadership* 44, no. 8 (May 1987): 26–32.

Counts, George S. *Dare the School Build a New Social Order?* New York: John Day Co., 1932.

Cronin, J. F. *Cardinal Newman: His Theory of Knowledge.* Washington, DC: Catholic University of America Press, 1935.

Culler, A. Dwight. *The Imperial Intellect: A Study of Newman's Educational Ideal.* New Haven, CT: Yale University Press, 1955.

Davis, Andrew, and Kevin Williams, "Epistemology and Curriculum." In *The Blackwell Guide to the Philosophy of Education*, ed. Nigel Blake, Paul Smeyers, Richard Smith, and Paul Standish, 253–270. Oxford: Blackwell Publishers, 2003.

Davis, Oren W., with Jennifer Dodge. "Liberationist Theology through Community Service-Learning at Trinity College of Vermont." In *To Serve and Learn: The Spirit of Community in Liberal Education*, ed. Joseph L. DeVitis, Robert W. Johns, and Douglas J. Simpson, 92–101. New York: Peter Lang, 1998.

Dearden, R. F., P. H. Hirst, and R. S. Peters, eds. *Education and the Development of Reason.* London: Routledge and Kegan Paul, 1972.

DeLaura, David J. *Hebrew and Hellene in Victorian England: Newman, Arnold, and Pater*. Austin, TX: University of Texas Press, 1969.

DeVitis, Joseph L., Robert W. Johns, and Douglas J. Simpson. "Introduction." In Joseph DeVitis, Robert W. Johns, and Douglas J. Simpson, eds. *To Serve and Learn: The Spirit of Community in Liberal Education*, 6–18. New York: Peter Lang, 1998.

Dewey, John. *Experience and Education*. New York: Collier, 1963.

——. *Democracy and Education*. New York: The Free Press, 1966.

Doughty-Jenkins, Bonnie-Marie. "The Connecticut School-to-Career System." EdD diss., Central Connecticut State University, 2005.

Dunne, Joseph. *Back to the Rough Ground*. Notre Dame, IN: University of Notre Dame Press, 1993.

——. "What's the Good of Education?" In *The RoutledgeFalmer Reader in the Philosophy of Education*, ed. Wilfred Carr, 145–160. London: RoutledgeFalmer, 2005.

Dunne, Joseph, and Padraig Hogan, eds. *Education and Practice: Upholding the Integrity of Teaching and Learning*. Malden, MA: Blackwell Publishing, 2004.

Egan, Kieran. *The Educated Mind: How Cognitive Tools Shape Our Understanding*. Chicago: The University of Chicago Press, 1997.

——. *Getting It Wrong from the Beginning: Our Progressivist Inheritance from Herbert Spencer, John Dewey, and Jean Piaget*. New Haven, CT: Yale University Press, 2002.

Elvin, Lionel. *The Place of Commonsense in Educational Thought*. London: Allen and Unwin, 1977.

Finn, Patrick J. *Literacy with an Attitude: Educating Working-Class Children in Their Own Self-Interest*. Albany: State University of New York Press, 1999.

Fitzpatrick, P. J. "John Henry Newman." In *Fifty Major Thinkers on Education*, ed. Joy A. Palmer, 100–104. London: Routledge, 2001.

Freedman, James O. *Liberal Education and the Public Interest*. Iowa City: University of Iowa Press, 2003.

Freire, Paulo. *Pedagogy of the Oppressed*, trans. Myra Bergman Ramos. New York: Herder and Herder, 1971.

Gardner, John N., A. Jerome Jewler, and Betsy Barefoot. *Your College Experience: Strategies for Success*. Boston: Thomson Wadsworth, 2007.

Garland, Martha McMackin. "Newman in His Own Day." In *The Idea of a University*, ed. Frank M. Turner, 266–281. New Haven, CT: Yale University Press, 1996.

Gary, Kevin. "Leisure, Freedom, and Liberal Education." *Educational Theory* 56, no. 2 (May 2006): 121–136.

Gauthier, D. P. *Practical Reasoning: The Structure and Foundations of Prudential and Moral Arguments and Their Exemplification in Discourse*. Oxford: Oxford University Press, 1963.

Gilman, Charlotte Perkins. *Herland*. New York: Pantheon Books, 1979.

Giroux, Henry A. "Modernism, Postmodernism, and Feminism: Rethinking the Boundaries of Educational Discourse." In *Postmodernism, Feminism, and Cultural Politics*, ed. Henry A. Giroux, 1–59. Albany: State University of New York Press, 1991.

——. *Pedagogy and the Politics of Hope*. Boulder, CO: Westview Press, 1997.

——. *Channel Surfing: Race Talk and the Destruction of Today's Youth*. New York: St. Martin's Press, 1999.

———. "Doing Cultural Studies: Youth and the Challenge of Pedagogy." In *After the Disciplines: The Emergence of Cultural Studies*, ed. Michael Peters, 229–266. Westport, CT: Bergin and Garvey, 1999.

———. "Education incorporated?" In *The Critical Pedagogy Reader*, ed. Antonia Darder, Marta Baltodano, and Rodolfo D. Torres, 119–125. New York: Routledge-Falmer, 2003.

Goals 2000: Educate America Act (PL 103–227). March 31, 1994.

Goodlad, John I. *A Place Called School*. New York: McGraw-Hill, 1984.

Gore, Al. *The Assault on Reason*. New York: Penguin Press, 2007.

Green, Nancy Stewart. "Training for Work and Survival." In *Cultures of Curriculum* by Pamela Bolotin Joseph, Stephanie Luster Bravmann, Mark A. Windschitl, Edward R. Mikel, and Nancy Stewart Green, 29–49. Mahwah, NJ: Lawrence Erlbaum Associates, Inc., 2000.

Green, Thomas F. "Needed: A Pedagogy Please!" In *The Condition of American Liberal Education*, ed. Robert Orrill, 238–243. New York: College Entrance Examinations Board, 1995.

Gregory, Marshall. "A Response to Mortimer Adler's *Paideia Proposal*." *Journal of General Education* 36, no. 2 (1984): 70–78.

Grumet, Madeleine R. "The Paideia Proposal: A Thankless Child Replies." *Curriculum Inquiry* 16, no. 3 (Autumn 1986): 335–344.

Gutek, Gerald L. *Historical and Philosophical Foundations of Education*. Upper Saddle River, NJ.: Prentice Hall, Inc., 2001.

Gutmann, Amy. *Democratic Education*. Princeton, NJ: Princeton University Press, 1999.

Gwiazda, Ronald. "The Peter Pan Proposal." *Harvard Educational Review* 53, no. 4 (November 1983): 384–388.

Hadot, Pierre. *Philosophy as a Way of Life: Spiritual Essays from Socrates to Foucault*, ed. Arnold I. Davidson and trans. Michael Chase. Oxford: Blackwell, 1995.

Halstead, J. Mark. "Liberal Values and Liberal Education," in *The RoutledgeFalmer Reader in the Philosophy of Education*, ed. Wilfred Carr, 111–123. London: RoutledgeFalmer, 2005.

Hansen, David T. "John Dewey on Education and the Quality of Life," in *Ethical Visions and Education: Philosophies in Practice*, ed. David T. Hansen, 21–34. New York: Teachers College Press, 2007.

Harvard University. *General Education in a Free Society*. Cambridge, MA.: Harvard University Press, 1945.

Henderson, Harold, and Barry Smith. "Introduction: A New Definition of Liberal Education." In *Liberal Education in a Knowledge Society*, ed. Barry Smith, 1–9. Chicago: Open Court, 2002.

Hinchliffe, Geoffrey. "Education or Pedagogy?" *Journal of Philosophy of Education* 35, no.1 (March 2001): 31–45.

———. "Work and Human Flourishing." *Educational Philosophy and Theory* 36, no. 5 (November 2004): 535–547.

Hirsch, E. D. *Cultural Literacy: What Every American Needs to Know*. New York: Vintage Books, 1988.

Hirst, Paul H. "The Contribution of Philosophy to the Study of Curriculum." In *Changing the Curriculum*, ed. John F. Kerr, 39–62. London: University of London Press, 1968.

———. *Knowledge and the Curriculum*. London: Routledge and Kegan Paul, 1974.

———. "Education, Knowledge and Practices." In *Beyond Liberal Education: Essays in Honour of Paul H. Hirst*, ed. Robin Barrow and Patricia White, 184–199. London: Routledge, 1993.

———. "The Foundations of the National Curriculum: Why Subjects?" In *Assessing the National Curriculum*, ed. Philip O'Hear and John White, 31–37. London: Paul Chapman Publishing, Ltd., 1993.

———. "A Response to Wilfred Carr's 'Philosophy and Education.'" *Journal of Philosophy of Education* 39, no. 4 (November 2005): 615–620.

Hirst, P. H., and R. S. Peters. *The Logic of Education*. London: Routledge and Kegan Paul, 1970.

Hogan, Padraig. "Teaching and Learning as a Way of Life." In *Education and Practice: Upholding the Integrity of Teaching and Learning*, ed. Joseph Dunne and Padraig Hogan, 18–34. Malden, MA: Blackwell Publishing, 2004.

———. "The Integrity of Learning and the Search for Truth." *Educational Theory* 55, no. 2 (May 2005): 184–200.

Holveck, Eleanore. *Simone de Beauvoir's Philosophy of Lived Experience: Literature and Metaphysics*. Lanham, MD: Rowman and Littlefield, 2002.

Howard, V. A., and Israel Scheffler. *Work, Education and Leadership: Essays in the Philospophy of Education*. New York: Peter Lang, 1995.

Humphreys, Debra. *Making the Case for Liberal Education: Responding to Challenges*. Washington, DC: Association of American Colleges and Universities, 2006.

Husen, Torsten. *The School in Question*. Oxford: Oxford University Press, 1979.

Hutchins, Robert. *The Higher Learning in America*. New Haven, CT: Yale University Press, 1936.

———. *The Great Conversation: The Substance of a Liberal Education*. Vol. 1. of Robert M. Hutchins, ed., *Great Books of the Western World*. Chicago: Encyclopedia Britannica, 1952.

Johnson, Tony. "Classicists Versus Experimentalists: Reexamining the Great Debate." *Journal of General Education* 36, no. 4 (1985): 270–279.

Joseph, Pamela Bolotin. "Connecting to the Canon." In *Cultures of Curriculum* by Joseph, Pamela Bolotin, Stephanie Luster Bravmann, Mark A. Windschitl, Edward R. Mikel, and Nancy Stewart Green, 51–71. Mahwah, NJ: Lawrence Erlbaum Associates, Inc., 2000.

Ker, Ian. *The Achievement of John Henry Newman*. Notre Dame, IN: University of Notre Dame Press, 1990.

Kimball, Bruce A. *Orators and Philosophers: A History of the Idea of Liberal Education*. New York: College Entrance Examinations Board, 1995.

———. "Introduction." In *The Condition of American Liberal Education*, ed. Robert Orrill, xxi–xxiii. New York: College Entrance Examinations Board, 1995.

———. "Toward Pragmatic Liberal Education." In *The Condition of American Liberal Education*, ed. Robert Orrill, 3–122. New York: College Entrance Examinations Board, 1995.

Kincheloe, Joe L., Shirley R. Steinberg, and Deborah J. Tippins. *The Stigma of Genius: Einstein, Consciousness, and Education*. New York: Peter Lang, 1999.

Kleiber, Douglas A. *Leisure and Human Development: A Dialectical Interpretation*. New York: Basic Books, 1999.

Kliebard, Herbert M. *The Struggle for the American Curriculum, 1893–1958*. New York: Routledge, 1992.

———. *Changing Course: American Curriculum Reform in the 20ᵗʰ Century*. New York: Teachers College Press, 2002.

Kohn, Alfie. "How Not to Teach Values: A Critical Look at Character Education." *Phi Delta Kappan* 78, no. 6 (February 1997): 428–439.

———. *The Case against Standardized Testing: Raising the Scores, Ruining the Schools*. Portsmouth, NH: Heinemann, 2000.

———. *What Does It Mean to Be Well Educated?* Boston: Beacon Press, 2004.

———. "NCLB and the Effort to Privatize Public Education." In *Many Children Left Behind*, ed. Deborah Meier and George Wood, 79–97. Boston: Beacon Press, 2004.

Koshar, Rudy, ed. *Histories of Leisure*. Oxford: Berg, 2002.

Kuhn, Thomas S. *The Structure of Scientific Revolutions*. Chicago: University of Chicago Press, 1996.

Leavis, F. R. *Education and the University*. London: Chatto and Windus, 1948.

Leitner, Michael J., Sara F. Leitner, and associates. *Leisure Enhancement*. New York: Haworth Press, 2004.

Levin, Benjamin. "*Changing the Educational Landscape*." Book Review. *Journal of Educational Thought* 30, no. 1 (April 1996): 79–81.

Lewis, Theodore. "At the Interface of School and Work." *Journal of Philosophy of Education* 39, no. 3 (August 2005): 421–441.

Lovelie, Lars, and Paul Standish. "Introduction: Bildung and the Idea of a Liberal Education." *Journal of Philosophy of Education* 36, no. 3 (August 2002): 317–340.

Lucas, Christopher. "*The Paideia Proposal: An Educational Manifesto*" Book Review. *Educational Studies* 14, no. 3 (Fall 1983): 282–285.

MacIntyre, Alasdair. "Practical Rationalities as Forms of Social Structure." *Irish Philosophical Journal* 4, no. 1 (1987): 3–19.

———. *Whose Justice? Which Rationality?* Notre Dame, IN: University of Notre Dame Press, 1988.

———. "Plain Persons and Moral Philosophy: Rules, Virtues and Goods." *American Catholic Philosophical Quarterly* 66, no. 1 (Winter 1992): 3–19.

MacIntyre, Alasdair, and Joseph Dunne, "Alasdair MacIntyre on Education: In Dialogue with Joseph Dunne." In *Education and Practice: Upholding the Integrity of Teaching and Learning*, ed. Joseph Dunne and Padraig Hogan, 1–17. Malden, MA: Blackwell Publishing, 2004.

Maritain, Jacques. *Education at the Crossroads*. New Haven, CT: Yale University Press, 1943.

———. "Thomist Views on Education." In *Modern Philosophies and Education*. 54th Yearbook of the National Society for the Study of Education, Part 1, ed. Nelson B. Henry, 57–90. Chicago: The University of Chicago Press, 1955.

Marsden, George M. "Theology and the University: Newman's Idea and Current Realities." In *The Idea of a University*, ed. Frank M. Turner, 302–317. New Haven, CT: Yale University Press, 1996.

Marshall, David. "The Places of the Humanities: Thinking through Bureaucracy." *Liberal Education* 93, no. 2 (Spring 2007): 34–49.

Marshall, James D. "Simone de Beauvoir: The Philosophy of Lived Experience." *Educational Theory* 56, no. 2 (May 2006): 177–189.

Marshall, James O. "Education and the Postmodern World: Rethinking Some Educational Stories." *Educational Theory* 50, no. 1 (Winter 2000): 117–226.

Marshall, J. Dan, James T. Sears, Louise Anderson Allen, Patrick A. Roberts, and William H. Schubert. *Turning Points in Curriculum: A Contemporary American Memoir*. Upper Saddle River, NJ: PearsonEducation Inc., 2007.

Martin, Jane Roland. "Bringing Women into Educational Thought." *Educational Theory* 34, no. 4 (Fall 1984): 341–353.

———. *Reclaiming a Conversation: The Ideal of the Educated Woman*. New Haven, CT: Yale University Press, 1985.

———. *The Schoolhome: Rethinking Schools for Changing Families*. Cambridge, MA: Harvard University Press, 1992.

———. "The New Problem of Curriculum." *Synthese* 94, no. 1 (1993): 85–104.

———. *Changing the Educational Landscape: Philosophy, Women, and Curriculum*. New York: Routledge, 1994.

———. "Women, Schools, and Cultural Wealth." In *Women's Philosophies of Education*, ed. Connie Titone and Karen E. Moloney, 149–177. Upper Saddle River, NJ: Prentice Hall, Inc., 1999.

———. *Coming of Age in Academe: Rekindling Women's Hopes and Reforming the Academy*. New York: Routledge, 2000.

———. *Cultural Miseducation: In Search of a Democratic Solution*. New York: Teachers College Press, 2002.

———. *Educational Metamorphoses: Philosophical Reflections on Identity and Culture*. Lanham, MD: Rowman and Littlefield, 2007.

McClelland, V. A. *English Roman Catholics and Higher Education, 1830–1903*. Oxford: The Clarendon Press, 1973.

———. "A Catholic Eton: By Hook or by Crook? John Henry Newman and the Establishment of the Oratory School." *Aspects of Education* 22 (1980): 3–17.

McCloskey, C. John. "Newman's University in Today's American Culture." In *Newman's Idea of a University: The American Response*, ed. Peter M. J. Stravinskas and Patrick J. Reilly, 55–65. Mt. Pocono, PA: Newman House Press, 2002.

McGrath, Fergal. *Newman's University: Idea and Reality*. London: Longmans, Green and Co., 1951.

McGucken, William. "The Philosophy of Catholic Education." In *Philosophies of Education*. 41st Yearbook of the National Society for the Study of Education, Part I, ed. Nelson B. Henry, 251–288. Bloomington, IL: Public School Publishing Company, 1942.

McKenzie, Floretta Dukes. "The Yellow Brick Road of Education." *Harvard Educational Review* 53, no. 4 (November 1983): 389–392.

McLaren, James. *Life in Schools*. White Plains, NY: Longmans, 1994.

Meier, Deborah. *Will Standards Save Public Education?* Boston: Beacon Press, 2000.

———. "NCLB and Democracy." In *Many Children Left Behind*, ed. Deborah Meier and George Wood, 66–78. Boston: Beacon Press, 2004.

Mitchell, Basil. "Newman as a Philosopher." In *Newman after a Hundred Years*, ed. Ian Ker and Alan G. Hill, 223–246. Oxford: The Clarendon Press, 1990.

Mitchell, Richard. *The Graves of Academe*. Boston: Little, Brown, 1981.

Molnar, Alex. "What the Market Can't Provide." In *The Critical Pedagogy Reader*, ed. Antonia Darder, Marta Baltodano, and Rodolfo D. Torres, 126–141. New York: RoutledgeFalmer, 2003.

Montessori, Maria. *The Montessori Method*. Trans. Anne E. George. New York: Robert Bentley, Inc., 1967.

Mulcahy, Cara M. "Emergent Possibilities for Diversity in Reading and Language Arts." In *Language and Cultural Diversity in U.S. Schools: Democratic Principles in Action*, ed. T. A. Osborn, 5–23. Westport, CT: Praeger, 2005.

———. *Marginalized Literacies*. Information Age Publishing. Forthcoming.

Mulcahy, Donal E. "John Dewey." In *The Praeger Handbook of Education and Psychology*, ed. Joe L. Kincheloe and Raymond A. Horn, 67–74. Westport, CT: Praeger, 2007.

———. "Progressive Education: The Legacy and Current Challenges." 2007 Yearbook of the South Atlantic Philosophy of Education Society, ed. Kurt Stemhagen, 36–44.

Mulcahy, D. G. "Cardinal Newman's Concept of a Liberal Education." *Educational Theory* 22, no. 1 (Winter 1972): 87–98.

———. "Newman's Retreat from a Liberal Education." *Irish Journal of Education* 7, no. 1 (Summer 1973): 11–22.

———. "Personal Influence, Discipline and Liberal Education in Cardinal Newman's Idea of a University." In *Internationale Cardinal Newman Studien*. Elfte Folge. Achter Newman-Congress Freiburg, ed. H. Fries, W. Becker, and G. Biemer, 150–158. Heroldsberg: Glock und Lutz, 1980.

———. *Curriculum and Policy in Irish Post-Primary Education*. Dublin: Institute of Public Administration, 1981.

———. "Is the Nation at Risk from *The Paideia Proposal?*" *Educational Theory* 35, no. 2 (Spring 1985): 209–221.

———. *Knowledge, Gender, and Schooling: The Feminist Educational Thought of Jane Roland Martin*. Westport, CT: Bergin and Garvey, 2002.

———. "Jane Roland Martin and Paul Hirst on Liberal Education: A Reassessment." *Journal of Thought* 38, no. 1 (Spring 2003): 19–30.

Mulcahy, D. G., and Ronnie Casella, "Violence and Caring in School and Society." *Educational Studies* 37, no. 3 (June 2005): 244–255.

National Commission on Excellence in Education. *A Nation at Risk*. Washington, DC: U.S. Department of Education, 1983.

Newman, Jay. *The Mental Philosophy of John Henry Newman*. Waterloo: Wilfrid Laurier University Press, 1986.

Newman, John Henry. *Fifteen Sermons Preached before the University of Oxford*. London: Rivingtons, 1887.

———. *Idea of a University*. London: Longmans Green, and Co., 1898.

———. *Discussions and Arguments on Various Subjects*. London: Longmans, Green, 1924.

———. *An Essay in Aid of a Grammar of Assent*, ed. Charles Frederick Harrold. New York: Longmans, Green and Co., 1947.

———. *The Idea of a University Defined and Illustrated*, ed. Charles Frederick Harrold. New York: Longmans, Green and Co., 1947.

———. *The Idea of a University*, intro. George N. Shuster. Garden City, NY: Doubleday and Company, Inc., 1959.

———. *University Sketches*, ed. Michael Tierney. Dublin, Browne and Nolan Limited, 1961.

———. *The Idea of a University*, ed. Frank M. Turner. New Haven: Yale University Press, 1996.

No Child Left Behind of 2001 (PL 107–110).

Noddings, Nel. "The False Promise of the Paideia: A Critical Review of the Paideia Proposal." *Journal of Thought* 19, no. 1 (Spring 1984): 81–91.

———. *The Challenge to Care in Schools*. New York: Teachers College Press, 1992.

———. *Happiness and Education*. Cambridge: Cambridge University Press, 2003.

———. "Is Teaching a Practice?" In *Education and Practice: Upholding the Integrity of Teaching and Learning*, ed. Joseph Dunne and Padraig Hogan, 159–169. Malden, MA: Blackwell Publishing, 2004.

———. *Critical Lessons: What Our Schools Should Teach*. Cambridge: Cambridge University Press, 2006.

Nussbaum, Martha C. *Cultivating Humanity: A Classical Defense of Reform in Liberal Education*. Cambridge, MA: Harvard University Press, 1997.

Oakeshott, Michael, J. *The Voice of Liberal Learning: Michael Oakeshott on Education*, ed. Timothy Fuller. New Haven, CT: Yale University Press, 1989.

O'Hear, Philip. "Coherence in Curriculum Planning." In *Assessing the National Curriculum*, ed. Philip O'Hear and John White, 15–24. London: Paul Chapman Publishing, Ltd., 1993.

O'Rahilly, Alfred. "The Irish University Question: V Newman on Education." *Studies* 50 (Winter 1961): 363–370.

Panel on Youth of the President's Science Advisory Committee. *Youth: Transition to Adulthood*. Chicago: The University of Chicago Press, 1974.

Pelikan, Jaroslav. *The Idea of a University: A Reexamination*. New Haven, CT: Yale University Press, 1992.

Perkinson, Henry J. *Since Socrates*. New York: Longman, 1980.

Perry, L. R. "Commonsense Thought, Knowledge, and Judgement and Their Importance for Education." In *Readings in the Philosophy of Education: A Study of Curriculum*, ed. Jane Roland Martin, 187–200. Boston: Allyn and Bacon, 1970.

Peterat, Linda. "Family Studies: Transforming Curriculum, Transforming Families." In *Gender In/forms Curriculum*, ed. Jane Gaskell and John Willinsky, 174–190. New York: Teachers College Press, 1995.

Peterburs, Wulstan. "Newman's *Idea of a University*, 'the Circle of the Sciences', and the Constitution of the Church." In *Victorian Churches and Churchmen: Essays Presented to Vincent Alan McClelland*, ed. Sheridan Gilley, 200–233. Woodbridge, Suffolk: The Boydell Press, 2005.

Peters, R. S. *Ethics and Education*. London: George Allen and Unwin, Ltd., 1966.

———. "Education and the Educated Man." In *Education and the Development of Reason*, ed. R. F. Dearden, P. H. Hirst, and R. S. Peters, 3–18. London: Routledge and Kegan Paul.

——. "Ambiguities in Liberal Education and the Problem of its Content." In *Ethics and Educational Policy*, ed. Kenneth A. Strike and Kieran Egan, 3–21. London: Routledge and Kegan Paul, 1978.

Peterson, Nadene, and Roberto Cortez Gonzalez. *The Role of Work in People's Lives.* Belmont, CA: Wadsworth/Thomson Learning, 2000.

Phenix, Philip H. *Realms of Meaning.* New York: McGraw Hill, 1964.

Pieper, Josef. *Leisure the Basis of Culture*, trans. Alexander Dru. New York: Pantheon Books, 1963.

Pinar, William F. *What Is Curriculum Theory?* Mahwah, NJ: Laurence Erlbaum Associates, 2004.

Plato. *The Republic*, trans. Benjamin Jowett. New York: Airmont Publishing Company, Inc., 1968.

Pratte, Richard. *The Civic Imperative: Examining the Need for Civic Education.* New York: Teachers College Press, 1988.

Pring, Richard. *Knowledge and Schooling.* London: Open Books, 1976.

——. "Liberal Education and Vocational Education." In *Beyond Liberal Education: Essays in Honour of Paul H. Hirst*, ed. Robin Barrow and Patricia White, 49–78. London: Routledge, 1993.

Purpel, David, and Kevin Ryan. "It Comes with the Territory: The Inevitability of Moral Education in the Schools." In *Moral Education... It Comes with the Territory*, ed. David Purpel and Kevin Ryan, 44–54. Berkeley, CA: McCutchan Publishing Corporation, 1976.

Reagan, Timothy, G. "Paideia Redux." *Journal of Thought* 38, no. 3 (Fall 2003): 21–39.

Religious Expression in Public Schools. Issued by the U.S. Secretary of Education. May 1998. <http://www.ed.gov/Speeches/08-1995/religion.html> (25 July 2007).

Richardson, Laurence. *Newman's Approach to Knowledge.* Leominster, Herefordshire: Gracewing, 2007.

Rickover, Hyman G. *Education and Freedom.* New York: Dutton, 1959.

Rifkin, Jeremy. *The End of Work: The Decline of the Global Labor Force and the Dawn of the Post-Market Era.* New York: Putnam, 1995.

Roberts, Arthur D., and Gordon Cawelti. *Redefining General Education in the American High School.* Alexandria, VA: The Association for Supervision and Curriculum Development, 1984.

Roberts, J. M. "*The Idea of a University* Revisited." In *Newman after a Hundred Years*, ed. Ian Ker and Alan G. Hill, 193–222. Oxford: Clarendon Press, 1990.

Roosevelt, Grace. "The Triumph of the Market and the Decline of Liberal Education: Implications for Civic Life." *Teachers College Record* 108, no. 7 (July 2006): 1404–1423.

Rorty, Richard. *Philosophy and the Mirror of Nature.* Princeton, NJ: Princeton University Press, 1979.

Rosenblith, Suzanne, and Scott Priestman. "Problematizing Religious Truth: Implications for Public Education." *Educational Theory* 54, no. 4 (Fall 2004): 365–380.

Rothblatt, Sheldon. *Tradition and Change in English Liberal Education.* London: Faber and Faber, 1976.

——. *The Modern University and Its Discontents: The Fate of Newman's Legacies in Britain and America.* Cambridge: Cambridge University Press, 1997.

Ryan, John K., and Edmond Darvil Benard, eds. *American Essays for the Newman Centennial*. Washington, DC: The Catholic University of America Press, 1947.

Sacks, Peter. *Standardized Minds: The High Price of America's Testing Culture and What We Can Do to Change It*. Cambridge, MA: Perseus Books, 1999.

Schall, James V. "Liberal Education and 'Social Justice'." *Liberal Education* 92, no. 4 (Fall 2006): 44–47.

Scheffler, Israel. *The Language of Education*. Springfield, IL: Charles C. Thomas, 1960.

Schiller, F. C. S. *Studies in Humanism*. London: Macmillan, 1912.

Schneider, Carol G. "Practicing Liberal Education: Formative Themes in the Reinvention of Liberal Learning." *Liberal Education* 90, no. 2 (Spring 2004): 6–11.

Schubert, W. H. *Curriculum: Perspective, Paradigm, and Possibility*. New York: Macmillan Publishing Company, 1986.

———. "THE BIG CURRICULUM." *Journal of Curriculum and Pedagogy* 3, no. 1 (2006): 100–103.

Shor, Ira. *Empowering Education: Critical Teaching for Social Change*. Chicago: University of Chicago Press, 1992.

Shuster, George N. "Introduction." In John Henry Cardinal Newman, *The Idea of a University*, 21–43. Garden City, NY: Doubleday and Company, Inc., 1959.

Siegel, Harvey. "Genderized Cognitive Perspective and the Redefinition of Philosophy of Education." *Teachers College Record* 85, no. 1 (Fall 1983): 100–119.

Simpson, Douglas J., Michael J. B. Jackson, and Judy C. Aycock. *John Dewey and the Art of Teaching: Toward Reflective and Imaginative Practice*. Thousand Oaks, CA: Sage Publications, 2005.

Sizer, Theodore R. *Horace's Compromise*. Boston: Houghton Mifflin, 1984.

Sizer, Theodore R., and Nancy Faust Sizer. "Grappling." *Phi Delta Kappan* 81, no. 3 (November 1999): 184–190.

Smith, B. Othanel, and Donald E. Orlosky, *Socialization and Schooling: Basics of Reform*. Bloomington, IN: Phi Delta Kappa, 1975.

Smith, Marshall S., Susan H. Fuhrman, and Jennifer O'Day. "National Curriculum Standards: Are They Desirable and Feasible?" In *The Governance of Curriculum*, ed. Richard F. Elmore and Susan H. Fuhrman, 12–29. Alexandria, VA.: Association for Supervision and Curriculum Development, 1994.

Soltis, Jonas F. *Education and the Concept of Knowledge*. New York: Teachers College, Columbia University, 1979.

Spencer, Herbert. *Education: Intellectual, Moral, and Physical*. Totowa, NJ: Littlefield Adams, 1969.

Standish, Paul. "The Nature and Purposes of Education." In *A Companion to the Philosophy of Education*, ed. Randall Curren, 221–231. Malden, MA: Blackwell Publishing, Ltd., 2003.

Stratemeyer, Florence, Hamden L. Forkner, Margaret G. McKim, and A. Harry Passow. *Developing a Curriculum for Modern Living*. New York: Bureau of Publications, Teachers College, Columbia University, 1957.

Tardivel, Fernande. *J. H. Newman Educateur*. Paris: Les Presses Modernes, 1937.

Taylor, Charles. *Sources of Self: The Making of the Modern Identity*. Cambridge: Harvard University Press, 1989.

———. Interview on PBS Newshour. March 20, 2007. <http://www.pbs.org/newshour/bb/religion/jan-june07/templeton_03-20.html> (25 July 2007).

The Great Ideas: The University of Chicago and the Ideal of a Liberal Education. An Exhibition in the Department of Special Collections, the University of Chicago Library, May 1–September 6, 2002. <www.lib.uchicago.edu/e/spcl/excat/ideas3 .html> (25 July 2007).

The Report of the Council of Education: The Curriculum of the Secondary School. Dublin: The Stationary Office, 1960.

Thompson, Audrey. "Caring in Context: Four Feminist Theories on Gender and Education." *Curriculum Inquiry* 33, no. 1 (Spring 2003): 9–65.

Tierney, Michael. "Catholic University." In *A Tribute to Newman*, ed. Michael Tierney, 172–206. Dublin: Browne and Nolan Limited, 1945.

Tozer, Steven E., Guy Senese, and Paul C. Violas. *School and Society: Historical and Contemporary Perspectives.* Boston: McGraw-Hill, 2006.

Triffin, John. "In Defense of Newman's 'Gentleman'." *Dublin Review* 239 (Autumn 1965): 245–254.

Tyler, Ralph W. *Basic Principles of Curriculum and Instruction.* Chicago: University of Chicago Press, 1949.

Waghid, Yusef. "Action as an Educational Virtue: Toward a Different Understanding of Democratic Citizenship Education." *Educational Theory* 55, no. 3 (August 2005): 323–342.

———. "University Education and Deliberation: In Defence of Practical Reasoning." *Higher Education* 51, no. 3 (April 2006): 315–328.

Walker, Decker F., and Jonas F. Soltis. *Curriculum and Aims.* New York: Teachers College Press, 1997.

Warnock, Mary. *Education: A Way Ahead.* Oxford: Basil Blackwell, 1979.

Weltman, Burton. "Individualism Versus Socialism in American Education: Rereading Mortimer Adler and *The Paideia Proposal*." *Educational Theory* 52, no. 1 (Winter 2002): 61–79.

Westheimer, Joel, and Joseph Kahne. "What Kind of Citizen? The Politics of Educating for Democracy." *American Educational Research Journal* 41, no. 2 (Summer 2004): 237–269.

White, J. *Towards a Compulsory Curriculum.* London: Routledge and Kegan Paul, 1973.

———. *Education and the Good Life.* New York: Teachers College Press, 1991.

———. "What Place for Values in the National Curriculum?" In *Assessing the National Curriculum*, ed. Philip O'Hear and John White, 9–14. London: Paul Chapman Publishing, Ltd., 1993.

———. "Education, Work, and Well-being." *Journal of Philosophy of Education* 31, no. 2 (July 1997): 233–247.

———. *Education and the End of Work: A New Philosophy of Work and Learning.* London: Cassell, 1997.

———. "Introduction." In *Rethinking the School Curriculum: Values, Aims and Purposes*, ed. J. White, 1–19. London: RoutledgeFalmer, 2004.

———. "Shaping a Curriculum." In *Rethinking the School Curriculum: Values, Aims and Purposes*, ed. J. White, 20–29. London: RoutledgeFalmer, 2004.

———. "Conclusion." In *Rethinking the School Curriculum: Values, Aims and Purposes*, ed. J. White, 179–190. London: RoutledgeFalmer, 2004.

Whitehead, A. N. *The Aims of Education.* New York: The Free Press, 1967.

Will, George, F. "Ed Schools vs Education." *Newsweek*, January 16, 2006. <http://www.msnbc.msn.com/id/10753446/site/newsweek/> (25 July 2007).

Williams, Kevin. *Faith and the Nation: Religion, Culture and Schooling in Ireland.* Dublin: Dominican Publications, 2005.

——. *Education and the Voice of Michael Oakeshott.* Exeter: Imprint Academic, 2007.

Willinsky, John. "Just Say Know? Schooling the Knowledge Society." *Educational Theory* 55, no. 1 (February 2005): 97–111.

Willis, G. H., W. H. Schubert, R. Bullough, C. Kridel, and J. Holton, eds. *The American Curriculum: A Documentary History.* Westport, CT: Greenwood Press, 1993.

Winch, Christopher. "The Economic Aims of Education." *Journal of Philosophy of Education* 36, no. 2 (February 2002): 101–117.

——. "Work, the Aims of Life, and the Aims of Education: A Reply to Clarke and Mearman." *Journal of Philosophy of Education* 38, no. 4 (November 2004): 633–638.

Wise, John E. "Newman and the Liberal Arts." In *American Essays for the Newman Centennial*, ed. John K. Ryan and Edmond Darvil Benard, 133–150. Washington, DC: The Catholic University of America Press, 1947.

Wolf, Alison. *Does Education Matter? Myths about Education and Economic Growth.* London: Penguin Books, 2002.

Wollstonecraft, Mary. *A Vindication of the Rights of Woman*, ed. Carol H. Poston. New York: W. W. Norton, 1975.

Wringe, Colin. "Is There Spirituality? Can It Be Part of Education?" *Journal of Philosophy of Education* 36, no. 2 (May 2002): 157–170.

Yale College, *Yale NEASC Self-Study of 1999.* <http://www.yale.edu/accred/standards/s1.html> (25 July 2007).

Yale Report of 1828, Part I. <http://collegiateway.org/reading/yale-report-1828/> (25 July 2007).

Yale University document. *<http://www.yale.edu/about/history.html>* (25 July 2007).

Index

action: practical, 167, 176n60;
purposeful, 167, 178
action research, 22
activism, 20
actvities of living, 8, 88, 157–61, 164,
166–67, 184–85, 188
Adler, Mortimer J., 135–38, 142n63;
and Aristotle, 169; and citizenship
education, 103n41, 148, 183; and
critical pedagogy, 99; education as
an end in itself, 98; and education
for social justice, 81, 99; and
education as preparation for life in,
99, 155–58; and Hirst, 118; and
liberal education, 10–11, 71–100;
and Martin, 107, 110–12, 126, 129;
and Newman, 59, 61, 71–72, 94,
122; and Noddings, 12; *and
Reforming Education*, 28n41, 75; and
same course of study, 76, 78, 83–86,
94, 99, 148; and school reform,
25n2; and Shor, 20, 152–53; and
the Great Books, 26n15; aims of
education in, 79–83; assessment in,
94–96; 100, 105n86; auxiliary
studies in, 76–77, 89–93, 166; basic
schooling in, 78, 86, 88; callings (or
vocations) of life in, 76, 98–99,

155–56, 160, 188; career education
in, 89; chief writings of, 100n1;
democracy in, 75–76, 78, 81, 83,
97, 99–100, 148; dichotomy in,
156; education for citizenship in,
90–93, 98–99,148; education for
work in, 90–93, 98–99; educational
objectives in, 76, 78, 83, 94;
enlargement of understanding in,
77; equality in, 71, 83–85, 99;
individual differences in, 78, 84;
knowledge and understanding in,
177; manual activities in, 89; moral
development in, 80–81; organized
knowledge in, 77 , 87–88;
participation in, 185; pedagogy in,
94–97; personal development in,
76, 79–82, 88–89, 156; physical
education in, 72, 77, 89–90;
practical education in, 90, 92, 168;
reform in, 79; religion in, 190;
sameness in, 78, 83–84, 94; socratic
teaching in, 15, 77, 91, 94, 102n30,
150; standards in, 94–96, 100;
teacher in, 79; teaching in, 78, 84,
87, 90, 94–97
Alberty, Harold, 28n29, 174n41
Aquinas, St Thomas, 72

211

Aristotle, 5, 42, 56, 169–70; and Adler, 72, 83; in Hirst, 23, 122, 124; in Newman, 45, 67n98, 67n99
Arnold, Matthew, 36–37
Association of American Colleges and Universities, 137
Athens, 4

Back to the Rough Ground, 23
Bantock, G. H., 102n36
Beecher, Catharine, 108, 112, 114–15, 126
Bereiter, Carl, 1, 21–22, 128, 150, 152, 177, 184, 187, 189, 195n32
Bergson, Henri, 52
"best education for the best . . .", 79, 83–85
Bestor, Arthur E., 9, 73
Birmingham, 36
Birmingham Oratory, 36, 62n8
Bloom, Allan, 10, 28n41, 31n95, 118, 152
Bobbitt, Franklin, 12, 157, 184
Bolton Joseph, Pamela, 17
Boyer, Ernest L., 10, 12, 73, 118, 150
Brameld, Theodore, 130, 183
Broudy, Harry S., 4, 152, 165, 170, 175n59; and Smith and Burnett, 5, 10, 59, 73, 76, 87, 118, 126; molar problems in, 19, 87, 130; uses of knowledge in, 76, 87, 170
Bruner, Jerome S., 9
Buchanan, Scott, 72
Burnett, Joe R., 5, 10, 59, 73, 76, 87, 118, 126
Bush, George H. W., 31n87
Bush, George W., 31n87
Bush, Jeb, 31n87

Cahn, Steven M., 90
callings of life, 13, 100, 157–61, 178, 188
Cardinal Principles of Secondary Education, 7–8, 27n26, 98, 157–59
care, concern, and connection, 60, 83, 114–15, 122, 128–32, 134, 136, 138, 187

caring, 12, 29n54; and service, 12; and service-learning, 14; and themes of, 12
Carnochan, W. B., 11, 47, 152
Catholic University of Ireland, 36–37, 50
Catholocism, 36
The Challenge to Care in Schools, 12
Changing the Educational Landscape, 108
Charters, W. W., 157
Church of England, 36
Cicero, 5
citizenship: and pragmatism, 24; education for, 57, 74, 90–93, 98–99, 183; in Adler, 3, 80; in DiVitis, Johns, and Simpson, 13; in Giroux, 18, 183; in Nussbaum, 13; in Waghid, 31n93; meaning of, 159
Clinton, William J., 83, 105n83; Administration of, 190
The College Board, 28n42
Columbia University, 72
Coming of Age in Academe, 108
Committee of Ten, 7
commonsense, 20, 181
Compte, Auguste, 16
concrete experience, 14, 20, 149, 192
Congress, 105n83
continuity and change in liberal education, 148–50; and Adler, 148–50; and Martin, 148–50; and Newman, 148–50
Corcoran, Timothy, 47
Cord, Robert L., 190
Counts, George S., 183
Critical Lessons, 15
critical pedagogy, 15–21, 149–50
critical thinking, 15
Cronin, J. F., 53
Culler, A, Dwight, 41, 64n37, 170
cultivation of the intellect: and liberal education, 35; in Adler, 79–83, 191; in Newman, 35, 47, 191
Cultural Miseducation, 108, 133–135, 141n57, 144n107
culture of positivism, 16

curriculum: academic disciplines in, 74, 184–87; aims and purpose in, 148, 150; design and development of, 86; of basic schooling, 86; of liberal education, 11, 150; of education as preparation for life, 186; pedagogical dimension of, 148; stance of Adler, 86–94, 98, 125

Davidson, Ellen, 21
Davis, Oren W, 14–15, 20, 185
Declaration of Independence, 77
demands of living, 8, 159–71, 173n21, 178, 188, 192; and unemployment, 164; education for, 182–89; philosophical, 169–71; origins of, 161; practical, 165–69; recreational, 164–65; work, 161–64
democracy, 31n90, 187; and self-actualization, 189; in Adler, 75–76, 78, 81, 83, 97, 99–100, 148; in Giroux, 17–18; in Martin, 133–34; values of in school and society, 189–90
Democracy and Education, 147
DeVitis, Joseph L., 12–15, 20, 30n64, 99, 184, 188
Dewey, John, 12, 15, 30n66, 173n31, 181, 187; and Adler, 99; and constructivism, 172n9; and *Democracy and Education,* 147; and method, 74; and Newman, 185; and Pring, 152–53, 172n6, 184–85; and Shor, 147–48, 152, 185; communication in, 181; in Martin, 132
discipline of mind, 35, 46, 48–49
Dodge, Jennifer, 14–15, 20, 185
domestic economy, 114
Dublin, 36
Dunne, Joseph, 23, 183, 194n23

Edinburgh Review, 6, 25, 36, 42
educated man, the, 101n7, 116–17, 127, 140n39
educated person, the, xii, 177–78; in Adler, 82; in Bereiter, 1, 150, 177; in

Hirst, 116, 123, 178; in liberal education, 82; in Martin, 82, 107–8, 117, 127–28, 138; in Newman, 43, 63, 177–78; in Peters, 116; liberally educated, 186
education: academic ideal of, 72; aim of, 73, 81, 156; and general education, 73, 178; and leisure, 4, 90, 157, 175n59; and liberal education, 73, 178; and schooling, 109, 141; and schooling in Martin, 109, 141; and social practices, 23, 185; as preparation for life, 153, 155–57, 159–60, 165, 167, 171, 173n21, 189; as personal development, 73; as value laden, 138, 188; content of, 74–75; for participation, 99; logical character of, 73; nature and purpose of, 8; places of, 25; practical, 23; purposes of, 25, 133
Educational Metamorphoses, 108, 133, 141n57, 144n107
Educational Reform Act of 1988, 183
Einstein, Albert, 181
Elementary and Secondary Education Act (ESEA), 9
empowering education: goals of, 19; as dialogic pedagogy, 20
Encyclopedia Britannica, 3, 71–72
England, 73, 143n87, 183
equality: in Adler, 71, 83–85, 99; in Martin, 129, 134, 138
Experience and Education, 147

Feminist theory, 109
Finn, Chester, 31n95
Franklin, Benjamin, 8
Franklin, Rosalind, 139n13
Freedman, James O., 37
Freire, Paulo, 15, 18, 20, 132, 152, 172n9

Gardner, Howard, 12,
Gardner, John N., 66n87
Gates Foundation, xiii
gender-sensitive education, 107–39

general education, xii; 8, 11, 35, 72, 138, 150, 155; aims of, 23, 152; and liberal education, 1, 73, 125–26, 154, 178; and the demands of living, 165, 178; as education, 125, 178; as preparation for life, 147–71; curriculum for, 2, 12, 153; idea of, 160, 184, 191; in Adler, 72, 79, 152; in Broudy, Smith, Burnett, 87; in Hutchins, 74; in Kimball, 24; in Noddings, 187; in schools and colleges, 44; in Shor, 20, 152, 187; in White, 23, 150; meaning of, 3–5; subject matter of, 87

General Education in a Free Society, 5, 8, 28n29

Gentleman: in Newman, 7, 37, 86, 121; in Nussbaum, 13

Gilman, Charlotte Perkins, 108, 112, 114–15

Giroux, Henry A.,15–18, 20, 183; and corporate culture, 17–18; and positivism and technical rationality, culture of, 15–17; scientific knowledge in, 16

Goals 2000, 94–95, 105n83

Grammar of Assent, 50; and experiential knowledge, 59–60; and Jay Newman, 55; and *University Sketches*, 45; reasoning in, 55, 58

Great Books program, 4, 26

great books of the Western civilization, 4, 74, 81, 98, 100

Great Books of the Western World, 3, 15, 72

Greece, 1, 6

Green, Thomas F., 150, 182, 187

Grumet, Madeleine R., 84, 103n53, 147

Guarasci, Richard, 13

Gutierrez, Gustavo, 14

Gutmann, Amy, 190

Habit of mind: imaginative, 20; philosophical in Newman, 40–43, 45, 49

Hadot, Pierre, 169

Harvard University, 5, 8

Henderson, Harold, 4

Herland, 112

The Higher Learning in America, 74

Hilton, Paris, xii

Hirsch, E. D., 19, 73, 118, 133, 152

Hirst, Paul H.: academic disciplines in, 104n65; and Adler, 118; and cultural pursuits, 165; and liberal education, 50, 59, 61, 98; and "Liberal Education and the Nature of Knowledge", 142n75, 54, 154–55; and Martin, 82, 108, 138; and Newman, 123; and Peters, 4, 10, 73, 108, 123, 125–26, 137–38, 154; and Plato, 126; and Pring, 179, 185; Aristotle in, 123; education as initiation in, 123; forms (or modes) of knowledge in, 59, 88, 118–20, 123–24, 151, 177–78, 192; investigation and proof in, 122–23; liberal education in, 88, 118–26, 129; knowledge and understanding in, 4, 123–24, 177; knowledge as logically basic in, 123, 142n67; practical reason in, 170; public discourse in, 122–23; religion in, 184; retraction of theory of liberal education in, 23, 56, 104n64, 126, 151, 179; Hogan, Padraig, 147, 183

Holveck, Eleanore, 169

home: educational work of, 128; ideal, 128; in Martin, 48, 107, 128, 132; in Montessori, 132; private world of, 107

Human tasks, 12, 156

Humphreys, Debra, 137

Hutchins, Robert M., 4, 152; and Adler, 72; and liberal education, 98; and the Great Books, 26n15; University of Chicago, 72, 74

Idea of a University, 6, 49–50; and Catholic University of Ireland, 36; and cultivation of the intellect, 59; and *Culture and Anarchy*, 36–37; and discipline of mind, 48; and Jay Newman, 55; and liberal education,

36; and reinterpretation of liberal education, 50; and University of London, 38; influence of, 35; philosophy in, 40; sciences in 39; teacher in, 45, 59; theory of knowledge in, 44
Industrial Revolution, 6, 38

Jefferson, Thomas, 99, 183
Johns, Robert W., 12–15, 20, 30n64, 99, 184, 188

Kahne, Joseph, 80
Ker, Ian, 40–41
Kimball, Bruce A., 10, 23–25, 29n42, 150, 170, 182
Kincheloe, Joe L., 15, 181
Kliebard, Herbert M., 173n33, 174n44
knowledge: and understanding, 7, 93, 165–66, 168, 177–79, 184, 192; as goal, 148; production, 21–22, 187; forms of in Hirst, 88, 93, 177–78; structure of, 35–36, 38–39, 44, 87, 123–24, 126, 151–52; structure of in Adler, 151–52; structure of in Hirst, 87, 118–19, 151–52; structure of in Martin, 118–19, 123; structure of in Newman, 35–36, 38–39, 44; uses of, 87
Knowledge, Gender, and Schooling, 121, 154
Kohn, Alfie, 106n87
Kuhn, Thomas S., 148

leisure, 90, 157, 159, 162, 164–65, 169, 175n55, 175n57
Levine, Harry, 10
Libby, Scooter, xii
Liberal education: aims or purpose of, 11, 151, 155; and Adler, 71–100, 137, 178; and citizenship, 3, 13; and critical pedagogy, 15, 187; and cultivation of the intellect, 35, 37; and gender bias, 3; and general education, 1; and Hirst, 118–126, 178; and knowledge production, 21–22; and Martin, 107–139; and

Newman, 35–61, 178; and pragmatism, 23–25, 150; and professional education, 5–7, 121, 162; and service-learning, 12–13; and vocational education, 4, 7, 43, 71, 74, 76, 124, 156, 162, 168–69, 191; as construct, 1, 3, 60, 107, 127; as cultivation of the intellect, 4, 47; as distinquished from liberal learning, 188; as a good education, 170; as education, 125, 154; as free and freeing, 123–24, 170; as general education, 125, 154; as guide, 147, 171; as honorofic label, 120; as leisure pursuit, 4; as preparation for life, 147–71; continuity and change in, 148–50; critique of in Martin, 107; curriculum or content of, 11, 151; defense of in Newman, 42; emergent conceptions of, 151, 155, 160, 170, 187; future of, 171; gender-sensitive, 107–39; goals of in Adler, 88; historical idea of, xii–xiii, 1–3, 11, 118, 122, 124, 130, 178–79, 187, 191; in Adler, 71–100, 116; in Martin, 107–39; in Newman, 35–61, 116; influences on, 11; limitations of for Martin, 149; limitations of for Newman, 149; mainstream tradition of, 57, 93, 98, 93, 98, 153; meaning of, 1–2, 3–5, 26–27n18, 142n68; new paradigm for, xiii, 128–29, 148, 150, 154–55, 177–93; origins of, 5–6; pedagogical dimension of, 150, 153; practical education in, 165–66, 180; reconceptualization of, 148, 155–60; redefining of, 3, 11, 25, 107, 116, 127, 136–39; redefining of and Adler, 137; redefining of and Hirst, 137; redefining of and Newman, 137; redefining of and Peters, 137; relevance of, xii, 1–3, 150; stipulative definition of, 122, 124; theories of, 68n135, 82, 93, 124, 154, 181; traditional idea of, 56, 60, 98, 128–30, 136–39,

148–51, 154, 171, 178–79, 191–92;
usefulness of, 5, 123, 127, 137, 150
"Liberal Education and the Nature of
Knowledge", 22, 142n75
Liberal education as a preparation for
life, 147–71, 187
Liberal education, a new paradigm for,
177–93; aims or objectives of, 177;
and demands of living, 177–78,
180; and Martin, 178, 192; and
philosophy of life, 178; and
practical education, 180; and
service-learning, 178, 191; and
student experience, 178, 180–81,
184, 192; and student voice,189–90;
and John White, 178; and many-
sidedness, 177–80; and pedagogy,
180–82, 184, 192–93; and
practicality, 177–78; and vocational
education, 191–92; as useful, 191;
caring in, 178–79, 183–84, 193;
curriculum content in, 182–88;
education for the philosophical
demands in, 184–86; education for
practical demands in, 183–84;
education for recreation in, 182–83;
education for social justice in,
182–83; education for work in,
182–88; empowering education in,
182–83; forms of knowledge in,
192; justification of, 177–78,
187–92; moral dimension of,
191–92; participation in, 193;
practical education in, 192
"Liberal Education in a Knowledge
Society", 21
life: as a practical affair, 166; as in 'the
good life', 23, 159–61, 169, 179–80,
188–93; as in 'ordinary life', 159–60,
169; liberal education as preparation
for, 147–71; meaning of, 159
life-adjustment education, 158, 160,
173n33
literacy, levels of, 102n40
The Logic of Education, 125, 141n59,
142n75, 154
Lovelie, Lars, 151

MacIntyre, Alasdair, 23, 32n126,
169–70, 183
male cognitive perspective, 117,
140n40
Mann, Horace, 99
Maritain, Jacques, 152, 184; and Adler,
72–75, 81, 86; and aim of
education, 81
Marshall, James D, 185
Marshall, J. Dan, 9,
Martin, Jane Roland, 20, 48, 87,
105n81, 192; academic disciplines
in, 91, 116–17, 120, 129, 135, 148,
172n8; aims of education in, 134;
and Adler, 107, 110–12, 126, 129;
and civic education, 183–84; and
curriculum philosophizing, 177;
and Hirst, 82, 138; and liberal
education, 3, 10–11, 107–39; and
mainstream curriculum theory, 118;
and mainstream libera education,
153; and Montessori, 60; and
Newman, 53, 61, 82, 107, 129, 149;
and new paradigm for liberal
education, 148; and Nussbaum, 13,
92, 130; and Peters, 138; as
development of the person in, 154;
critique of Hirst in, 118–26,
154–55; critique of in Levin,
144n118; critique of liberal
education in, 121–26; cultural
wealth in, 108, 129–30, 132–34;
curriculum in, 132–34, 139n15;
curriculum of gender-sensitive
education in, 134–36; democracy in,
133–34; Dewey in, 115; domestic
tranquility in, 115, 130–31, 133–34;
domesticity in, 114–15, 126–27,
129, 131–33, 135–38; educated
man in, 101n7, 116–17, 127, 138,
140n39; educated person in, 107;
educated woman in, 108–16, 127,
138; education and schooling in,
109, 141; education for action in,
119–20, 129, 141n61; education for
boys in, 112; education for family
in, 122, 126, 129–30, 134, 137;

education for girls in, 112;
education for participation in, 15,
92, 99, 129, 150, 176n60, 188;
educational agency in, 130, 132–34;
educational thought of, 148;
epistemological critique in, 108,
118; epistemological fallacy in,
118–19, 124–26; equality in, 129,
134, 138; gender in, 110; gender
critique in, 108, 118; historians of
education in, 110–11; home
economics in, 136; identity
postulate in, 110; ivory tower people
in, 118–22, 125, 179, 193n5;
knowledge-how in, 119–20;
lopsided human beings in, 119;
mind and body dualism in, 120,
124, 154; noncognigive states in,
119–20, 126; personal development
in, 126; physical education in, 119;
Plato in, 108–13, 115, 117, 121–26;
private world of home in, 122, 128,
130–31; productive processes in,
109–10, 128–29, 139n6; public
world of work in, 122, 128, 130,
139n6; redefining of liberal
education in, 107, 116, 127,
136–39; reproductive processes in,
109–10, 117, 127–29; role
opportunity in, 110; role occupancy
in, 110; Rousseau in, 111–12, 115;
Rousseau's Emile in, 111–13, 117,
140n19; Rousseau's Sophie in, 111,
113, 140n19; School as home in,
131, 143n94; The U.S. Constitution
in, 115, 190; valuable education in,
142n71; vocational education in,
119; whole of education in, 124–25,
129, 154
McGrath, Fergal, 68n144
McGucken, William, 74
McLaren, Peter, 15
Meier, Deborah, xiii
Middle Ages, 72
middle college, xiii
Mitchell, Basil, 54
Montessori, Maria, 108, 131–32

moral development, 12, 80
moral imperialism, 189
Mother Teresa, 86

A Nation at Risk, 26n6, 73, 94, 183
National Aeronautics and Space
Administration (NASA), 9
National Defense Education Act
(NDEA), 9
National Education Association, 7
National Resource Center for the First-
Year Experience, 66n87
"Needed: A New Paradigm for Liberal
Education", 124, 127, 192
Newman, Jay, 55, 68n130, 68n135,
149
Newman, John Henry, 62n6, 127, 129,
150–56; and Adler, 59, 61, 71–72,
94, 122; and Aristotle, 64n53; and
Birmingham Oratory, 62n8; and
Cambridge University, 65n67,
65n77; and cultivation of the
intellect, 35, 43, 59, 61; and Dewey,
59; and Jay Newman, 68n130,
68n135, 149; and knowledge as
truth, 74; and liberal education,
3–4, 6–7, 11, 35–61, 116, 137; and
Martin, 53, 61, 82, 107, 129, 149;
and Noddings, 60; and Oxford
University, 65n67, 65n77; and
Rousseau, 59; and Yale, 63n22;
apprehension in, 50–51, 60;
architectonic science in, 40–41, 170;
as rector, 66n92; assent in, 50–51,
54; Athens in, 46; care in, 60;
certitude in, 54; circle of the sciences
in, 39–40, 88, 123; college as home
in, 48, 58 149; concept of mind in,
41–44, 48; connatural qualities of
liberal education in, 57; defense of
liberal education in, 42; discipline
of mind in, 35, 46, 48–49, 66n92;
education for action in, 59;
educational implications of his
thought, 57–61; educational
thought of, 148–49; experiential
knowledge in, 59–60; good sense in,

54–55; idea of, xii–xiii; illative sense in, 50, 67n99; inference in, 52–56, 60; intellectual formation in, 37, 57–58, 74; knowledge and understanding in, 19, 42, 48, 177; liberal education and concrete reasoning in, 60; logic in, 52–53, 56; moral education in, 36, 47, 57–58, 59, 59–61; notional knowledge in, 53, 55–56, 138, 148; notional propositions in, 50; Olympic Games in, 42; on literature, 63n29; on science, 63n30; on university and church, 66n82; personal in, 45–46, 65n74, 66n92; personal knowledge in, 61, 185; philosophy in, 38, 40, 62n20, 64n38; philosophical habit of mind in, 40–43, 45, 49, 58; philosophical knowledge in, 38, 40–41, 123, 170–71; philosophical stance, 63n31; practical knowledge in, 61; real knowledge in, 53–54, 56, 138; real propositions in 50; reasoning in, 51–52, 54, 56–58; reinterpretation of, 50; religious education in, 36, 47, 57–58, 60, 149, 184; retreat from liberal education in, 36, 49–57, 60, 138; Rome in, 46; science in, 39–41; scientific knowledge in, 39, 55–56, 61; theology in, 39, 46, 93, 123; theoretical knowledge in, 55–56, 58, 60–61, 138, 149, 185; theory of knowledge in, 35–36, 38–43, 44, 55, 61, 64n50; the teacher in, 44–49, 65n64; university education in, 7, 36, 45, 47, 57–58, 60–61, 191
"Newman's Retreat from a Liberal Education", 36
No Child Left Behind (NCLB), 31n87
Noddings, Nel, 4; and Adler, 12, 98; and *Cardinal Principles of Secondary Education,* 27n26, 158; and civic education, 183–84; and emergent conceptions of liberal education, 187; and Newman, 61; and personal

development, 79; critical thinking in, 15; human tasks in, 12, 156; liberal education as a false ideal in, 12, 154–55
Nussbaum, Martha C., 5, 13, 92, 130

Oakeshott, Michael, J., 4, 23, 42, 143n75, 170, 173n20, 194n23
O'Hear, Philip, 143n87
orator, 5
Oriel College, 36
Oxford movement, 36
Oxford University, 7, 25, 36, 46
Oxford University Sermons, 50; and experiential knowledge, 59; reasoning in, 55, 58

The Paideia Group, 75
Paideia Problems and Possibilities, 74, 80, 95
The Paideia Program: An Educational Syllabus, 75, 84, 92
The Paideia Proposal, 103, 105–6, 147, 156; and auxiliary studies, 89–93; and equality, 81; and Grumet, 147; and objectives of schooling, 79, 83, 153; and same course of study, 83; basic schooling in, 71, 84; context of, 72–75; pedagogy in, 94–97; scope of, 75–79; significance of, 97–100
Panel on Youth, 97
performativity, 183
personal development, 2, 93, 158–60, 177, 180, 185, 192
personal influence, 35, 65n74
Peterburs, Wulstan, 43
Peters, R. S. 142n67; and Hirst, 4, 10, 73, 108, 123, 125–26, 137–38, 154; and Martin, 138; in Martin, 101n7, 108, 116–17, 125, 127, 140n39
Phenix, Philip H., 10, 59, 61, 73, 87, 118, 126, 136, 152
philosopher king, 109–10, 113, 121–22, 125, 170
philosophy as a way of life, 169, 171
Philosophy of Education Society, 116

philosophy of lived experience, 185, 195n32
phronesis, 23, 67n99
plain persons, 185
Plato, 5, 139n9, 170; and Adler, 72, 86, 93; and Hirst, 126; and Newman, 45, 56; divided line in, 123; educational thought of, 139n9; in Martin, 108–13, 115, 117, 121–26; just state in, 110
Popper, Karl, 22
the practical, 21–25; and practices, 21–25; moral dimensions of, 166–68; nature of, 166–67; practice in, 169
practical action, 167, 176n60
practical judgment, 167, 169, 176n60
practical knowledge, 90, 93, 179, 181, 193, 193n8, 194n23; in Newman, 61, 185
practical reason, 23, 170, 176n62, 188; need for education in, 170
practical subjects, 166
pragmatism, 73; and liberal education, 23–25
Pratte, Richard, 12
Pring, Richard, 19–20, 84, 168, 176n60, 181, 185; and constructivism, 172n9; and Dewey, 152–53, 172n6, 184–85; and Hirst, 179, 185; and Newman, 61, 185; and Shor, 152–153, 172n6, 184; liberal education in, 168–69; practical knowledge in, 179, 181; vocational education in, 168–69
The Process of Education, 9
progressive education, 73
Purpel, David, 138

"The Radical Future of Gender Enrichment", 129
Ravitch, Diane, 31n95
Reclaiming a Conversation, 108, 112, 115–16, 127–28
recreation, nature of, 164–65
Reforming Education, 75
The Relevance of Education, 9

religion in school and society, 184, 190–91
The Republic, 110
Rickover, Hyman G., 9, 73
Rifkin, Jeremy, 164
Roberts, J. M., 63n35
Rome, 1, 6
Roosevelt, Grace, 17
Rorty, Richard, 74
Rousseau, 86, 111, 126, 152, 172n9
Ryan, Kevin, 138
Ryle, Gilbert, 194n23

Scheffler, Israel, 124
Schiller, F. C. S., 52
Schniedewind, Nancy, 21
schooling: and education, 75–76, 188–91; and preparation for life, 155–58, 167, 169–70, 184; in Adler, 75–84, 86, 88, 94–96, 98–100, 153, 156, 169; in Martin, 109, 117, 120, 130–31, 137; loss of confidence in, 10; government involvement in, xi; privatization of, 18
school-to-career movement, 92, 97
The Schoolhome, 108, 115, 129, 131–33, 143n94
Schubert, W.H., 17, 31n90
self-actualizing, 189
service, 12
Service-learning, 12–15, 187–88; and heightened understanding, 14–15; and liberation theology, 14; faculty opposition to, 14
seven liberal arts and sciences, 93, 123
Shor, Ira, 84, 150, 152–53, 174, 188; and Adler, 20, 152–53; and constructivism, 172n9; and critical pedagogy, 15, 18–22, 174n41; and Dewey, 147–148, 152; and empowering education, 18–21; and education for activism, 152; and education for democratic citizenship, 152; and education for empowerment, 152; and education for participation in, 99; and emergent conceptions of liberal

education, 187; and Pring, 152–53,
    172n6, 184–85; themes in, 19, 152
Simpson, Douglas J., 12–15, 20,
    30n64, 99, 184, 188
Sizer, Theodore R., 73
Smith, Barry, 4
Smith, B. Othanel, 5, 10, 59, 73, 76,
    87, 118, 126
social efficiency, 8
Snedden, David, 157
Spencer, Herbert, 8, 28n27, 157
Sputnik, 2, 9, 158
St Augustine, 6
St Jerome, 6
standards, 105n83
standardized testing, 95–96
Standish, Paul, 151, 162
Steinberg, Shirley R., 181
Stratemeyer, Florence, 8, 158
student experience, 19, 84, 148, 152
Studies in Humanism, 52

Taylor, Charles, 159, 195n35
theoretical knowledge, 151, 178–79,
    184–85, 194n23
third idiom, 20
three Cs, 60, 107, 114–15, 118,
    126–27, 129, 132, 134–37, 187
three Rs, 6, 81, 83, 88
Tippins, Deborah J., 181
"Toward Pragmatic Liberal Education",
    23
A Treatise on Domestic Economy, 112
Trinity College of Vermont, 14–15
Turner, Frank, 42

University of Chicago, 4, 72
University of London, 7, 36, 40

University Sketches, 49; and Catholic
    University of Ireland, 36; and
    discipline of mind, 49; and
    Grammar of Assent, 45; and *Oxford
    University Sermons*, 45; Newman in,
    66n94; reasoning in, 58; the college
    in, 46–47
The U.S. Constitution, 77, 115, 131
The Uses of Schooling, 3

Van Doren, Charles, 72
A Vindication of the Rights of Woman, 112
vocational education, 74

Waghid, Yusef, 31n93, 176n60
War on Poverty, 9
Washington, 9
Wegener, Charles, 1
Weltman, Burton, 98
Westheimer, Joel, 80
White, J., 29n43, 118, 162
Whitehead, A. N., 187
Winch, Christopher, 156
Wollstonecraft, Mary, 112–13, 115
"Women, Schools, and Cultural
    Wealth", 132
women, voices of, 107
Women's Ways of Knowing, 186
work: and identity, 162; education for,
    57, 74, 80, 90–93, 98–99, 182; end
    of, 164; kinds of, 162; meaning of,
    159; nature of, 161–64;
    objectionable, 163–64
World War II, xi, 8, 29n47, 72

Yale, 46, 48, 63n22, 65n77
Yale Report of 1828, 6, 74
Youth: Transition to Adulthood, 97

About the Author

D. G. Mulcahy is professor in the School of Education and Professional Studies at Central Connecticut State University and formerly professor of education at University College, Cork, Ireland. Earlier books of his include *Curriculum and Policy in Irish Post-Primary Education* (1981), *Irish Educational Policy* (co-edited with Denis O'Sullivan, 1989) and *Knowledge, Gender, and Schooling* (2002). He is a past president of the Educational Studies Association of Ireland and of The New England Philosophy of Education Society and twice a recipient of Fulbright awards.